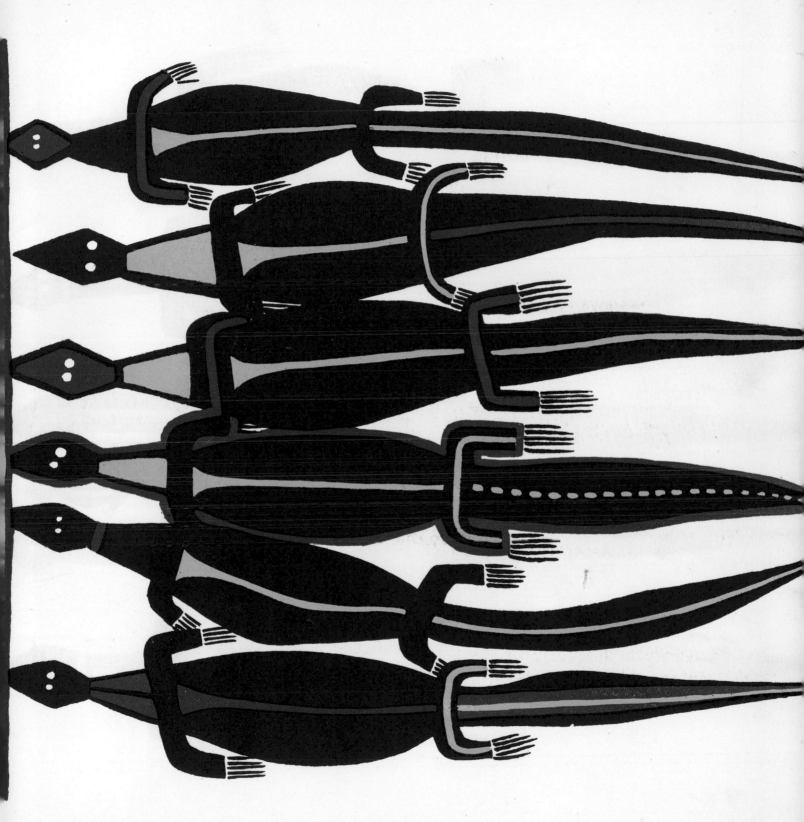

Australian Aboriginal Art

Australian Aboriginal Art

edited by **RONALD M. BERNDT**
with chapters by **R. M. BERNDT, A. P. ELKIN, F. D. McCARTHY**
C. P. MOUNTFORD, T. G. H. STREHLOW, J. A. TUCKSON

The Macmillan Company, New York
Collier-Macmillan Ltd, London
1964

First published in the United Kingdom 1964 by
Collier-Macmillan Ltd, London

Published in the United States of America by
The Macmillan Company, New York

Published in Canada by
Collier-Macmillan Canada, Ltd, Toronto

Library of Congress Catalog Card No. 64–12214

Manufactured in the Commonwealth of Australia

CONTENTS

v

Plates

Plates within the text

facing page

x

Emeritus Professor A. P. Elkin occupied the Chair of Anthropology in the University of Sydney from 1933 until his retirement in 1956, and during that period he deeply influenced Australian anthropology. Since that time, he has continued his active interest both in writing and in research, and has remained editor and manager of the well-known Australian anthropological journal *Oceania*.

Professor Elkin, the foremost authority on the Australian Aborigines, has had a distinguished career. He has held many important academic and scientific posts, and among the numerous honours bestowed upon him have been the James Cook Medal of the Royal Society of New South Wales (1955), and the A.N.Z.A.A.S. Mueller Medal (1957), and the Herbert E. Gregory Medal of the Bernice P. Bishop Museum, Honolulu (1961). He has carried out considerable anthropological research in various parts of north-western Australia, central and South Australia, Arnhem Land, eastern New South Wales, and south-eastern Queensland, as well as in New Guinea.

Several of Professor Elkin's many publications are noted in the Bibliography of this volume and need not be mentioned again here. In this connection, one may note only his *Australian Aborigines: How To Understand Them* (first published in 1938), which has become widely acknowledged as a classic work on the Australian Aborigines. Over the years, he has been extremely interested in Aboriginal art, which he first studied in the field in the northern Kimberleys in 1928. It was then that he found, for the first time, the ritual significance and underlying meaning of the now famous Wandjina paintings which George Grey had discovered early in the nineteenth century. Since then he has sought to understand the function of Aboriginal art in relation to ritual and mythology on one hand and religious philosophy on the other. In Arnhem Land, too, he has been vitally concerned with Aboriginal art, and in 1950 published (in conjunction with R. and C. Berndt) *Art in Arnhem Land*.

Charles P. Mountford, O.B.E., Dip. Anthrop., has been actively interested in Aboriginal art for close on forty years, and indeed has pioneered this subject. Much of his work has been carried out under the auspices of the South Australian Museum. He has been a member of, and led, many field trips to various parts of Australia—for instance, to the Warburtons in 1935, to Central Australia in 1936, 1942, 1951, 1952, 1956 and 1960, as well as to Arnhem Land and Melville Island (1948 and 1954). In nearly all cases, his primary focus has been on art, myth and symbolism; and over the years he has built up an international reputation in that direction.

Charles Mountford has published widely on Aboriginal art, among other subjects, and some of his works are mentioned in the Bibliography to this volume; his *Brown Men and Red Sand, The Art of Albert Namatjira, Art, Myth and Symbolism of Arnhem Land* (the result of field work he carried out in 1948, when he led the American-Australian Scientific Expedition to Arnhem Land), and *The Tiwi* are widely known. Closely associated with his work on Aboriginal art have been his outstanding contributions in the field of photography: he has produced several documentary films on the Aborigines, for which he has received awards. He has also been a recipient of the John Lewis Gold Medal (Royal Geographical Society, South Australian Branch), the Founder's Gold Medal (Royal Geographical Society, Queensland Branch), and the Franklin Burr Award of the National Geographical Society of America, among others, and was a Nuffield Research Scholar between 1957–59.

Frederick D. McCarthy is, and has been during many years, Curator in Anthropology at the Australian Museum, Sydney. For the past thirty years he has specialized in the study of Australian Aboriginal prehistory, art, material culture, and economic life. His archaeological work has involved excavations in eastern and western New South Wales and in Arnhem Land. More particularly, in connection with the focus of the present volume, Mr. McCarthy has recorded and analysed extensive series of rock engravings and cave paintings in those areas, as well as in north-western Australia. Most of this research has been under the auspices of the Australian Museum, but some of it has been financed by the Wenner-Gren Foundation for Anthropological Research (New York), the Nuffield Foundation, and the recently established Australian Institute of Aboriginal Studies. He has also accompanied

several research parties, most notably the American-Australian Scientific Expedition to Arnhem Land in 1948, and his interest in the problem of external and alien contact influencing Australian Aboriginal life took him to Indonesia and Malaya in 1937 and 1938.

His publications on the subject of Australian Aboriginal art, prehistory, and so on, number over two hundred papers. Among these his two Australian Museum handbooks on *Aboriginal Decorative Art* and *Rock Art*, both profusely illustrated, have won him world recognition as an authority in these fields. His more general work (1957) on the Aborigines, too, demonstrates his wide interests and competence in Australian ethnology. Mr. McCarthy has held, over the years, many offices in scientific bodies in Australia — including the Royal Society of New South Wales, A.N.Z.A.A.S., the Anthropological Society of New South Wales, the Far Eastern Prehistory Association, and the Historical Monuments Committee of Unesco.

T. G. H. Strehlow, M.A., is Reader in Australian Linguistics at the University of Adelaide. Earlier he had been a research worker under the Australian National Research Council; a patrol officer and then Deputy Director of Native Affairs for the Northern Territory (1936–42); Instructor, L.H.Q. School of Civil Affairs, Duntroon, 1945; Research Fellow in Australian Linguistics and lecturer in English Literature, University of Adelaide, 1946; and Research Fellow, Australian National University, 1949–51. He has travelled and lectured extensively in Europe.

Mr. Strehlow was born at the Hermannsburg Mission, Central Australia, where his father was pastor, and in childhood acquired an intimate knowledge of Aranda dialects. It was this initial interest which later inspired him, after the appropriate training, to take up systematic research in this field. As a result, he has become the recognized authority, both in Australia and overseas, on the Aranda region, having specialized on linguistics and religious life (including myth and ritual). His insight into and knowledge of Aranda life are such that his position in Australia is virtually unique — he has achieved an understanding and feeling for Aranda life which has rarely been equalled by other workers in others parts of this continent. The ethnographical material he has collected is considerable, ranging from extensive genealogical data to the detailed recording of poetry and music. His colour films (on sacred Aranda ritual) are outstanding in their beauty. For instance, he has recorded 4,000 song verses and photographed 850 secret totemic acts. His publications include *Aranda Traditions* (1947), as well as many articles and pamphlets, and his classic study of *Aranda Phonetics and Grammar* (*Oceania* monograph, 1944). He has also held a number of offices in academic and scientific organizations.

J. A. Tuckson is the Deputy Director of the Art Gallery of New South Wales, where he has been on the staff for twelve years. He started his art training in London and completed it after the war at East Sydney Technical College. Mr. Tuckson is a member of the Contemporary Art Society of Australia, with which he occasionally exhibits.

In 1958 and again in 1959 he went with Dr. Stuart Scougall to Melville Island and Yirrkalla, where grave posts, bark paintings, and carved figures were acquired for the collection as a gift from Dr. Scougall. In 1960 Mr. Tuckson organized, on behalf of the Australian State Art Galleries, an exhibition of Aboriginal art which toured the Commonwealth of Australia.

The Editor, **Professor Ronald M. Berndt,** at present occupies the Chair of Anthropology in the University of Western Australia. His interest in anthropology grew out of an early association with the South Australian Museum, and his initial training was carried out under Professor A. P. Elkin at the University of Sydney, followed by postgraduate study under Professor Raymond Firth at the London School of Economics (University of London). He has held a number of appointments both in Australia and overseas; for instance, he lectured for some years at the Department of Anthropology, University of Sydney, was a Nuffield Foundation Fellow in 1953–4, and a Carnegie Corporation Travelling Fellow in 1955–6.

Professor Berndt's social and cultural anthropological research, the first of which was undertaken in 1939, has (since 1941) been carried out in conjunction with his wife (Dr. Catherine Berndt) and, within Australia, has extended over much of the Northern Territory (particularly in Arnhem Land), western and northern South Australia, western New South Wales, and Western Australia. His actual field work in Aboriginal Australia, in terms of time, covers a period of approximately 77 months. He has published widely on the Aborigines and on the Eastern Highlands of New Guinea, and is internationally recognized as an authority in these fields. Especially he has concentrated his attention on problems of Aboriginal religion, social organization, law and order, and social and cultural change. Apart from numerous articles, he has published *Kunapipi*, *Djanggawul*, and *An Adjustment Movement in Arnhem Land*, along with several volumes written in conjunction with his wife, among them *The First Australians* (1952) and a detailed study of traditional Australian Aboriginal life to be published in 1964 under the title of *The World of the First Australians*.

Professor Berndt has been awarded the Edgeworth David Medal for Anthropology (Royal Society of New South Wales, 1950), and the Wellcome Medal for Anthropological Research (Royal Anthropological Institute, 1958). He is a member of a number of professional and academic committees, and has held several important offices in these (for example, as President of Section 'F', A.N.Z.A.A.S., 1962; Chairman of the Australian Branch of the Association of Social Anthropologists, 1962–64; etc.). He is also general editor of a new journal entitled *Anthropological Forum*.

The Growth of Interest in Aboriginal Art:
Australian Aboriginal art is becoming better
known these days, or at least more widely
known, than ever before. Once it was relegated
to the ethnological section of a museum, and
treated along with artifacts and material objects
of other non-literate peoples. Now it is not unusual to find such things as Aboriginal bark
paintings taking their place alongside European and other examples of aesthetic expression.
And because they rub shoulders with all forms
of art, irrespective of cultural origin, the infer-
ence is that they are being evaluated in more
general terms: that there is not only wider
appreciation of Aboriginal endeavour in this
respect, but that it is, almost imperceptibly,
taking its place in the world of art.

Fifteen to twenty years ago few of us would have
envisaged this meteoric rise in popularity, within
Australia and overseas. Prices asked for the
more outstanding work of Aboriginal artists
have been sky-rocketing. At the same time
examples of traditional Aboriginal art are increasingly difficult to obtain, as people of Aboriginal descent all over the continent become more
and more Europeanized.

Interest in this field has been stimulated by the
publication of several volumes dealing directly
or indirectly with Aboriginal art. (See, for instance, Barrett and Croll, 1943; Elkin, 1938/56;
Elkin and R. and C. Berndt, 1950; McCarthy,
1938/58, 1957a, 1958; Mountford, 1954b, 1956,
1958a, 1961a.) Exhibitions have helped in this
direction, too. (See Chapter Five.) Part of a
large collection, which I obtained in Arnhem
Land, was shown in Sydney (at the David Jones'
Art Gallery) in October, 1949; in 1951 a Jubilee
Exhibition of Australian Art, of twenty-six
items, appeared in all capital cities; and in 1957
an exhibition of Arnhem Land bark paintings
and carved human figures (70 paintings and 10
other objects) was held in Perth. The Australian
National Committee for U.N.E.S.C.O. prepared a display of Australian Aboriginal culture, which visited all Australian States in
1957–8. The Adelaide Festival of Arts in 1960
held its own exhibition; and there have been
others as well, not only in this country, but also
in the United States, Britain, and Europe.

In 1960–1 an exhibition, the largest of its kind
yet planned, was arranged by the State art
galleries of Australia and toured all States.
Broadly conceived, it included bark paintings,
carved figures, and sacred and secular objects—

1

115 items altogether. Mr. J. A. Tuckson, Deputy Director of the Art Gallery of New South Wales (who contributes Chapter Five of this volume), was responsible for its organization and presentation.

This exhibition has served as a framework for the design of the present volume. Because it was so important, bringing together as it did a wide range of Aboriginal art styles from many sources, the decision was made to record it on a more permanent basis. The most outstanding of the bark paintings and other objects were selected for the purpose, together with others not previously available. The result is the presentation, in colour, of a much larger collection of Aboriginal art than has hitherto been possible. It does not claim to provide a complete coverage, to deal exhaustively with this many-faceted subject; but it does focus attention on some of the most striking and aesthetically exciting examples of Aboriginal art, and on their significance both for the Aborigines and for ourselves. Even though the various contributors have approached this material from differing perspectives, there is, necessarily, some overlapping in content; and the cross-referencing which this involves should add to the over-all interest of the volume.* Five of the contributors have had wide experience in the Aboriginal field, have published works on the Aborigines, and have carried out anthropological field-work in various parts of Aboriginal Australia. The sixth, whose concern with this broad topic was evidenced in the leading role he played in arranging the 1960-1 exhibition, approaches it from a rather different perspective—from the standpoint of an artist, looking at the Aboriginal world from the outside, but with sympathy and regard for its traditions.

An Approach to the Subject: The growing interest in Aboriginal art has not always entailed a similar appreciation of what it means to the artists themselves. Members of the public see examples of such art displayed in galleries, or purchase them for their own homes, usually with little or no information that would help them to understand the traditional or current meaning of these things. In this they are conforming, naturally enough, to what we ordinarily do with paintings and with art objects. We hang them in our galleries, collect them, beautify our homes with them, are vulnerable to fluctuations in taste, think in terms of what they are likely to bring on the open market, and evaluate them as good or bad, masterpieces or daubs, depending on circumstances. Perhaps this is the fate of all art, including Aboriginal art, once it has been removed from its own socio-cultural environment.

As far as Western-European art is concerned, the argument runs that to appreciate the works of particular artists, to recognize what they are attempting to do, calls for a synthesis of two, not necessarily coincident, points of view. One is the artist's own subjective or personal interpretation: an artist is said to be expressing himself individually, although in doing so he conforms broadly to the dictates of a particular school. The other is the provision of a label, which nevertheless leaves the way open to the viewer to draw his own conclusions. The fact that Western-European artists are influenced by their own social and cultural setting, and can never get too far away from this if they want to sell their products, or at least create something meaningful to themselves or to others, is often overlooked. In other words, within its own socio-cultural environment, art is a form of language, and if it fails to communicate in some way it is not art, but something else. Art which is appreciated, which is aesthetically pleasing to us, and which is part and parcel of our cultural heritage—not only traditional, but also con-

*A point in regard to Aboriginal names: because these languages were not traditionally recorded in writing by the Aborigines themselves, and because some of their sounds have no exact equivalent in English, there have been differences of opinion in regard to the most appropriate spelling. Many Aboriginal words have, therefore, been written in a variety of ways: for instance, the tribal name Kakadu or Gagadju; the ritual and myth of Kunapipi or Gunabibi; the mythical beings Wandjina or Wondjina—and so on. In addition, in phonetic transcription *j* has the sound of the English *y*, so that *jiridja* should be pronounced as *yiridya*, Julunggul as Yulunggul.

2

temporary art—does communicate, or can communicate, because the language is there if we go to the trouble to learn it.

Let me put it another way. If a picture is to be more than an unintelligible design, however pleasing to the eye, it must have social relevance: people looking at it must be able to understand, to some degree at least, what the artist is trying to say and why he is saying it. This is true of Aboriginal art, no less than of other varieties. Generally speaking, an item of art produced within a certain area, assuming it is contemporary and not prehistoric, will make sense to local Aborigines; sections of it may have to be explained to some of them, and interpretation may vary according to such factors as age, sex, and social status—but most people who see it will know something about its background.

When such an object is taken away from its home surroundings into our own, immediately the problem of *translation* is involved. If there is no interpreter available, and usually there is not, we can merely look at the designs, and find them either pleasing or otherwise. Much depends on whether they conform to our canons of aesthetic taste, themselves the product of social and personal experience.

Art and the Traditional Aboriginal Environment: The place of traditional Aboriginal art was very different to that of its counterpart in Western-European-type society. There were no professional artists, only some who were recognized as being more outstanding, or more competent, than others. They were mostly men, not women, and they did not constitute an occupational category who made their living solely in this way. Art productions were not specifically sold, but in some contexts they did have economic significance. With a few outstanding exceptions (for example, the *tjurunga* discussed by T. G. H. Strehlow in Chapter Four), they were not intended to be kept permanently. This was particularly the case with nearly all ritual and ceremonial regalia and emblems. Some of them concerned only a particular ritual sequence, and when that sequence was completed they were destroyed or abandoned. Probably only the rock carvings and paintings, the sacred *tjurunga*, and carved and incised boards, were expected to remain more or less intact over a long period of time.

Approximating our own usage was the Arnhem Land practice of decorating the bark walls or the roofs of small huts, built flat on the ground or raised on stilts during the wet season in country subject to flooding. This was bark painting as it was traditionally known in that area. Its subject-matter, in coloured ochres, was quite extensive although usually of a non-sacred kind; there were hunting scenes, and incidents from stories, or from real-life situations. These lasted for as long as did the houses themselves, which was rarely more than a couple of seasons. In contrast to this informal activity, in western Arnhem Land particularly, exhibitions of bark paintings of a sacred character were an integral part of initiation rituals. Novices were taken from one to another, and each was described to them by fully initiated men. Later the paintings were left to rot or deliberately destroyed. In this area, too, stories were sometimes illustrated on bark, and some of the specimens collected by Sir Baldwin Spencer in 1912 may have been used for that purpose. (See Plates 30 and 64.)

Aboriginal art was both sacred and secular, the first probably far more important than the second. There is no question that most Aboriginal art can be classified as sacred art, and this is stressed by Professor Elkin and Mr. Strehlow. It is painting or carving which generally, through its symbolic representations, conveys some aspect of myth. Usually this has to do with the great spirit beings of the Eternal Dreaming, the creative era. These beings set the pattern of living for all the natural world, including man. In Aboriginal belief they are still alive today, in spirit, much as they were at the beginning of time. And art, in one form or another—a bark, ground, or cave painting, an especially constructed emblem, a carved and decorated pole or figure, an incised stone or board—is the medium through which their power or influence is brought to bear on everyday affairs. The material symbolic representations which are used in ritual, through which that sacredness itself is expressed, and which actors in those performances use as a connecting link between themselves as ordinary persons and those sacred beings, are not simply works of art in the ordinary sense of the phrase. Aborigines themselves do not evaluate them in that way. It is what they stand for, which is important: there is an emotional connotation here. They are constant reminders of the reality of the myth, a tangible expression of its contemporary relevance.

Because of this close religious significance of much of Australian Aboriginal art, and because it was largely symbolic and concerned the perpetuation of the past in the present, there was a minimum of innovation. The emphasis, generally speaking, was on non-change, in the sphere of myth, ritual, and its material representations. The creative beings, the ancestors, or the spirits, had shown how these were to be told, acted out, or made, and too much deviation from the stipulated form would inevitably damage their efficacy. For this reason, as Strehlow notes in his chapter, the traditional designs used in the *tjurunga* and in other objects seem to have been virtually static. In another context, Mountford (in Marian W. Smith, ed., 1961*b*: 8) speaks of ceremonial art as being 'almost completely fossilized'. In a way, this gives a wrong impression of sacred art. It is true that, as far as we know, the sacred art of any one area has not changed radically over a very long period indeed. However, although there is repetition in this sense, with fairly strict adherence to a particular art style, this has not inevitably meant artistic rigidity. There was some scope for individual treatment, for the production of a masterpiece, so to speak, even though the rules or conventions were limiting and the subject-matter stereotyped. As far as this point is concerned, it is Central Australian art which has mostly been viewed as unimaginative and inflexible. Yet, as Strehlow points out, there is in fact a very wide range of different designs—numerous variations on a common theme, revealing considerable ingenuity and subtlety. Although the designs

used may appear to be simple in character, actually they are extremely complex.

The same variety is apparent in Aboriginal cave and rock art (see McCarthy), and this is especially rich in the Kimberleys and in Arnhem Land, where some of the most remarkable cave paintings are to be found. In the sacred art of the ritual ground, too, there was some provision for innovation. However, this gives rise to two questions, which I shall touch upon very briefly. One concerns style, the other the influence of sacred upon non-sacred art. I shall look first at the second of these.

Sacred and Non-sacred Art: The dominant pressures of sacred art have everywhere on the continent influenced other forms, which relate either to magic or to mundane affairs. Nevertheless, it is in these last that innovation is more obvious. Bark and cave paintings which deal with such topics as hunting, fishing, camp scenes, various creatures and human beings, love magic and sorcery, are much more flexible and susceptible to individual treatment. At the same time the artist painted or carved according to a recognized style or convention. In any one area, the difference between sacred and secular art lies not so much in style as in subject-matter. Furthermore, the boundaries between sacred and secular art are by no means clearly defined. We find mythological subjects, of directly sacred origin or significance, appearing, for instance, on a Kimberley pearlshell, or an everyday spear-thrower, or in the designs used at a camp ceremony. Sacred art is not confined to the ritual ground.

Style: The matter of style is particularly significant. There is no one style relevant to the whole continent, although Australian Aboriginal art productions can, in general, be distinguished from those of other peoples, in New Guinea, Indonesia, and so on. Within the continent itself are, or were, many art styles or traditions; and, in fact, several might be present in the one region, either simultaneously or over a period of time. Mountford and McCarthy bring this out quite clearly as far as cave painting and engraving are concerned: paintings are super-

4

imposed on others, and carvings of different style appear on the one rock outcrop, or in the one gallery. In western Arnhem Land, for instance, is the well-known X-ray art, in which the internal organs of the subjects are depicted (see Plates 22, 33 and 60); and, as well, there are the very beautifully and delicately drawn stick-like figures, which have collectively been called *mimi*, although they concern a range of subject-matter not confined to these *mimi*, or spirits (Plates 39 and 42). (See Mountford, Chapter Two.) Real *mimi* art is not produced today, and is probably quite ancient; but contemporary *mimi* art, as illustrated in Plates 36 and 37, is possibly derived from this earlier form, as are the outstanding sorcery and love-magic figures. (See Plates 20 and 56; Elkin and R. and C. Berndt, 1950; and R. and C. Berndt, 1951.) Yet these do, in fact, constitute different styles.

A comparison of Plates 24, 57, 26, 32, 55, 58, 34 and 53, which depict bark paintings from Melville and Bathurst islands, western and north-eastern Arnhem Land, and Groote Eylandt, will demonstrate at a glance the existence of four different art styles in this part of Aboriginal Australia. If western Arnhem Land art is compared, impressionistically, with north-eastern, we can observe that in the first there seems to be a preference for open spaces, a concentration on the central figure or figures against a plain background; detail is subordinated to the main design; and there is an impression of suddenly arrested motion. Naturalism is emphasized, with a minimum of stylization; roundness and curves are favoured, rather than angles and straight lines (see Plates 32, 56 and 60). On the north-eastern side of Arnhem Land (as illustrated in Plates 25, 35, 55, 58 and 61), in contrast, the bark canvas is almost completely covered with design; the drawing is shaped to fit into the imposed boundaries of the bark sheet, and in most cases the artist himself supplies a border as well. Careful attention is paid to the main figures (as in Plate 25). But here, although spaces are occasionally left, the tendency is to fill in the ground with cross-hatching or criss-crossing of lines, even to the extent of design

repetition. There is little in the way of movement or action; and in some examples the duplication of central and subordinate figures, as well as of minor motifs, bears striking resemblance to a textile-type pattern. Several others (as in Plates 25, 35, and 66) have a cartoon-like quality, when, for example, several events in the life of a particular mythical character are shown on the one bark, irrespective of sequence. The art of this region shows, too, a concentration on stylization, much more specialization of design, and a corresponding absence of emphasis on naturalism.

Such comparisons could be made for a large number of art areas throughout the continent. Elsewhere (Berndt, 1958*b*: 26–43) I have attempted to relate the art styles of western and north-eastern Arnhem Land to other features of their social and cultural contexts, and suggested a certain closeness of fit in each case.

Art, whether naturalistic or stylized, is always an abstraction from reality—from the empirical situation which is observed or perceived. It is a statement about something, framed in such a way that it is readily identifiable within its social environment. Although variation is present at any one period within an art tradition, just as it is through time, a particular style should provide us with a key to the basic values current among the people who sponsor it; it should tell us something about the ethos of that society, offering a shorthand summary of at least some of its main features.

Aesthetic Perspective: An artist, as we have seen, is ordinarily obliged to work within a particular tradition, conforming to dictates which are already established. Variation outside these recognized limits is likely to meet with disapproval, if not condemnation, especially if this falls within the religious sphere. Looking at the illustrations in this volume, it is as well for us to remember that certain conventions had to be followed by the artist, and that these were not the conventions of, for instance, Renaissance art in Europe.

Large genitalia attached to human figures (as in Plates 20, 30, 38, 56 and 64) express qualities of maleness or femaleness, or obliquely indicate themes of fertility. A small human hunter is shown alongside a comparatively large creature (Plates 3, 4, 22 and 52), or major mythical characters may be drawn much larger than are minor ones. This is a common and widespread device, which not only projects onto a drawing local views about gradations in status, but also underlines the relative importance of the figures. In X-ray art, internal organs are depicted in the drawings of both animals and human beings. This is a conventional way of demonstrating completeness—indicating that there is more to man, or to an animal, than his (its) outward appearance. The artist in this case is not satisfied with an outline sketch: he wants to show what makes his subject live. Although this style is reported only from the central part of the Northern Territory, from the Katherine River across into western Arnhem Land, in north-eastern Arnhem Land I have seen examples of carved human figures where designs of horizontal and vertical lines on the forehead signify the thoughts of the subject.

In much Aboriginal art the designs or figures are drawn flat, not placed within a landscape setting. This is particularly the case with the Wandjina, or Wondjina, drawings (see Plates 19 and 44), and the cave paintings of Central Australia and New South Wales (see Plates 2, 3 and 4). But there are many exceptions, as in Plate 37, where a landscape and hills are suggested. In north-eastern Arnhem Land specimens, for instance, human and animal figures are incorporated within the land and seascape, not superimposed on it.

In relation to techniques there is the question of how designs and figures are painted. As far as bark painting is concerned, the sheet is held on the artist's knees, or placed flat on the ground. In painting, he moves it around or, alternatively, moves about it himself. To appreciate most eastern Arnhem Land examples one needs to do the same—not only to look down at the painting, but to move around it. Strehlow illustrates this very well in relation to *tjurunga* art; according to him, the motifs themselves are derived from looking downward at tracks and marks on the ground. There have been suggestions that some designs are intended merely to be decorative, and have no meaning attached to them. Sir Herbert Read (in Marian W. Smith, ed., 1961 : 17) speaks of the 'complex meander designs on pearl shells' or the 'intricate patterns on ceremonial message sticks' as arising from horror vacui, 'an instinct to obliterate empty meaningless space'. This is not necessarily so when all designs have meaning. The pearlshell patterns, for instance, can mean different things: tracks of an ancestral being, tidal marks on a beach, rising clouds, and so on. In the case of a message stick, each mark may be interpreted. Apart from this, without looking more closely at the local situation, one needs to be cautious in imputing to the artists a distaste for undecorated space as such—as I have done in our north-eastern Arnhem Land example. Western Arnhem Land is a case in point, while Strehlow has observed that undecorated *tjurunga* are often regarded as being more important than those bearing conventional designs.

The Maturity of Aboriginal Art: Aboriginal artists all over the continent had few tools and techniques at their disposal, and this fact in itself imposed limits to artistic development. The way in which they overcame these in some instances is nothing short of genius. Basically, there were four colours. In painting they used their fingers, small twigs, and brushes of various kinds. For carving and incising they used stone knives, axes, adzes, chisels, hammer stones, and so on; in the north, after Indonesian contact, iron and shark-skin sandpaper were added to this list. They painted on stone, on flesh, on bark, and on the carved wooden objects they made. They also constructed a wide range of emblems of various kinds; and for decoration they had such things as blood, feathers, flowers, wild cotton, and twine made from human hair, animal fur, or vegetable fibres. In short, they used almost everything at their disposal. Some of their productions are roughly done—mere daubs—but others are outstanding masterpieces. Not all Aborigines are natural artists. Just as

6

in our own society, there are some who are more competent than others.

There is a tendency for many writers, even for art historians, to speak of Aboriginal art generally as being comparable to European palaeolithic art: to suggest that in some way it represents a 'primitive survival' which will provide us with information about the origins of art. Sir Herbert Read (Marian W. Smith, ed., 1961: 14-21), in a recent assessment, accepts this approach on the grounds that 'there does not seem to be any valid reason why (the philosophical and social life of palaeolithic man of Europe) should have differed greatly from that of the primitive man of Australia. . . .' He goes on to ask, and answer, a number of questions about prehistoric art, on the basis of Australian Aboriginal material. But valid answers cannot be obtained by such means, because the Aboriginal art available to us today is contemporary, or almost so, and no more prehistoric than the people who are responsible for it. It is true that certain cave paintings and rock engravings may indeed be quite ancient, and may legitimately be termed prehistoric (see Plates 2, 10, 45, 47, 48 and 49); more recent designs have been superimposed on these, and there are no living people who are able to tell us about the meanings of those that appear to be earlier, except to make guesses about them. But, apart from this, nearly all the illustrations in this book refer to *contemporary* Aboriginal art; and this has no special associations with the art of palaeolithic, or stone-age man. To speak of Aboriginal art in this sense, as primitive, is misleading. Aboriginal societies over the centuries developed their own particular styles, just as has been the case in other parts of the world. We should not evaluate them against our own. We have many art styles; the Aborigines also had many, with differences between one part of the continent and another. The bounds within which Aboriginal artists worked (in relation to the range of material and technical equipment available to them, and the demand for conformity to traditional standards) did not prevent the development of sophisticated art forms. What we see is in no sense raw experimental art, or art in its early stages of development. In Sir Herbert Read's view (*ibid.*: 21), Aboriginal art 'remains at a childish stage of development'. Enough has been said to demonstrate the gross inadequacy of such a statement. On the whole this is a mature, adult art, reflective of a people's social and cultural life, and of their underlying values and view of the world. It is also deeply satisfying to both artist and others: not simply because it is aesthetically pleasing and conforms to canons of local taste, but, more importantly, because in designs and subject-matter it is closely integrated with both the religious and secular life of the people.

Significance of Aboriginal Art: All Aboriginal art is basically utilitarian. It is specifically planned to have some use, some direct or indirect purpose, or effect. This is particularly so with paintings, carvings, objects, or emblems, used in sacred ritual. Over and above their decorative interest, these are tangible representations of the sacred mythological past in the present, the bridge that links man with his gods. In addition, much Aboriginal art is of magical intent. Part has to do with the increase of the natural species —the belief that a drawing, either alone or in conjunction with some ritual action, or song or chant, will release the spirit inherent in its subject-matter. This aspect, because it is closely related to religion, has been called magico-religious. It is brought out clearly by Professor Elkin in connection with the Wandjina. (See Plates 19, 43 and 44.) Many of the paintings and carvings in the galleries of Aboriginal Australia were prepared for such a purpose. Some of the great totemic beings, at the end of their travels during the creative era, are said to have made themselves into Dreaming—made themselves spiritually immortal, or eternal—and left their images in the shape of paintings on a cliff-face, or on the wall of a shelter. In local belief, retouching the painting released the spirit that was latent in it, and so ensured the increase of that particular species.

Other drawings and carvings had more obviously magical aims: a hunter, shown in the act of spearing an animal; a desired woman, designed to attract her attention and entice her magically toward the artist; a sorcerer's image of his intended victim. There were paintings recording noteworthy incidents in everyday life—an outstanding hunting, or fishing expedition; a ceremony, or ritual; or scenes illustrating stories and myths, serving as statements to 'verify' them.

Art and Leisure: Although there are examples of doodling, there is little evidence that Aborigines drew or carved entirely for pleasure, to fill in an idle moment. The nearest approach to this would possibly be the bark hut 'murals' of Arnhem Land. It is more likely, however, that most secular art was an aspect, or an accompaniment, of story-telling—as in the Aranda sand drawings described by Strehlow (Chapter Four). Undoubtedly, there would have been much enjoyment associated with this. In this respect we could probably say that there is a close relationship between art and leisure.

In their traditional environment the Aborigines were faced with the almost constant task of foraging for food. Even so, they seem to have had a certain amount of time left for other things. One obvious illustration is provided by the elaborate ceremonies, or festivals, which were held seasonally, and usually covered a number of weeks. These required a great deal of preliminary planning and effort, not only in the preparation of objects and emblems, but also in making sure that there was sufficient food for that period. Then, again, there are the miles of cave paintings and carvings scattered throughout the continent—inevitably raising the question of the time that must have been spent in putting them there.

These Aborigines were not sedentary, but semi-nomadic. Nothing stood between themselves and their physical environment. Every man was a hunter, every woman a food collector. In the circumstances, the fact that they were able to produce carvings, paintings, and objects of various kinds, in large quantities, is even more remarkable. The answer lies not so much in the availability of leisure, enabling them to do so, but in the realm of stark necessity. This brings us back to the religious significance of most of Aboriginal art. To live securely within their natural and physical environment, it was necessary for these people to come to terms with it. Religion (of which art was one external manifestation) gave this security. But to cope with the ritual and other demands they associated with it called for a form of social organization that emphasized interdependence, one in which all persons within the confines of a particular social system were closely linked, with reciprocal obligations and responsibilities, allowing for a maximum of co-operation. This provided some with the opportunity to paint or carve, while others carried out more mundane tasks; but the division was a fluctuating one. It did not harden into a separation of identity between 'art specialists' and 'others'.

Representational and Abstract Art: Aboriginal art, whether in a religious, magical, or secular context, is frequently representational. But just as frequently, especially where religious art is concerned, it is what we might call abstract, or highly conventionalized. Observers unfamiliar with various Aboriginal styles often classify items of purely representational and naturalistic art as abstract. But a particular tradition itself prescribes, at least in broad terms, just how certain subjects should be depicted. Aboriginal artists did not work from nature, or employ human models to pose for them. They did not endeavour to reproduce photographically what they actually saw. Rather, they made use of existing codes to express what they wanted to say. In some cases the results are strikingly realistic, as in the case of drawings of natural species in western Arnhem Land and elsewhere. In others, where the accepted ways of representing men and women as well as animals and other things were more highly formalized, the result was not a complete description of an event as it might be seen by an onlooker, but a stylized or compressed statement about it. Thus in northeastern Arnhem Land special designs indicate clouds, others rain falling, water, leaves, and so on. (See Plates 53, 59 and 69.) This conventionalization is even more marked in Central Aus-

8

tralia, with its relatively narrow range of basic symbols standing for particular things. But all designs, whatever their degree of abstraction, were intended to be understood by someone. The artist was not simply talking to himself. The formalized is no more difficult to comprehend than the realistic,when both stem from the same tradition: when both are part of a familiar local pattern, even though the one may correspond much more closely than the other to its counterparts in the real physical world. Although some Aboriginal art is symbolic, much can be understood immediately in terms of its subject-matter: there is a great deal which can be readily identified, whether it be a realistic or highly stylized representation.

Nevertheless, although the actual figures or shapes or drawings themselves may be easily recognizable to members of the social unit to which the artist belongs, the context in which they appear, singly or in combination, may have to be explained. They may refer to myths, told only to certain sections of the community at certain times—during an initiation sequence, for instance. Or if they have further symbolic associations, perhaps esoteric or secret ones, these too will have to be taught, and learnt. Sex differentiation, social and ritual status and prestige, are involved here: thus art-as-communication can tell us something about social positioning and social relations. But, generally speaking, all Aboriginal art is designed to convey meaning, either to the community as a whole, or to a specific category within it. And it can succeed in that intention only among those belonging to that society, or sharing its particular tradition.

External Influences: Aboriginal art, then, has probably been subject to some changes over the years: styles have altered, individual artists have introduced innovations. In some cases, there is a tolerance of adaptation and of subject-matter differing from what was regarded as traditional. There is also the problem of diffusion; McCarthy mentions this in relation to some styles. The most striking examples come from north-eastern Arnhem Land. Carved human figures (illustrated in Plates 68 and 69; see Chapter Two) show the influence of Macassan (Indonesian) traders who visited that coast over a period of some hundreds of years up to the beginning of this century. So do many of the designs or patterns found in Arnhem Land art. But in their translation they have become Aboriginal.

Carved Figures: The actual carving of a complete human figure in the round is a fairly recent development. Traditionally such objects in north-eastern Arnhem Land were post-figures, made to represent human beings, but very highly conventionalized. As a rule they were shaped from a solid log of wood, the top chipped to represent a head, of sorts, the trunk painted and incised with totemic designs. The figures from this area are almost unique for Aboriginal Australia, especially in their more elaborately developed form as illustrated in this volume. In Arnhem Land the art of wood carving and shaping was much more highly developed than in the rest of Aboriginal Australia, with a wide range of naturalistic and stylized figures of various creatures used, particularly, as ritual emblems. There were also painted log coffins, human skulls, and a number of other objects (see Plate 73).

Tall carved and painted mortuary poles were common along the north coast and on adjacent islands—for instance, the mortuary posts of Bathurst and Melville islands. (See Plates 5, 6, 7 and 8, and also Spencer, 1914: Plate X; Mountford, 1958a.) In the central and inland regions, too, poles were used, but mainly for sacred ritual. (See Chapter Four.) In the Kunapipi (Gunabibi)—Gadjari rituals of the Northern Territory, primarily concerned with fertility (see Chapter One, and R. Berndt, 1951a), large constructions up to eighteen or twenty feet high were made of bushes, grass, and sapling poles, bound closely together, and superimposed with designs marked out in feather down stuck on with blood. These *jelmalandji*, as they were called in some places, represented either the Great Mother, or a monstrous rock python, or both. In one part of the Territory they were tipped with bunches of feathers, with pearlshells to represent eyes.

Although human figures carved in wood have been reported from other regions, too, they were not common. Nor were human figures moulded from ochre or clay. The ochre head and bust shown in Plate 69, from Oenpelli in western Arnhem Land, is a development of a more simple and roughly made form used in sorcery (black magic). In north-eastern Arnhem Land moulded beeswax human figures and creatures were used for hunting or love magic, or for sorcery. And throughout Arnhem Land, as well as in the Kimberleys, human images of paperbark, or stringy-bark, or bound fibre were made for sorcery, for mortuary signposts, or to provide company for the corpse of a newly dead person alone on its mortuary platform.

Criteria of Appreciation: When we, as outsiders, approach Aboriginal art, we should keep in mind several basic points that undoubtedly influence our appreciation of it. Firstly, we should try to view it without prejudice, and to refrain from evaluating it, in the sense of judging it or assessing its merits and defects, on the basis of standards and specimens from our own, or any other society. Secondly, all such art is the mature product of a long tradition; the apparent exceptions are merely examples of poor work, or poor craftmanship. Its very simplicity is often deceptive—most notably as far as Central Australian art is concerned. It is much more sophisticated than it seems. At its best, in some of the northern cave or bark paintings, for instance, there can be no doubt that we are in the presence of great art, having a vitality and a beauty of its own.

Thirdly, there are a number of different styles or art traditions throughout the continent, and within any one of these a limited range of variation may be discerned. Fourthly, all Aboriginal art had (or has) meaning. Appreciation of any example of such art is dependent on what it means, or what it has to convey or say to its viewer, and on what it is supposed to do. It is not simply a matter of a pleasant pattern, or bizarre figures. Behind every painting, every object, every decorative design, lies a story of some sort: some explanation is called for. Unless we know something about this, we cannot pretend to understand Aboriginal art. Fifthly, because an artist draws or carves according to certain conventions, he does not try to capture, or reproduce, an exact replica of the real or natural situation. The natural world is all about him, and it would be pointless to attempt to encapsulate it on a sheet of bark, on a rock surface, or in a lump of wood. He aims at something different. The form, of course, needs to correspond to the original, in either a naturalistic or stylized way, but it is the essence of the thing which really interests him, and which he strives to set down.

Significantly, the Aborigines had no separate words which we can translate as 'art', or as 'artist', although there were words for painting, for carving, for incising, and so on. There was no need to separate this form of activity, which we call art, from other forms, and to give it a special name. They took for granted the beauty of the world around them, of which they themselves were part; and what they produced was essentially in harmony with their surroundings.

CHAPTER ONE

Art and Life

A. P. ELKIN

In Western-European-type society, painting and sculpture, music and ballet are usually the interest of small groups, almost esoteric in composition, and have little significance for the vast majority; the art gallery, the conservatorium, and the high-priced theatre are the temples of the arts, and only a minority of citizens enter therein. Fortunately, some religious organizations make the arts part of the context of their worship and instruction, and so keep them before the consciousness of their members.

Art, and Aboriginal Life: The situation, however, is very different among a people of relatively simple culture, in which the pattern of life is the same for all and is visible to all. The Australian Aborigines are such a people. They exist solely on what they gather and catch, and do so in an environment which for the most part is not bountiful and, indeed, is often very difficult. Therefore they are constantly on the move in small groups, each in an area well-known to it. Only in the few more favourable regions, and occasionally elsewhere when times are good, can a number of groups camp and hunt together for a period, arrange marriages, exchange goods, perform ceremonies and rituals, and so enrich their tribal and intertribal life.

This semi-nomadic, food-gathering economy prevents the development of permanent settlements and even of houses, except of simple and temporary form, and puts a heavy discount on impedimenta. The life of each family and individual is an open book, read by all members of the clan and of any associated group. This is true not only of general social behaviour and economic pursuits, but also of art in its several forms. Even the most abstruse symbols and doctrines of the men's secret cult are revealed in due time to all males, and the women's secret rites and chants to all females. Everyone in the vicinity sees the camp or public dances, and the designs painted or arranged on the dancers' bodies and on the symbols they wear or carry. Indeed, all may take part at least by joining in the singing, or beating the time—the accompaniment of the dancing. As the eyes of the children gradually close and sounds grow fainter and fainter in their ears, they drop off to sleep in a context of song and dance, of symbol and design; and a little later, moving to their camp-fires close by, the adults do likewise. They sleep, not just dreaming, but *in* the Dreaming. Thus art, as represented in music and ballet, on painted body and emblem, is an inescapable

11

element in their lives. They do not choose it; it comes to them and enters the depths of their minds.

Later on, too, as the years go by, the males are admitted, amidst impressive solemnity, into the secret and sacred archives of the tribe. These may include, according to the region, engravings on rock or on trees, designs drawn or raised on the ground, and paintings on rock galleries, in addition to engravings and paintings on movable objects. Then it is they realize that art forms of painting and engraving, as well as of chanting and dancing, are a ritual expression of traditionally moulded desire and also a sacramental means of satisfying it.

Appreciation of Aboriginal Art — A Tardy Development: A century was to pass from the time of the first European settlement in Australia, before observers stepped over the threshold into the shrine of meaning within the natural temple of Aboriginal art. And yet specimens of this art were the earliest fixed signs and memorials of the Aborigines which the newcomers saw. The usual outward forms of an indigenous culture were as elusive as the natives themselves, but rock engravings were found near Port Jackson in the first years of settlement, and rock paintings on Chasm Island in the west of the Gulf of Carpentaria in 1803; on Clack's Island, far North Queensland, in 1827; in the south-western corner of the continent in 1830; and in the northern Kimberley in 1838. Indeed, into whatever region explorers and settlers pushed, sooner or later rock galleries of paintings or engravings were found. And although these were often described as uncouth, yet they were 'specimens of Australian taste in the fine arts' (King, 1827), 'proof of (the natives') ingenuity', exhibiting 'tolerably strong likenesses' (White, 1790), and 'showing that the natives were not without notions of sculpture' (Stockdale, 1789-90). Perhaps too, the galleries held some special significance; at least, Captain Stokes (1846) reflected 'on the curious frame of mind that could induce these uncultivated people to repair, perhaps at stated seasons of the year, to this lonely picture gallery . . . (on Depuch Island,

Western Australia) to admire and add to the productions of their forefathers.' And by 1853 Flanagan, a brilliant young contributor to Henry Parkes' journal, *Empire*, saw in this painting, however rude, 'a systematic longing after the development of the sublime capabilities of humanity', which seems to contradict the doctrine 'that man in a primitive state of barbarism does not possess within himself the power of attaining the most elevated status of the human race'. (Flanagan, 1888: 27.)

This is fundamental. A people may seem to possess no cultural forms on which civilization can be built—no houses, gardens, flocks and herds, no markets, and no temples. In such case their humanity may be assigned to a low evolutionary phase, as indeed was done by some observers as far as the Aborigines were concerned. But once their art is recognized as the urge to represent the world around and within them, to record the objects and creatures which have interest and meaning for them, and also to express in pictorial form their feelings and desires, their humanity is revealed as of the same order as our own. On rock, on wood, on bark, on the human body and on the ground, on weapons, utensils, ornaments, and on sacred paraphernalia, everywhere in Aboriginal Australia there is, or there has been, this expression of the mind in line, colour, and form, in the language of symbolism.

Moreover, as we have slowly learnt during the past seventy years, these art forms and patterns have grown up within the cultural development and traditions of centuries and, maybe, millennia; they have become a bond through time, witnessing to, and contributing to, the continuity of spiritual life and aspiration. In addition to being time-binding, these forms override spatial frontiers; for their 'prettiness', their visual appeal, and the generalized meaning enshrined in them educe reactions of appreciation and often, too, of reverence. The patterns and their interpretation may vary from tribe to tribe, but those patterns so carefully engraved or painted are basically symbols of the fundamental doctrine of the Dreaming, of the formative, life-ensuring

12

period of the past, which, however, is always potentially present; it is indeed the context of life from generation to generation, from north and south, and east to west. Art is a means of expressing the timeless and non-spatial spirit of man, be he dubbed primitive or civilized.

Adaptation and the Challenge of the Contingent: The Aborigines, being utterly dependent as food-gatherers and hunters on what nature provides, built up a systematic body of knowledge regarding their tribal and regional environments. Modified by experience in changing conditions through time, this heritage has been passed on from generation to generation by example and instruction. They know *where* and *when* and *how* to get the food they need. They can read the signs and anticipate the seasons. They make implements and weapons and other accessories for use in the food-quest. And, in addition, their social organization and behaviour are correlated with the semi-nomadism, which is inherent in food-gathering and hunting. In other words, their adaptation is intellectual, technological, and social.

In spite, however, of the Aborigines' accumulated knowledge and skill, and in spite of living according to their appropriate social order, droughts and floods and other untoward circumstances occur; food and water become scarce and life is threatened. In the course of generations the Aborigines have learnt that these undesirable contingencies are an aspect of the environment, and that, although they are unpredictable, they are almost certain to happen some time, somewhere. Therefore, they must be met and, if possible, prevented.

Appearance and Reality: Without irrigation and conservation, however, and without cultivation and animal husbandry, the Aborigines can do no more than express their desire and their need in thought and word, and in action which is social and ritual, but, as we see it, without effect on natural growth and reproduction. *Their* interpretation is different. They come to terms with their environment and 'all that is therein'. Natural species and phenomena are the present-day outward signs, the varied sacramental forms

of 'personal' creatures who were active as such in the Dreaming, along with human beings of heroic proportions—that is, culture-heroes and even deities. The Dreaming, however, is not just a heroic period in the past; it is timeless. The essential life of the beings and creatures of that age is always present, though seemingly inactive. When their heroic course was run, they became 'shades' associated with relics—with memorials in paintings and engravings, with stones or other objects and phenomena. But as shades, they are still potent, for it is in the shade within, not in the external form, that power and the life-giving principle reside. Consequently they, or emanations from them, are expressed, incarnated as it were, from age to age, in human beings and in natural species and phenomena. And it is the purpose of a great class of Aboriginal rituals to ensure the continuity of this process.

The Bond of Symbolism: Thus, as man and nature belonged on the heroic level to the one order of life and action in the Dreaming, so it is now, although on an everyday level. As the outward sign of this, Aboriginal social groups, among which the clan into which a person is born is fundamental, include both human beings and also, in each case, certain natural species and objects. These latter are the totems, usually referred to by the Aborigines as 'flesh' and in specified cases as Dreamings. They are regarded as relatives, and at the same time as symbols of the genealogical relationship which exists between the human members of that particular group, and ultimately as symbols of a mythological relationship between man and those natural species and objects—that is, between the shades of each.

Therefore, on the one hand, all persons with the same totem are brothers and sisters, and also mothers and children if membership of the clan (or moiety or phratry) be determined through the mother (that is, by matrilineal descent), or fathers and children if membership be patrilineal. For them to intermarry would be incestuous and fraught with disastrous consequences, and therefore traditionally punishable with death, no matter how distant their genealogical relationship as we would reckon it. On the other hand the totemic animal or plant, bird, or insect is not simply a natural species; it is a symbol of the association of man and such species in the Dreaming, and indeed of the transformation of one into the other.

This symbolic or, indeed, sacramental bond between man and nature is even clearer in the belief regarding the passing of spirit-children to the mothers' wombs. This may occur through plant or animal, water-pool or whirlwind. The food which a woman eats, the billabong into which she steps, the rushing column of wind which she fails to avoid, or the mythological totemic centre, a Dreaming, in the vicinity of which she passes by: any one of these may at any time be the medium of spirit-children. And so, too, may be the animal or fish or bird, which the husband spears at the time of his wife's 'conception'—it changes before his eyes into a pre-existent child, and goes with him to his wife. Here again things are not merely what they seem. The human shade within the outward plant or animal appearance, or at the totemic centre, the rainbow snake within the pool or whirling wind: these constitute the significant ideas.

With this background the Aboriginal artist is not basically concerned with representing, or reflecting as in a mirror, natural things just as they appear. He may sometimes do so quite skilfully. His approach, however, is through myth and doctrine to the shade or spirit within the creature or object represented. The significance of the symbol, not the portrait or image, is the important thing; and for this purpose, abstract, geometrical, and conventional representation will serve as well as naturalistic—perhaps better. Through it communication is made with the Dreaming, with the ever-present channel of life in man and nature. For man's need is to secure the passing of the pre-existent spirits and the 'living shades' or 'germs' into objective form, so that children may be born, animals and plants increase, and rain fall.

This is ensured by appropriate behaviour and by appropriate ritual: by correct behaviour toward one's clansmen and kinsfolk; by circumspect behaviour toward one's totem and, indeed, toward the totems of others also; and by caring for the mythological or Dreaming centres, by preserving the myths, chants, emblems, and designs, connected with these, and by performing the associated rituals.

It is only in these ways that the Dreaming becomes sacramentally and effectively present, and the future assured.

Art and the Contingent: Here the artist's contribution is of vital significance. His immediate purpose, or nearer goal, is to re-present myth and belief in order to preserve continuity with the Dreaming, to make the unseen cause and context of life and action 'in some way tangible and visible', and so bring each generation into conscious and continuous relationship with it. This is done with tremendous dramatic effect in the arid, central regions, and in a more restrained but no less effective manner in the kinder north. In the former region, as the scene rises before me, so vivid is my recollection, I see again a group of men, the chorus, chanting for hours; suddenly there appears an actor, on whom sacred designs have been applied and emblems attached in deep secrecy; excitement rises; the chanting becomes more accentuated; members of the chorus rise, draw blood from themselves, and dance in a vigorous, backward slide until they are on the verge of collapse. And why? Because the Dreaming has become manifest in the decorated figure who performs his ritual act. Nietzsche saw this with the eye of genius as he analysed the 'Birth of Tragedy' in the Greek chorus and drama: 'The Chorus is now assigned the task of exciting the minds of the audience to such a pitch of Dionysian frenzy, that, when the tragic hero appears on the stage, they do not see in him an unshapely man wearing a mask, but they see a visionary figure, born as it were of their own ecstasy'. And this, he adds, is nothing else than 'the Apollonian dream-state, in which the world of today is veiled, and a new world, clearer, more intelligible, more vivid and yet more shadowy than

14

the old, is, by a perpetual transformation, born and reborn before our eyes'. (Nietzsche, 1871: 218–19.) It is this 'new world', the real world, the Dreaming, which through ritual art — painting, engraving, chanting, and dancing—is reborn before the eyes of the initiated in the totemic and major cult-ceremonies of the Aborigines. In this way the future is believed to be assured. The contingent has been faced. Tragedy has been averted.

These rituals of the Dreaming include much visual art, such as body paintings representing totemic motifs; wooden objects, painted or engraved, or composite ones built up out of wood, bark, and string, and decorated and painted to represent totemic and heroic themes; and engravings of the rainbow serpent on the walls of the symbolic earth-womb of the 'mother goddess' in the Kunapipi (Gunabibi) cult of southern Arnhem Land. Moreover, the engraving and painting of such objects are ritual acts, forming part of the total ritual.

In the northern Kimberley, however, the painting is not simply part of the over-all ritual. It *is* the ritual. From the King Leopold Ranges to the Drysdale River area, there are very many caves and rock-shelter galleries, in which the main paintings are of a certain type, called Wandjina, or Wondjina. (See Plates 19, 43 and 44.) The Wandjina were heroes of the Dreaming era, who at the end of their travels and exploits 'died' and became paintings; that is, they left their shades on rock-walls. They are usually depicted with eyes and nose, but no mouth. To retouch a painted Wandjina causes rain, and to paint or retouch figures of animals, birds, reptiles, and plants in a Wandjina gallery ensures the increase of the particular species in due season. The painting or retouching *is* the ritual; it is a sacramental act, through which life is mediated to nature and to man. Each local group, always a patrilineal clan, has its gallery or galleries, knows the myth of the gallery's Wandjina, and is responsible for the painting ritual there. The species represented in it are the clan's totems.

This association of rock art and the food-supply is not limited to northern Kimberley. Passing east through the north of the Northern Territory, there are scores of rock galleries of paintings, in which natural species are represented, and also, in many of them, obvious culture-heroes. (See, for example, Plate 38.) In the latter case there is, or must have been, mythology, making the figures permanent manifestations of the Dreaming. But, even if only natural species or hunting and fishing scenes be represented, it does not necessarily follow that the paintings were, or are, done solely for pleasure, to while away the time, or to record a past occurrence. The reference may be to the future, or to both the past and the future. Painting the fish or bird or animal or reptile may express the native's desire for success in the hunt, and also his belief that drawing the picture gives certainty, and even a power over the creature sought. A man sees a fine fish in the river; he paints it on the gallery, and then is sure he will see it again and spear it. So I was told by a native when visiting a gallery in Arnhem Land.

Throughout western and southern Arnhem Land there are many galleries, in which not only is the available surface covered with figures, but figures are painted over each other. (See, for example, Plates 3, 4, 38, 39, 40, 41, 42, 51.) Clearly, the important thing was, and is, the act of painting the figures—not contemplating them afterward as works of art. The painter expressed himself, his desire, and his beliefs. His painting was not rubbed out, and so remained effective. Painting over it did not matter. His symbolic art was there for all time. Indeed, one native friend of mine said that a person liked to paint something on a gallery in his clan country, for then those who saw it when he was away or dead would remember him and feel sorry.

There is nothing in the known mythology, beliefs, and values of Aborigines from east to west and north to south to lead us to suppose that the significance of rock galleries varies in general meaning. We may, therefore, interpret those in regions in which the Aborigines had died out before we studied them, along the same lines as those we know in the centre and

15

in the north. For example, the galleries in the Port Jackson-Hawkesbury River region (see Plates 9, 10 and 11), in western New South Wales, and at Port Hedland, Western Australia, are almost certainly records in stone of doctrine and myth, and of ritual acts for ensuring success in the food-search and continuity of the species on which the tribes depended for life. The grooving and regrooving, or the pecking until an intagliated surface was produced, was surely the renewed, seasonal expression of man's need, and of his belief in the efficacy of the myths and beliefs on which his hope was based, and which were indicated on the rock.

Through Art to Faith: Hope, as mentioned earlier, springs from right conduct and right ritual. These are the prerequisites for well-being in man and nature. And this is the twofold lesson and vision which the individual learns during childhood and adolescence, and, especially in the case of males, during the years of initiation. He does so partly through direct precept, but more impressively through song and chant, through legend and myth, through representations in dance and drama, and through painted or engraved designs and figures, both temporary and permanent. In other words the whole gamut of art is brought to bear on adolescence and early adulthood. Through it the young man absorbs the moral sanctions, is caught up in the myths and doctrines which are the source of those sanctions, and senses the symbolic relationship which exists between himself and nature. The visual art patterns and forms, be these naturalistic, conventional, 'geometrical', or abstract, are a tracing board, a symbolical key to life as it has been, and should be, traced. The meander and the maze; the spiral; the concentric circles and diamonds; the wavy or the angled lines; the U and the arc; the tracks and other markings; and often, too, the figures of man, animal, plant, and inanimate objects: what are these but symbols of the deeds of ancestors and culture-leaders, and signposts along the way they followed—the way which must be followed by each generation of men, even as they rub their fingers along the grooves

and over the paint, chanting as they 'go'!

'The blackfellow doesn't make a mark that has no meaning', said an old Aboriginal. To him with esoteric perception, the geometrical, conventional, and abstract patterns may indicate camp or water-place, road or river, cloud or sky, hill or tree, man or animal, a direction or a warning. They are doors opening out of the expanse of myth and doctrine, of sanction and belief. And this is, of course, true also of the naturalistic figures and designs. In symbolic effort Aboriginal man reaches beneath, or beyond, the external forms to the permanent Ideas of Plato's philosophy, seeking laws of nature and life, and sure, though unseen, grounds of hope. He passes from the particular and ephemeral to the general and lasting. It is thus that he can 'live on even terms with Time'. In his art, to use the words from Emerson's essay on art, 'All the weary miles and tons of space and bulk (are) left out, and the spirit or moral of it contracted into . . . the most cunning stroke of' his painting or engraving tool.

Art, Skill, and Purpose: We must not hastily think that the Aborigines resorted to lineal designs or, in painted and engraved naturalistic figures, represented parts or organs out of proportion, because of lack of knowledge, technical skill and equipment, or because of the intractable nature of the surface to be painted or the material to be engraved. Of course, native artists accommodate their work to the material on and with which they work. Curr (1886, I: 96) observed eighty years or so ago that 'as long as the carver cut pretty well across the grain of the wood, he (might) incline his line to a curve', but when his bone, shell, or flint implement had 'to take a direction nearly the same as the grain, it (was) almost impossible to prevent it following the grain, especially perhaps, when the wood (was) green'.

Such difficulty or restriction, however, did not prevent the engraver in wood from producing on weapons and sacred emblems effective and attractive designs, with contrast of light and shade, built up of grooved straight lines and angles. This was the case in south-eastern Australia and over a wide region of Western Australia, whereas in south-western Queensland and in central and north-central Australia, including east Kimberley, curved, and circular, and spiral engraved designs were typical—and not only in wood, but also, in the last named region, on secret stone emblems of *tjurunga* type. (See Plate 70.)

Engraving on stone surfaces with stone tools is no easy matter, but the crudeness, or uncouthness, which sometimes appears is not necessarily attributable to technical difficulties, and certainly not to lack of patience. The skill with which a north-central or far north-western Aboriginal selects his material and then makes the long, three-sided, flaked spear-point, or the artistic, pressure-flaked spear-point, respectively, leaves no doubt on this. The Aboriginal artist surely selected a suitable stone-face to be his gallery of petroglyphs, and also suitable stone tools with which to bore, cut, groove, or peck into it. Moreover, the apparent defects, which often appear in naturalistic designs on petroglyph galleries, such as crudeness of outline, lack of proportion in depicting certain organs, and inexactness regarding fingers and toes, appear also in paintings on rock and even on bark and wooden objects, where the artist has few technical problems.

In any case, why should we expect the Aborigines to be over-anxious about these details? Ruskin (1873), declaring that Holbein drew 'skeleton after skeleton, in every possible gesture', but never so much as (counted) their ribs, commented that 'nothing has ever more pleased me than this grand negligence'. And of Albrecht Dürer's engraving he wrote, 'The dots are not all measured in distance; the lines not all mathematically parallel or divergent. He has even missed his mark at the mouth in one place, and leaves the mistake, frankly. But there are no petrified mistakes . . .' So, too, the Aboriginal engraver and painter sometimes misses the mark, or does not count the fingers carefully. He is concerned with something wider and deeper.

We must remember that the Aborigines are pre-eminent observers of natural species and objects, and that some of their artistic work is far from crude and uncouth, even in our eyes. If, then, they represent their subjects crudely and with inaccuracies, the reason is that they have no need to be exact; the engraving or painting or shaped piece of wood is the symbol of the shade of the species, not the replica of an individual member of it. Further, when they draw or engrave a culture-hero or other mythical being with an unnatural massiveness, or with an organ or feature accentuated, they may be focusing attention on a significant theme in the myth, the meaning of which will be known to instructed viewers.

Moreover, it is this priority of meaning which enables the artist freely to blend and modify his subjects in a painting in accord with the total design, or the amount and configuration of the area of rock, tree-trunk, bark, or emblem. What Agnes Schulz (1946: 55) says of certain Wandjina galleries in the northern Kimberley has been noted in many parts of Australia: 'It is remarkable how ingeniously the paintings are interwoven with the rock formations. Particular figures are accented by means of bulges and projections. Nowhere is there any inconsistency; all representations are so co-ordinated with one another and with the rocks that the effect is organic and magnificent.'

Thus, because his purpose is symbolic—that is, to indicate value and meaning—the Aboriginal artist can let himself go, and express 'his innate desire for shape and order', for prettiness as he sees it, without interfering with that purpose.

Motive and Origin: This emphasis on symbolism does not imply that, in pre-European conditions, Aborigines painted or engraved only when ritual or tradition required such activity. They may have done so merely because they wanted to; but the evidence for this, except in northern Arnhem Land, is meagre. I certainly saw none either in south-central arid regions, or in the northern Kimberley at a period, over thirty years ago, when contact was very slight.

Further, the problem of whether Aboriginal art was religious and magical in origin, or arose out of an innate urge to express in material form what was seen and felt, is probably insoluble. Perhaps the two are but aspects of man's adaptation to his environment. We do know that this art derives meaning from the magico-religious sphere. Engravings and paintings on weapons and implements may seem to be done from aesthetic motives only, but actually the decoration is an essential and required part of the finished article, and when studied in the living situation turns out to be of mythological significance: it endows the article with heroic—that is, with Dreaming—effectiveness. This may have been the case everywhere. Of course, we do not know, because early, and indeed later, observers were lacking or simply failed to inquire. We do know, however, that sacred designs are depicted both on secret paraphernalia and on everyday articles, indicating that 'Dreaming virtue' is not absent from secular contexts.

Similarly, in northern regions the designs which are painted on the bodies of ritual actors in an atmosphere of solemnity and secrecy, often to the accompaniment of chanting, are left on them when the ritual is over. They go to the general camp, where everybody sees the designs and knows they are a visible break-through of the secret and sacred. In parts of Arnhem Land, also, as Baldwin Spencer saw in 1912, a person may paint designs on the walls of his hut, itself a temporary, seasonal structure. (Spencer, 1928: 792–3; Elkin and R. and C. Berndt, 1950:13.) He may do this because he wants to while away an idle hour, to leave his mark, or to have something aesthetically pleasing around him. At Oenpelli in the same region, the walls of some caves up in a hill where people sometimes passed the nights beyond mosquito range were 'decorated with quaint but often very realistic drawings of the animals on which they fed' (Spencer, 1914: 32). Some Aborigines confined in Palmerston (Darwin) jail toward the end of last century transferred this type of artistic endeavour to the walls of their cells. (Worsnop, 1897: 37.) Howitt also reported that the Gippsland natives used to bend a sheet of bark across the middle, 'set it up like a tent, and then draw figures inside with charcoal, or perhaps red-ochre' (Smyth, 1878, I: 292.) In other words, home art was not unknown.

However, we must notice that what we may term home art and painting in a secular, or non-ritual context has been observed almost solely after the Aborigines have been in contact with, and influenced by, Europeans. (For example, Smyth, 1878, I: 268–88.) As a result of such contact there has been some change in attitudes and values. The logical end-result is seen in Arnhem Land, where artists are busy preparing bark paintings for a ready market, at times using bark canvases sixfold the traditional size; they cover the enlarged surface with traditional designs, although sometimes incorporating introduced motifs, and command high prices for this work. Still, this is genuine Arnhem Land art, done with indigenous ochres and 'brushes'. It differs from the introduced water-colour painting of the Hermannsburg School of Aranda artists in Central Australia. Forsaking the geometrical and naturalistic art of their region, and inspired by the work of a visiting European artist, Albert Namatjira and his followers developed a thriving business, painting scenes from the local environment with its mountains, trees, and striking colours.

In all their art, however, be it secret, sacred or secular, indigenous or introduced, the Aborigines reveal a feeling for design, for line and

1 Rock-pool with adjacent shelter, at Mulyareena Creek, western New South Wales. Aborigines lived in such shelters, and there made their paintings **2** Section of a gallery at Mulyareena Creek, showing human figures holding boomerangs and shields **3** Part of a cave or shelter at Mulyareena Creek. There are various human figures, possibly referring to hunting or fighting, a kangaroo or wallaby chase, and two stencils **4** Cave paintings at Iona Station, western New South Wales; among other designs are sets of small human figures

curve, for balance and colour, for composition and movement. Whether they paint, engrave, or carve, sing or dance, they are artists, not fumblers.

Variety—its Significance: This fact of sureness and efficiency suggests some antiquity for Aboriginal art, and undoubtedly archaeologists will be able, through modern methods, to determine the approximate and relative ages of the various galleries, and to work out time-phases in the techniques of rock carving, grooving, and pecking, and in the use of colours as well as in the designs of both petroglyphs and rock paintings. Indeed, there is already some advance.

In the meantime we can record and seek the significance of the variety in Aboriginal visual art according to regions and, even, schools. There is no space here to analyse the variations, and to attempt systematic correlations with the different environments and available media, and with variations in social organization, ritual, and mythology. A few suggestions must suffice. The culture-hero concept of eastern Australia does seem to be associated with the rock carvings of this vast region, with the carved trees (dendroglyphs, as they are called) around some ceremonial grounds, and probably, also, with the well-developed polished and pecked stone-implement technique of the same region. Similarly, the rock engravings of the Port Hedland region may well be associated with the Bagadjimbiri type of sky culture-hero mythology of that part of the continent.

A different theme appears in the rock paintings of northern Kimberley, which are an expression of the Wandjina clan-hero mythology, while in the crowded galleries of western and southern Arnhem Land the dominance or, at least, the prevalence of female subjects may be correlated with the centrality of the cult-heroine and fertility-mother concepts of that region. Again, the designs on bark and on sacred wooden objects as on the human body, which are symbolic in character, having only occasional naturalistic features, are associated with the doctrine of the shade, that unseen and eternal double which man and nature possess, clan by clan.

On the other hand, the predominantly geometrical patterns of the arid regions, especially the concentric circles, squares, and diamonds, and the parallel lines joining them, may surely be correlated with the travellings of the earth-bound heroes of the Dreaming from water to water, the sources and sustaining centres of life. And the large rock paintings of the rainbow snake in appropriate rock shelters express the desire for that link with the world on top, without which there would be no rain, and consequently no water present in the 'wells' and rock-holes.

Finally, the variety in Aboriginal art, as represented both on weapons, implements, and ritual paraphernalia, and also on bark and rock, shows that, although there are traditional, tribal, and regional and ritual patterns, new ideas and new techniques have been worked out or obtained in some way and accepted. The Aborigines are no more hidebound in their art, be this painting, engraving, chanting, or dancing, than in their artifacts, their social organization, their ritual, or their ceremonies. The virtuoso, the dreamer, the innovator, the leader, is part of the social system. Through him, modifications of the old and also new themes are revealed. These are not 'something-nothing', matters of little or no account; they are the welling-up of the Dreaming, and therein lies the path of life.

CHAPTER TWO

The Art of Arnhem Land

C. P. MOUNTFORD

The Aboriginal practice of painting or scratching simple pictures on bark appears to have been widespread wherever the Aborigines used sheets of bark to construct their wet-weather shelters. Few examples of this art from southern Australia and none from Tasmania have survived. This is probably due, in the first place, to the fact that the early settlers took little or no interest in that aspect of Aboriginal life, and, secondly, that in those early stages of colonization there were no institutions in which such perishable materials could be stored.

Nevertheless, as early as 1807, a sketch by Péron's artist (Péron and Freycinet, 1807: Plate 15) illustrated sheets of bark, with symbolic designs painted on them. Bunce (1857: 49, 50) and several other early travellers in Tasmania also refer to them. Massola (1958:124–7) has shown that the art of painting or scratching designs on the sheets of bark that made up the Aboriginal wet-weather shelters was common throughout Victoria. One of these sheets, described by Brough Smyth (1878, I: Fig. 40), is in the collection of the National Museum of Victoria, and another, recently described by Massola (1958: 128), in the British Museum. Mathews (1896: 155) quotes many examples of

bark paintings having been used in the Bora initiation ceremonies of the eastern coast of Australia, while Dunbar (1943: 146) refers to the Aborigines of the Darling River painting designs on the trunks of trees adjacent to these initiation grounds.

Although there are no bark paintings from central or northern Queensland in museum collections, it is probably safe to assume that here, as elsewhere in Australia, wherever Aborigines built their huts with sheets of bark, they would also have painted designs on their inner surfaces. There, are, however, no records, nor any examples of bark paintings in the central part of the continent. This is probably due to two factors: firstly, that few of the trees are large enough to provide suitable sheets of bark with which to build shelters and, secondly, that the low rainfall and the semi-nomadic life of the Aborigines of this area made permanent shelters unnecessary.

It is in northern Australia, and particularly in Arnhem Land and the adjacent islands, that Aboriginal art as expressed through bark painting has reached its highest development. Campbell (1834: 151) was the first to make reference to bark paintings in northern Australia, when he described some shelters on Melville Island. He wrote, 'Some of them were ornamented with figures drawn in white pipe-clay, one, in particular, being neatly and regularly done all over, resembling the cross-bars of a cell'. This design was similar to a Melville Island bark painting collected and illustrated by Mountford (1958: Plate 52 D). Cox (1878: 155) illustrated a series of bark paintings from Port Essington, a military settlement abandoned in 1849 on the Cobourg Peninsula, western Arnhem Land. More recently I located, in the British Museum, two additional examples of bark paintings from the same locality. I also described (Mountford, 1957: 87–8) six bark paintings collected by Captain Carrington in 1887 from a deserted camp on Field Island, at the mouth of the East Alligator River.

There are a few records of bark paintings from northern Western Australia: the head of a Wandjina figure in the Western Australian Museum (see Plate 19), several depicting reptiles in the National Museum of Victoria, and some with Wandjina figures and reptiles in the British Museum. Petri (1959: Plate 35), leader of the 1938 Frobenius expedition to north-western Australia, illustrates several bark paintings from that area.

Although Worsnop (1897: 87) and Basedow (1925: 38) made passing reference to the bark paintings of northern Australia, it was Sir Baldwin Spencer who first recognized their aesthetic quality and revealed that a rich mythology lay behind them. In 1914 (Plates 72 to 92), and again in 1928 (Figs. 519 to 535), Spencer illustrated a number of such paintings from western Arnhem Land, and recorded the associated myths. Three of Spencer's bark paintings are illustrated in this volume (Plates 22, 30 and 64).

There was little or no research on the art of bark paintings of northern Australia from the time of Spencer's visit to Oenpelli in 1912, until Mountford (1939: 365) illustrated thirty-nine bark paintings collected on Goulburn Island by Miss M. Mathews.

During 1946–7 R. M. and C. H. Berndt first obtained approximately four hundred bark paintings and the relevant myths from the Aborigines of north-eastern Arnhem Land, and more were collected from this region over the years until the present time; also, in 1947, 1949, 1950, and later, a couple of hundred or more were obtained from Oenpelli, and Goulburn Island, in western Arnhem Land. Some of these were illustrated in Elkin and R. and C. Berndt (1950). Illustrations of seven of these bark paintings are included in this volume (Plates 17, 20, 26, 32, 36, 37, and 56).

While in charge of the 1948 National Geographic Society-Commonwealth Government expedition to Arnhem Land, and during two subsequent short visits to the same area, I collected and later described four hundred bark paintings from three localities: Groote Eylandt, north-eastern Arnhem Land, and Oenpelli, western Arnhem Land. (See Mountford, 1956.)

When, in 1954, I was the leader of the second National Geographic Society expedition, this time to Melville Island, I obtained a further one hundred and eighteen bark paintings. These were later illustrated and described. (See Mountford, 1958.) This large collection of over five hundred and fifty bark paintings, illustrated with the meanings of their designs and the relevant myths in books and a number of scientific journals, has all been deposited in art galleries and museums throughout Australia. More recently Dr. Stuart Scougall made a gift to the Art Gallery of New South Wales of an attractive series of bark paintings from north-eastern Arnhem Land.

It will be seen, then, that, owing to the efforts of Sir Baldwin Spencer, Drs. Ronald and Catherine Berndt, Miss M. Mathews, Dr. Stuart Scougall, odd donors, and myself, there are a thousand or more bark paintings available for study in the various art and scientific institutions of Australia. This collection and the accompanying scientific descriptions form a veritable storehouse of Aboriginal art and myth for artists and scholars of this and many succeeding generations.

The Bark Paintings of Arnhem Land and Melville

Island: Within the compass of Arnhem Land, and Melville and Bathurst islands, there are four distinct art regions: (i) north-eastern Arnhem Land; (ii) western Arnhem Land; (iii) Groote Eylandt; and (iv) Melville and Bathurst islands.

Techniques: Before describing the individual bark paintings from these localities, we will examine the materials and techniques employed in their production. They are (i) colours; (ii) fixatives; (iii) brushes; and (iv) flat, dried sheets of bark.

(i) Colours: The Aboriginal artist uses red, yellow, black, and white pigments to paint the designs on the sheets of bark. On Groote Eylandt, where there are no deposits of red ochre, this material must be obtained by trade from the adjacent mainland. But the other colours, yellow, white, and black (a form of manganese ore), are obtained locally. In north-eastern Arnhem Land, there is a plentiful supply of red, yellow, black, and white pigments. Here, however, there is an interesting division in the ownership of colours. Red and white belong to the *dua* moiety of the tribe, and yellow and black to the *jiridja*: only *dua* men collect the red and white, and exchange these for yellow and black pigments. As most of the ochre deposits in western Arnhem Land are of poor quality, the local people obtain the major part of their supplies through trade with adjacent tribes. (See also R. Berndt, 1958a: 251.) On Melville Island there are ample supplies of red, yellow, and white ochres; but in the place of a black pigment, which is unobtainable there, the Aborigines use powdered charcoal.

Throughout Arnhem Land the pigments are ground with water or fixative on flat, coarse-textured stones, until they are of a creamlike consistency. On Melville Island, however, where the ochres are more friable, they are crushed in large cockle-shells and mixed with water and fixative.

(ii) Fixatives: On the mainland the sap of a tree-orchid bulb is commonly used as a fixative. In north-eastern and western Arnhem Land, for example, the broken bulb is rubbed directly on the inner surface of the bark sheet; on Groote Eylandt it is usually mixed with the pigments on the grinding-stone. The Melville Islanders use three different fixatives to ensure that the painted designs on the bark sheets and burial poles are as permanent as possible. They are: the gelatinous sap of one of the tree-orchids, the wax and honey of the wild bee, well mixed together, and the yolks of the eggs of the sea-going turtle.

(iii) Brushes: In Arnhem Land three types of brush are normally used.

(a) A narrow strip of bark, usually from a stringy-bark tree, chewed at one end. (Fig. 1, F.) This is held as in Fig. 1, C, and used for the broader lines. (b) A cylindrical stick, Fig. 1, E, about 3/32nd of an inch in diameter and about three inches long. The brush is held as in Fig. 1, B. (c) The third brush, made either from a few fibres of palm-leaf, or from a small feather, Fig. 1, G and H, demands considerable skill in its use. It is long and flexible, resembling the lining tool used by the coach painters of the last gen-

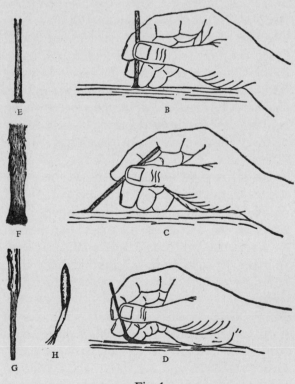

Fig. 1

eration. The brush, held delicately between the fingers as in Fig. 1, D, is drawn away from the body. The intricate cross-hatchings of north-eastern design, and the broken and parallel lines of Groote Eylandt, are all made with this brush. It is not used by the Melville Islanders. Berndt (1958a: 251, Footnote 5) mentions two other brushes used in north-eastern Arnhem Land— a human-hair brush, as well as burred orchid-tuber.

(iv) Sheets of bark: The sheets of bark on which Aborigines paint their designs are stripped from stringy-bark trees. Having selected a tree free from knots and cracks, the Aboriginal makes two cuts around the circumference of the tree, usually about three feet apart. Then, loosening a narrow strip of bark at the bottom of the cut, he pulls it upward. This leaves a narrow vertical opening, into which he inserts a stick, gently levering the bark from the tree and then putting it on a blazing fire. Removing the bark from the fire after a few minutes, he strips the outer fibrous surface until the inner, denser portion of the bark is approximately three-sixteenths of an inch thick. In this condition the bark, which is flexible, is easily flattened and dried.

The procedure I adopted (and, without doubt, other investigators, except Sir Baldwin Spencer, did the same) was to ask Aborigines to make bark paintings for me, seldom suggesting the subject. At the end of the day the artists brought their finished paintings to my tent, related the myths, and explained the meanings of the designs.

The Artists: It has been suggested by some writers (for example, by Adam, 1951: 163) that only a few Aborigines are permitted to become tribal artists. This is not so. I have yet to meet an Aboriginal, who could not and did not want to paint at one time or another, although, naturally enough, some are more skilled than others.

North-eastern Arnhem Land Art: The art of north-eastern Arnhem Land differs quite mark-edly from that of the rest of Arnhem Land, Groote Eylandt, and Melville Island. While, in general, the art of Groote Eylandt, and that of

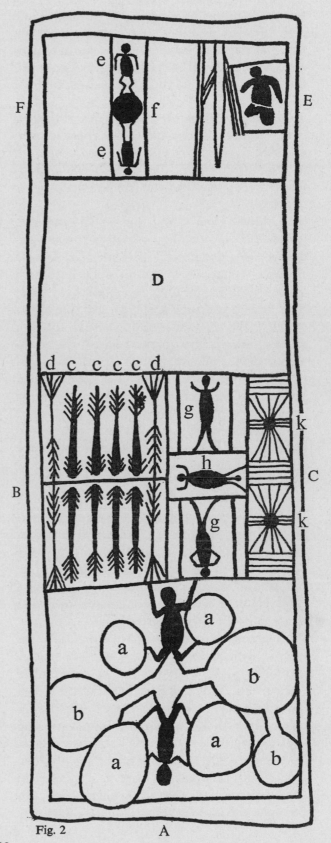

Fig. 2

23

western Arnhem Land, consists of single or multiple figures on a plain ground, that of north-eastern Arnhem Land is made up of a wide range of naturalistic and abstract motifs, skilfully and interestingly arranged within the painting area. Eleven bark paintings from this area are illustrated, seven from Yirrkalla on the extreme north-eastern corner of Arnhem Land, and four from Milingimbi, an island off the north-central coast. These bark paintings are grouped together, because in both areas the art forms and underlying beliefs are similar: both places belong within the same cultural bloc, The following is a brief description of some of these, demonstrating the direct linkage between mythology and art.*

Plate 25 illustrates a particularly complex and beautiful example of a bark from Yirrkalla. It concerns the Djanggawul, Djanggau (or Djankgowa) and his sisters. (See Warner, 1937/1958; Berndt, 1952.) It was painted by Mauwulan (or Mawulan), a ritual leader of one of the linguistic units which own a part of the extensive Djanggawul myth cycle. According to the mythical story, Djanggawul and his two sisters left some place far beyond the sunrise and, travelling westward by canoe, eventually landed at Jelangbara, on the eastern shores of the Gulf of Carpentaria. From this point the creative beings walked across a great part of Arnhem Land, creating the topography, the hills, the creeks, and the waterholes. At one place the two sisters gave birth to many children, ancestors of the present-day people. The bark painting portrays this section of the myth, along with other episodes.

The general story relating to the bark painting, as explained by Mauwulan, tells of incidents during this epic journey of the Djanggawul and his sisters across the Gulf of Carpentaria, of their landing on the eastern coast of Arnhem Land, of the two sisters giving birth to large numbers of children, and of the death and

*Relatively detailed descriptions of all plates discussed by Mr. Mountford are contained at the end of this volume under the heading, 'Descriptive Annotations to the Plates' (Ed.).

burial of the women. The accompanying sketch (Fig. 2) will facilitate the description. In the bottom panel, A, are the two sisters; the circular design, a, a, a, a, adjacent to their hands and feet, represents the conical-shaped mats, which these mythical beings placed over their newly-born children to protect them from mosquitoes. The meaning of the circular designs, b, b, etc., is not known. The vertical designs, c, c, etc., on the centre of panel B signify eight sacred objects decorated with feathers, and those on the outside, d, d, d, d, four trees which Djanggawul and his sisters saw when they landed at Jelangbara. The designs on the opposite panel, C, illustrate the sunrise and sunset, which the brother and his sisters watched while on their canoe journey across the Gulf of Carpentaria. At h, in the centre of the left-hand side, is the Djanggawul brother himself, and above and below him at g, g, are his two sisters. The design, k, k, represents the sunrise and sunset. The central disc is the sun; the radiating, cross-hatched designs are the lines of light in the clouds; and the horizontal parallel lines above and below these designs are the light reflected from the crests of oncoming waves.

The human figures in the large square, D, represent the Djanggawul sisters giving birth to male and female children, whose descendants now live in the country around Milingimbi, the males being painted in yellow and the females in black. The designs in panel F show the two sisters, e, e, in their grave, f, and those in panel E the artist, Mauwulan, holding the sacred object of the goanna totem in his hands, and chanting the song cycle of the Djanggawul myth. (Compare this drawing with those which are illustrated in Berndt, 1952: Plates 3, 13, 23, and 24.)

The simple bark painting from Milingimbi, in Plate 55, depicts an immense python, Julunggul (or Yulunggul), who is a principal figure in one of the most important myths in Arnhem Land —the myth of the Wawalag sisters. (See Warner, 1937/1958; Berndt, 1951a.) These two women came from a locality far away to the south. As they travelled, they collected and named various edible plants, yams, and fruits, as well as many creatures used for food—kangaroos, for instance, and bandicoots, lizards, snakes, and so on. One day, when they reached a waterhole named Mirirmina (or Miraramina, or Muruwul), the elder sister, who was pregnant, asked the younger to build a bark hut, because she was about to give birth to her child. The other did as she was asked, and no sooner was it completed and her sister inside, than the child was born.

When Julunggul, who lived at the bottom of the nearby waterhole, smelt the afterbirth blood, he became angry and emerged from the depths to punish the women for intruding on his domain. The younger sister, who saw him coming, chanted many powerful songs and performed many powerful dances, hoping thereby to drive Julunggul back to his waterhole. Finding this was of no avail, she retreated into the hut, blocking the openings with grass to keep him out. But Julunggul pushed these barriers aside and after swallowing first the child, then the two sisters, returned to his waterhole.

Plate 63 illustrates a number of mythical goannas who, during a severe drought in mythical times, dug a hole in the ground until they were stopped by a layer of rock (the central division). When this happened, the goannas died, and their bodies were transformed into a goanna-shaped mountain at Arnhem Bay. The eggs of five female goannas on the lower section of the painting are shown within their bodies. The designs on this bark painting are almost identical with those illustrating the mythical freshwater goannas who, when digging nesting burrows near Caledon Bay, unearthed the yellow and black pigments, which, as mentioned earlier, may be collected only by members of *jiridja* clans and linguistic units.

The bark painting in Plate 65 is a simple arrangement representing large and small human footprints and handprints, although some of the smaller designs on the left-hand edge may represent the fore-paws of kangaroos. The crescent shapes on the right-hand edge probably refer to the livers of sharks, stingrays and other marine creatures—a favourite food of these Aborigines.

Plate 59 illustrates a myth that tells of two beings—Wuluwaid, the man, and Bunbulama, the woman. When they wanted rain, they tied bundles of grass together and soaked them in swamp-water. After the bundles had been in the water for a day or so, the clouds would form and the rain fall. The rain continued until the bundles were removed from the swamp. The two figures shown in the bark painting are the rain-makers, Wuluwaid and Bunbulama, with the magic rain-making bundles in their hands. Above them is a rainbow, with the rain (cross-hatched vertical panels) falling across it. The vertical lines on the side of the painting, and those from the bundles held by the rain-makers, also indicate falling rain.

Plate 31 illustrates the myth of the moon-man, Ngalindi (or Nalimba), and his sister, the dugong-woman, Balwogman (Bulunggu, Bulungani, or Mangguldji). (See Warner, 1937/1958: 523–4; Berndt, 1948: 16–50.)

In the creative era, the moon-man spent much of his time digging jungle yams for food, while his sister, the dugong-woman, searched for spike-rush, *ragai*, bulbs growing in an adjacent swamp. One day the dugong-woman inadvertently walked through a patch of 'itch weed', which, as soon as her body became dry, caused intense irritation. After trying several unsuccessful remedies she dived into the sea. On finding that this stopped the itching, she said to her brother, 'I'm going to change myself into a dugong, and stay in the sea for ever'. 'If you do,' replied Ngalindi, 'I'll always live in the sky.' True to his word, he went into the sky, taking with him the yams he had gathered. In the centre of the painting is Ngalindi himself, the torpedo-shaped designs representing the yams he took with him. The dugong-woman is shown to the left of the lower panel, the footprints on the right being those of the mangrove-man, Gurungurun, who once tried to capture her.

Although there is no definite information where the painting illustrated in Plate 67 was obtained, the fine cross-hatching on the one hand, and the X-ray motifs on the other, suggest that it is possibly the work of Aborigines living in an area intermediate between north-eastern and western Arnhem Land. According to the accompanying description, the designs represent Aborigines who, having caught a large sail-fish, are sitting with their companions enjoying the result of their labours. In the right-hand panel are women and children seated before a fire, waiting for their share of the food.

The painting in Plate 62, collected by Lloyd Warner during 1926–9 in the Milingimbi region, depicts five different kinds of snakes and a number of oval designs that have not been identified.

Western Arnhem Land Art: The art of western Arnhem Land is neither as complex, nor as colourful, as that of the north-east. Nevertheless, in many respects it is more interesting, because the Aborigines use two distinct and possibly unrelated art forms on both their bark and cave paintings.

The first is what has now become known as X-ray art, in which the artist depicts, in polychrome, not only the external forms of the creatures he wishes to represent, but also the internal details, the skeleton, as well as the internal organs, the lungs, the heart, the stomach, and so on. The second art form depicts, almost exclusively, single-line monochromatic drawings of tall, thin-bodied men and women usually in action, running, frolicking, or throwing spears. The local people say that such paintings in the caves of the Arnhem Land plateau are the work of the Mimi, one of the many kinds of spirit beings said to live in the surrounding country. The homes of these spirits are in many places—in the clefts of the rocks, at waterholes on the flood plains, in termite mounds, hollow trees and holes in the ground, as well as in the sky. Although the characteristics and dwelling-places of each one of these beings is known, the Aborigines have not seen them. However, they maintain that in the past there were men, native doctors, much cleverer than those of the present generation, who often caught a glimpse of them.

Very broadly indeed, the Aborigines divide spirit beings into two main classes, although there are some not so easily grouped under those two headings: the Mimi, shy, harmless folk who do not as a rule interfere with human beings (although there are exceptions), and the Namandi, malignant, ill-disposed demons, who are always in conflict with them. These Namandi are feared, but the danger of attack by them is lessened, so it is said, if two or more persons travel together.

Five of the bark paintings illustrated in this volume concern spirit people. I will mention these, along with some others.

Plate 66 depicts a number of spirits performing a ceremony. In the lower right panel, one blows a long wooden trumpet and the other, standing beside him, beats two clapping-sticks to mark the rhythm of the dance. The remaining three panels depict a number of the spirits performing a lively dance.

Two of the harmless spirit people, a man and a woman, called Yerobeni, are pictured on Plate 30. During the hours of darkness the Yerobeni sleep either in holes in the ground, or among the tangled roots of banyan-trees. At sunrise they leave their hiding-places and search for food, the man collecting honey from the hives of the wild bees, carrying this in a bag slung across his shoulders: the woman, with a digging-stick (not shown), digs for freshwater tortoises in swamp mud, or for yams in the jungle.

A spirit man, probably named Auenau, is depicted in Plate 64. A long spine grows from the

5	
6	7 8

5 Part of a group of grave-posts from Bathurst and Melville islands **6** Graveposts of Bathurst and Melville islands *in situ* **7** Grave-post of Bathurst and Melville islands being painted by an artist who is decorated for the *bugamani* mortuary rituals **8** A group of Bathurst and Melville island posts demonstrating the wide range of style and decoration

back of his neck, and there are leg bones of dead men hanging from his elbows: Auenau has taken these from the tree and platform burials, which are common in this area. The long, tail-like appendage represents lightning, which may be seen on the hilltops when Auenau is prowling about. This spirit man, whom the local people fear, can be frightened away only by a native doctor.

Plate 20 depicts a female spirit, named Manubi, with feathers hanging from her elbows. This figure is a historical character, and is related to sorcery. However, what may have been the same woman, but in this case known by the name of Dadubi, formed the subject of a cave painting I recently found in western Arnhem Land. The Aborigines are particularly afraid of this being, who is a sorceress: her homes are in the low scrub that surrounds the springs at the base of the Arnhem Land plateau. Should one of the Dadubi women see a man drinking from a spring, or travelling by himself in the scrub, she will sneak up behind him and, by shooting one of her barbed spines into his body, make him ill. If the friends of the sick man know that he has been near the haunts of the Dadubi women, they will call on a native doctor magically to remove the spine. Sometimes this succeeds, and the victim gets well; more often, he dies.

The left-hand figure of the bark illustrated in Plate 37 is of a man who has been captured, and is about to be eaten, by a number of Mimi spirits living in the rocky country of western Arnhem Land. The central figure is the Mimi who made the capture; and, on the upper right, three others dance with pleasure in anticipation of the forthcoming feast. On the lower right is one of these spirits preparing to dismember the victim.

Plate 36 illustrates a continuation of the same story. From the left to the centre of this painting, six Mimi are dancing with pleasure over the meal that awaits them. The dismembered body of the victim (*right*) is being guarded by another spirit; on the upper left is a yam, the normal food of these spirit people.

There is a belief among the people of western Arnhem Land that a sorcerer can, by painting an image of his victim on a sheet of bark and chanting over it the appropriate magical songs, bring about his illness, or even his death. Plate 56 illustrates such a bark on which a sorcerer, desiring to kill his victim, has painted his portrait, transfixing it with a number of stingray spines.

Plate 17 represents a yam which, so the Aborigines believe, is the food of the Mimi spirit people who live in the rocky hills. There is a close resemblance between the design and a highly conventionalized female figure—suggesting that, during the creative period, this particular yam was indeed a mythical woman.

The two men (Plate 32) wearing feather head-dresses are impersonating mythical red-eyed pigeons. They are participating in one of the sacred *ubar* rituals. Between them is the hollow gong which, beaten with the shredded stump of a pandanus root, takes a central part in some of the most colourful rituals of western Arnhem Land.

The bark painting of the kangaroo (Plate 60) from Goulburn Island is a particularly fine example of X-ray art. It is possible to distinguish the spine, ribs, leg, and arm bones of this animal, as well as the heart, lungs, liver, and stomach. Two eyes are shown on one side of the head; this adheres to the conventions of this particular art form.

Another example of X-ray art from the same locality (Plate 33) depicts a wading bird, probably a jabiru or native companion, and three fish. The skeleton of the upper fish, and the alimentary canal and spine of the jabiru, are shown.

Groote Eylandt Art: Although the art of north-eastern Arnhem Land is particularly decorative and rich in design, that of Groote Eylandt, although separated from the nearby mainland by only a few miles of comparatively narrow sea channels, is much simpler. Generally, it consists of single or grouped figures on a plain black ground. This difference is an example not only of the effect of relative isolation, but also

27

of a distinct art style. The following two examples will suffice. although other examples of Groote art are illustrated here.

The bark painting of the barracouta (Plate 23) is typical. Instead of using broad splashes of colour, most Groote Eylandt artists tend to use broken lines and groups of dots. Plate 34 illustrates an unusual motif. This bark painting portrays two mythical stories. The central and right-hand panels concern the travels of the stingray and sawfish people, and the left-hand panel, those of a mythical man, Jundurana (or Yunduruna). These mythical stingray and sawfish initially camped, during the creative period, on the eastern shores of the Gulf of Carpentaria. Later they decided to leave, and make a new camp on Groote Eylandt. Landing on the western shore of this island, they continued their journey eastward, the sawfish (note its saw) cutting out the channel of the present-day Angoroko River. The figures on the right of the painting represent the stingray and sawfish people on their way to Groote, and the central panel two sawfish creating the channel of the Angoroko River. The mythical man, Jundurana, who once lived at the mouth of the Roper River in southern Arnhem Land, became dissatisfied with his surroundings. Leaving this place, he travelled northward along the eastern shores of Arnhem Land, creating many waterholes on the way; finally, by way of Bickerton Island, he came to Amaliba, on the eastern shores of Groote Eylandt, where he camped. Today, large pillars of rock mark his camping-sites. The oval and the small rectangle on the left of the bark painting represent these pillars of rock at Amaliba, while the intricate designs in the long rectangle signify, in detail, his travels from the Roper River, across to Bickerton Island, and on to his final resting-place at Amaliba.

Melville Island Art: Melville and its companion island, Bathurst, are separated from the rest of Australia by the turbulent waters of the narrow Dundas and Clarence straits. This water barrier has isolated the Aborigines of these islands to some extent from the cultural influences of the

Fig. 3

mainland for an unknown period. Consequently we may expect the art motifs of either side of the strait to bear little relationship one to the other. In western Arnhem Land, art style is focused almost entirely on the representational: on Melville Island, it is so highly formalized that the designs themselves are difficult to correlate with the subjects they are said to represent. This island art, to an even greater degree than is the case with Groote Eylandt art, demonstrates quite nicely how its style tends to become less complex when isolated over a period from external influences—or, conversely, more complex, in abstract terms. The following two examples demonstrate the typical design for this area.

The bark painting illustrated in Plate 57 shows the totemic place of the woman, Puruliangkala, who was responsible for the first bush-fire on Turiturina Island, western Bathurst Island. In

Fig. 4

Fig. 3 the central white circle is Turiturina Island, once the camp of this mythical bush-fire woman. The smaller yellow circles, a, a, now low rocks on the coast, were her camp-fires; b, b, the black circles, the freshwater springs which provided her with water; the red circles, c, c, c, are deposits of red ochre; d, d, of white ochre, and e, e, milkwood-trees. The sap of this tree, mixed with the red and white ochres, was used by this woman and her companions to decorate themselves for the initiation ceremonies, which were performed during those creative times.

The next is a particularly decorative bark paint-ing (Plate 24), representing sea creatures which the artist saw during a canoe journey. Although the design as a whole appears as if it were an abstract one, once the meanings are known it is possible to recognize a passing resemblance to the creatures which the artist had in mind. As in other cases, because the patterning is complex, I have included an outline drawing (Fig. 4) so that the designs can be more readily identified. The design, a, represents a shark; b and f are large sea-snakes; e is a smaller sea-snake; and g, another variety of snake that lives in the man-grove swamps. A sawfish is represented by c; d is a dolphin, and h is a sea-slug. Designs, m, m, etc., are shells; l, boulders on the sea bot-tom; k, a creek in the mangrove swamp, and j, a sandbank.

The Wandjina Painting: Plate 19 illustrates the only bark painting in this volume that does not belong to the Northern Territory. Collected at Walcott Inlet in the Kimberleys, Western Aus-tralia, by Dr. Helmut Petri, it depicts one of the now well-known Wandjina cave paintings, which belong only to that part of Australia. There is an interesting history behind the disco-very and later interpretation of these remarkable figures. In 1837 Sir George Grey (1841:201–3), when exploring north-western Australia, dis-covered and afterward published an imperfect illustration of some of these Wandjina cave paintings. Later this was to give rise to many strange theories and controversies about their origin: controversies which continued for almost ninety years, until Love (1930: 35) and Elkin (1930 and 1948) showed conclusively that these figures had been painted by Aborigines, and were part of their religious life. The general belief associated with these paintings is that during the early days of the world the Wandjina, who were mythical human beings, created a part of the country. At the completion of these tasks each Wandjina—and there were many—left his likeness in the form of a painting in a cave within the area he had made, and then entered a nearby waterhole. But before doing this the Wandjina decreed that, prior to the onset of each wet season, their paintings must be touched or renewed by ritual leaders. If this responsibility were evaded, it would cause drought and consequently hunger: once the painting on the rock shelter becomes dim, the Wandjina vanish, and with them go also the rain and fertility of the countryside. (See Chapter One.) The body of a Wandjina painting is believed to be a receptacle partly for blood, and partly for water. The blood makes men and other creatures strong, and this is symbolized by the red-ochre bows surrounding the heads of such paintings, while the water, which is essential for all forms of life, is symbolized by their white faces and bodies.

Carved Human Figures: Human figures in the round, carved in wood or stone, moulded in wax or clay or shaped from bark, have a wide, if sporadic, distribution in Australia. They are, however, more numerous in north-western Australia and in Arnhem Land. As early as 1876 Cox (1876: 1223) illustrated two full-length human figures moulded in wax, which were collected in an Aboriginal camp at Rockhampton, Central Queensland. McConnel (1953: Plate 17 F) also provides an example from Cape York, northern Queensland. In the Pitt-Rivers Museum at Oxford there is a small but well-carved human head on the handle of a South-Australian spearthrower, while in the National Museum of Victoria there is a human face carved on a wooden bucket made from a gnarl of a gum-tree. In the South Australian Museum are also some striking examples of human figures carved in kaolin by an Aranda man, Injarupma, of Charlotte Waters, on the border of South and Central Australia. Goddard (1939: Plate 9) illustrates a number of figures carved in soft stone, the work of an Aboriginal woman named Kalboori, of the Pitta-pitta tribe of south-western Queensland, while R. Berndt (1951*b*: 350–3, Plates 1 to 10) collected in 1949–50 an interesting series of fifteen heads, moulded in white and red ochre, from Oenpelli in western Arnhem Land: ten of these have been described and illustrated.

Human figures and heads in wood, stone, or bark are widespread throughout north-western Australia. In the Kimberley area, for example, full-length human figures made from wood or grass are used in the *Gurangara* (or Goranara) ceremonies. (Worms, 1942: Plates 4 and 7.) Petri records two heads, one in wood (1957: Plate 2) and one in stone (1959: Plate 67), while

Mountford (1954*a*: Plate 1) illustrates a full-length wooden figure from the Durack Range. There is also a well-made mask from Western Australia, said to be associated with initiation rituals. This specimen is now in the Historical Museum of the Wellcome Institute in London, and a small, but particularly well-carved, figure of a woman from La Grange Bay is in the Western Australian Museum. It is possible that further research will yield additional information about these carved figures of Western Australia.

Although a large range of human figures is found in the north-eastern part of this continent, we do not know much about their associated mythology, nor about their significance in ritual or ceremonial terms. The matter is very different when we turn to Arnhem Land and the adjacent Melville and Bathurst islands.

The first oblique reference to carved human figures in Arnhem Land was made by Warner (1937: 504) who, during his field-work between 1926–9, noted that a grave post might have '. . . a series of incisions . . . made at the top of it to give it the appearance of a carved "head" with one or more necks'. During 1938 the Reverend F. W. Chaseling presented a human-headed burial post from north-eastern Arnhem Land to the Australian Museum. This is a unique example of Aboriginal craftsmanship, which went unrecorded for many years. (See Mountford, 1956: 416, Plate 138, C, D.) During 1946–7 fifty-one carved human figures were collected by R. Berndt at Yirrkalla. Some of these have been discussed and illustrated (see R. and C Berndt, 1948, 1949), and a few redescribed, together with a small group of hitherto unrecorded carved heads (see Elkin and R. and C. Berndt, 1950) and the information relating to these. During 1948 and 1951 I collected, and obtained the associated myths of, thirteen wooden, full-length human figures (Mountford, 1956: Plates 130 to 132, 135 to 137), nine wooden heads (1956: Plates 139 and 140), two human figures modelled in bark (1956: Fig. 65 C, D), and two in wax (1956: Plate 10a, e, f). While on Melville Island during 1954 I saw, and later described

(1958*a*: Plates 40 and 41), six full-length human figures, which the local people had placed on the graves of their dead, together with three human-headed burial poles (1958*a*: Plates 38 and 39). The four figures illustrated in this volume were carved by north-eastern Arnhem Landers. In my view this art form does not appear to have been part of the local culture for more than two generations. However, R. Berndt holds that it is possibly of earlier introduction, and was influenced by the Indonesian traders to this northern coast. But the complete figure, with arms and legs, is a recent development. (See R. Berndt, 1958*a*: 259–60.) Mauwulan (mentioned previously), who is now about sixty years of age, states that he remembers as a small boy, seeing an old Malay trepanger, Bobalinda, teach his father how to carve a human head on the top of a burial post. Mauwulan—so he says—learnt this art from his father, and himself showed others how to make such objects. As time went on, the Aboriginal craftsmen, without the help of Europeans, improved their techniques, until today they are producing some outstanding examples.

Plate 68 shows a carved figure of the spirit being named Laindjung, who in one of his manifestations is Banaidja (barramundi). In one version of the copious mythology about him, Laindjung made his camp at Blue Mud Bay on the western shores of the Gulf of Carpentaria: here his huge size and loud voice so terrified the local people that they attacked and threw many spears into his body, until in desperation he dived into a nearby waterhole to escape. While Laindjung was resting at the bottom, waiting for his wounds to heal, he painted special designs on parts of his body. Then, changing his name to Banaidja, he rose from the water and called the people together. Once they had assembled, he pointed to his body designs and explained to each linguistic unit the significance of these, allocating them for use in sacred rituals. In this way everyone would know to which country each belonged. These designs can be seen on the carved figure illustrated in Plate 68. A different version is given by R. and C. Berndt, 1948.

The myth of the two Wawalag sisters and their encounter with the mythical rock python, Julunggul, has already been related in association with a bark painting illustrated in Plate 55. In Plate 68 two further carved figures are shown. The first is a representation of the elder Wawalag sister, with pendulous breasts, indicating that she has borne a child. The horizontal bars incised and painted on the figure, above and below the breasts, are cicatrices. The other designs on the trunk of the figure represent, among other things, the blood that caused Julunggul to emerge from his waterhole and swallow the two sisters. The second figure depicts the younger Wawalag, whose breasts are those of a young girl, the ridge between them being an ornamental scar. She also wears a red-ochred, jungle-string girdle as decoration. The painted designs on her body represent a number of different things relevant to the myth, but principally blood.

In Plate 69, a carved figure of a Wurumu (Wuramu) man is shown. Such figures are often placed on graves. When the bones are disinterred at the close of the mortuary rituals, relatives, taking the Wurumu post from the grave, run from camp to camp, collecting food and other goods for the main participants. It is thus called a 'Collection man' and owes its origin to Indonesian contact.

The carved head illustrated in Plate 69 represents one of the spirit beings who live in the jungles of north-eastern Arnhem Land. In this case it is the head of Ranjara, or Kultana (Guldana), whose special duty is to send the cold north winds to the mainland. The designs on the head signify wind and clouds. Elkin and R. and C. Berndt (1950: Plates 3B and 9) and Mountford (1956: Plates 139 and 140) illustrate a number of these little heads. Although the Aborigines have been carving such heads for a comparatively short time, they show evidence of much skill and artistic appreciation. The second head in Plate 69, made at the request of R. Berndt (1951*b*: Plate 9), after he had seen a small, roughly made head used in sorcery, was moulded in ochre by Aborigines at Oenpelli.

The triangular face is that of a man, with eyes, wrinkles and moustache, beard and teeth, etched and worked with a small twig. Although such delightful examples of Aboriginal art do not refer to the religious and ritual background of these people, they are traditional—in the same way as is the work of Injarupma of Charlotte Waters, and Kalboori, of the Pitta-pitta tribe, mentioned before.

The future of Aboriginal art may be viewed in two ways: in relation to the Aborigines themselves, and from the standpoint of its contribution to the world of aesthetics. As far as the former is concerned, two questions are raised. Will these people continue with their traditional and time-honoured art forms in the face of increasing pressures, which are exerted toward assimilating them into the wider Australian community? If they do, to what extent will it be possible for them to retain the vitality and beauty that it now possesses? For one thing, the art of these Aborigines is very closely bound up with their age-old beliefs. (See Chapter One.) In fact, as these are changed or destroyed through assimilation, the art forms which we have been discussing will themselves change, or be destroyed.

At present, under the stimulus of the Arnhem Land missions and commercial enterprise generally, the Aborigines of that region are producing bark paintings for sale. In north-eastern Arnhem Land some of these paintings, particularly those produced by the older artists, are works of considerable merit. (See Plates 25 and 35, for instance.) However, with the passing of the older generation the younger men, in adopting the ways of the white man, will discard their ancient art and its part in sacred and everyday life. They will use it, not to record the rich heritage of their culture in the form of mythology, but only as a means of supplementing their income. Under such conditions, under the pressures of commercialism, their art is bound to deteriorate until it has little or no aesthetic value. If, therefore, the indigenous art is likely to disappear and, indeed, under present conditions this does seem to be inevitable, it is imperative that, while the opportunity still remains, we should spare no effort in recording all aspects of the living art for the benefit of future generations.

From the standpoint of aesthetics generally, the contribution the Aborigines can make to the world of art is considerable. There is, for instance, in contemporary Western-European-type life, a constant demand for new motifs. And there is an exciting store of such motifs in Aboriginal art—particularly in the art of the bark paintings. These could provide a rich source of stimulus to both artists and designers the world over. If they are to derive the utmost value from this art, however, it must be reinterpreted, accepted, and finally integrated into the new environment. Aboriginal art is not just a series of strange, exotic symbols designed to attract the curious. It is an expression of beauty in its own right: an art that will take its place alongside the art of other cultures, and in so doing must, inevitably, enrich them.

CHAPTER THREE

The Art of The Rock-Faces

FREDERICK D. McCARTHY

The semi-nomadic Aborigines, despite their adherence to a hunting and gathering economy followed by man for over a million years before he became a pastoralist and cultivator, are prolific artists, and their rock engravings and paintings occur in a surprisingly large number of places in Australia. The literature on this rock art includes more than two hundred papers and several monographs, but it was not until the last two decades that study of the sites became systematic and scientifically based. Close links exist between the engravings and paintings in many localities, but for clarity they will be described separately.

Engravings: Laymen and scientists alike have evinced considerable interest in the engravings, the existence of which was noted as early as 1788 by the First Fleet chroniclers. As the Aborigines were not asked to interpret the motifs, and Europeans had not witnessed their fashioning, the great variety of techniques, motifs, and styles puzzled students considerably. Little progress, therefore, was made in the understanding of their history and significance until recent times, when a sequence of phases, prehistoric to modern, was established.

Hale and Tindale (1930) distinguished three phases in the Devon Downs cave on the Lower Murray River, linked with the middle and late occupation periods of the site. Worms (1954) recognized outline and pecked strata in the galleries of north-west Australia. The present author, as a result of widespread field-work, defined four phases by a study of the engraving or superimposition of techniques, motifs, and styles over one another at traditional sites, where artists had worked for generations. (See McCarthy, 1957*b*, 1962; McCarthy and Macintosh, 1962.)

The first phase consists of abraded grooves, either scattered irregularly over a rock-face, or arranged in simple designs which include parallel, gridded, and radiate sets, associated with bird tracks and crosses. Rounded holes bored into the rock are commonly found with them. At the Black's Palace near Tambo, the Carnarvon and Drummond ranges, and other sites in central Queensland, a deep oval gash with a groove around it, barred and other simple designs, together with abraded grooves, cover vertical rock-faces hundreds of feet long. (See Plate 49.) This phase of engraving is widely distributed in Australia, and the rows of short lines and solid circles among the rock paintings of eastern Australia are believed to have all had a similar function. Aesthetically, this phase is of little interest. As the earliest known type of engraving, its archaeological value is considerable. The grooves are commonly called tally marks to represent people, and it has been suggested that they were also shaping grooves for bone and wooden spearheads, or barbs. At Delamere, in the Northern Territory, Aborigines interpreted them as cicatrization patterns. They occur on several types of prehistoric stone implements.

The second, or outline, phase of engraving is represented by tortoises, circles, and other simple motifs whose grooves are abraded into the limestone walls of, for example, the lower River Murray rock shelters, and by the conjoined puncture technique at Burra, in South Australia. The finest displays, however, are in the Sydney-Hawkesbury River district of eastern New South Wales, and at Port Hedland and other sites in north-west Australia. At these sites the pits and punctures are up to an inch wide and half an inch deep, but are usually smaller. They either overlap one another to form a continuous groove, or make an outline of separated pits. To achieve the relatively fine control of line, which can be attained in this medium only with a laborious technique, it is thought that the artists first drew their subjects on the rock in pigment, or scratched them in with a stone, before fashioning the groove by percussion. In a number of important figures in the Sydney-Hawkesbury district the groove has been abraded and smoothed by successive generations.

The Sydney-Hawkesbury series is an outstanding corpus of rock art. (See Plates 9, 10 and 11.) In this area of some 6000 square miles of rugged sandstone ridges and gorges, over 600 groups, embracing over 4000 figures, have been located. (See McCarthy 1958: 17-20.) There are, for instance, from one to over a hundred and fifty figures in a site, and they occur at all levels from the creek-beds to the saddles and higher terraces of the ridges, and in the marshes. Some groups cover an acre or two of rock surface; and it is probable that the large size of the figures, from life-size to gigantic proportions, has been influenced to some extent by the immense areas at the disposal of the artists.

One difficulty facing the student of Aboriginal art of this variety is to decide how much of it is sacred and mythological, and to what extent it is simply a secular record of events in the everyday lives of the local people. At the core of this art is the widespread belief, over much of southeast Australia, in what has been termed by some writers an All-Father. (See, for instance, Howitt, 1904: 488–508.) Baiami, to cite one of his names, was viewed as the heroic spirit creator of the world, of its human and animal inhabitants, and of their customs and ways of life. In addition, he was the source of the magical power possessed by native doctors (see R. Berndt, 1947: 334–8): and he was the one upon whose life that of ordinary people was modelled. This supreme being had several wives. Living in the sky, he sent his emissary, a one-legged hero known as Daramulun, among other names, to visit the initiation grounds on earth, there to take away the novices and return them as initiated men. Both types of hero are featured in these engravings, usually in a static pose. (See, for instance, Plate 9.) The Baiami type is shown facing the viewer as a giant anthropomorph, while the Daramulun type is in profile and is often a composite being, partly human and partly animal. Thus such a portrait may have the body and one leg of an emu, and a human foot; but the head varies from human, to bird, snake or mammal. This suggests its totemic character, shown in the combined form of human spirit and totem animal.

The mythology of these sandstone tribes has not been recorded in any detail, and the relative importance culturally of these two heroes is not known. Along the coast the Daramulun type was regarded as supreme; to the west of the Great Dividing Range the Baiami type assumed major importance. Among the engravings, both heroes hold clubs, hafted axes or boomerangs, often in the left hand. They are decorated with rows of cicatrices, or ornaments like strings of kangaroo teeth. Although their wives are sometimes shown with them, very few spirit heroines are engraved singly. Men predominate among the human figures, but they are shown with women, and in a few instances in sexual intercourse. Undoubtedly the most important compositions embody these heroic beings with humans, weapons, and tracks. The tracks are those of the hero; and the assumption is that they were followed during the historical and totemic re-enactments performed, in the shape of ritual, at these sites. Such tracks often point from one group of engravings to another, and it is probable that whole series of separate groups formed part of one saga, of which unfortunately we have no record.

The second important theme among the engravings is that of what can be termed totemic animals—those regarded as potential food predominate. (See Plate 11.) Fish, for example, constitute one-quarter of the total engravings of this type found in the coastal areas. North of the Hawkesbury River, however, they are not so common. Kangaroos and wallabies are the dominant mammal motifs, just as the emu stands out among the comparatively few birds, the goanna among the reptiles, the boomerang and shield among the artifacts. Such important food mammals as the possum and bandicoot, however, are rare figures, and the wombat rather more so; but the koala is a subject frequently found in the upper-Hawkesbury bush country. Apart from single figures, among which the kangaroo is the principal one, a school of fish, or series of wombats, echidnas, or weapons, occasionally form the only subject in an engraving group. Plants, shells, and articles relating to women's economic tasks are represented scarcely at all, while insects are unusual. Circles, ornaments, gnarl containers and baskets, stone axes, and topographical diagrams are other subjects depicted; but the range of motifs does not include many animals and artifacts of ritual, as well as everyday, significance.

The wide range of hunting and ritual compositions in this art is of considerable aesthetic interest. The simplest kind consists of a mixture of hunters and game. Others illustrate, in addition, the spearing or killing of emus and kangaroos with hunting-spears or boomerangs, and the tracks of hunter and game are often included. Fishing-parties carrying bark canoes and fish, ceremonial activities, and whale feasts are notable compositions. Subjects with a sexual connotation do not appear to any great extent in this art.

Outline engravings of the same kind occur also at Port Hedland, where over fifteen thousand figures are engraved on eight miles of ridges. (See McCarthy, 1962.) Fish and boomerangs predominate in the range of subjects, which include mammals, birds, goannas, snakes, and artifacts. There are few compositions involving a number of subjects, and very few ancestral beings or human figures. An outstanding anthropomorph is the so-called Minjiburu: this is an outline figure with pecked hands and feet, and either short grooves or circles, or natural potholes, for the eyes, mouth, breast, and genital organs. Males and females are represented, sometimes in pairs, with various animals and artifacts, and the human figure is often shown in an alert or dancing posture. Many fully pecked human tracks lead to the Minjiburu engravings, and it is believed that these constituted focal points of ritual activity. Such engravings range from the simple outline to the more involved pecked phases of engraving, all of which are represented in this traditional gallery. To the outline engravings were added striped, barred, and other line designs, which cover the whole surface of turtle, dolphin, whale, and ritual designs, as well as those of weapons and sacred boards; and these display very well the changes in style.

Plain and decorated outlines occur also on Depuch Island (see McCarthy, 1961), at Abydos, and other sites in the north-west of Western Australia; and there is a remarkable figure of what appears to be a crocodile's head at Panaramittee North in the Flinders Range in South Australia, which may belong to this phase: the interpretation, however, has been questioned by Berndt, who has information suggesting that it represents a magical object. (See Elkin, 1949: 150.)

The outline naturalistic phase of engraving is not of a very high artistic standard. The swimming, feeding, watchful, and action poses, in which the artists engraved the relevant animals, illustrate well how much they were concerned with these creatures among which they lived, and on which they depended for food; and associated with these are representations of weapons and artifacts. The figures are commonly shown, too, as the hunters themselves saw them, either moving, or about to be struck with a weapon. Anatomical details and body contours are often inaccurate; posture and the general form of the subject have been accorded first preference. The artists had a high appreciation of line, but were technically unable to master their medium to the same extent as were, for example, the upper-palaeolithic artists of Western Europe. This is not a matter of comparison in broad cultural terms, but has to do simply with the techniques used. There were undoubtedly reasons why some of these Aboriginal engravings appear crudely executed.

In the third phase of engraving in Australia an abrupt change took place in the motifs, but not in the technique. The motifs changed to the formal, the conventionalized, and the symbolic. Linear and geometric designs include the full and half concentric circle, the arc, parallel sinuous lines, meandering line and maze, barbed spearhead, radiate, pubic apron, feather-plume ornament, and animal tracks. They all occur in north-west Australia, where it is thought they were introduced during the diffusion of bronze-age techniques and art designs some two thousand years ago from South-East Asia into Indonesia and Oceania. More work is needed to establish this linkage. However, it is plain that such designs spread from the north-west, south-eastward into Central Australia, South Australia, and as far east as the Great Dividing Range in New South Wales and Queensland. As a rule, they are haphazardly engraved, often close together, and compositions are almost unknown among them. Although this is, as it were,

a prehistoric phase of engraving, some of the motifs, including the full and half concentric circle, parallel sinuous lines, animal tracks and others, survived to become an essential element in the ritual art of the living people of Central Australia. Harney and Elkin both obtained interpretations of some of these linear-design engravings from Aborigines, but Mountford has cited most of the south and central Australian sites as being either non-interpretable by, or unknown, to local Aborigines.

Detailed examination of the numerous known sites is called for to establish the full range of motifs in this phase, and more information, too, must be obtained about them from living Aborigines. As most of these figures are small and easily fashioned, vast numbers of them have been engraved on the rocks, boulders, and shelters of these sites. The barbed spearhead and pubic fringe are numerically the commonest in north-west Australian sites, but the fringe is rare in those of southern Australia. Until recently the linear designs were incorrectly lumped together as pecked geometric engravings; they are not pecked, and some of them can be interpreted in naturalistic terms.

The fourth or pecked phase of engraving is artistically perhaps the most interesting. It, too, represents another abrupt change in aesthetic values and style. On this occasion there is a change from the formal symbolic art of the second phase to a representative art, in which a classical type developed and spread as far southeast as the Flinders Range and western New South Wales, and south-west only as far as the Murchison district in Western Australia. (See Plates 45 to 48.) The thousands of pecked intaglios scattered over Depuch Island, for instance, depict fish, dolphins, whales, turtles, dingoes, emus and wading birds, praying mantis, snakes, lizards, clutches of eggs, weapons, and other artifacts. Hunting compositions include men spearing kangaroos, mangrove crabs and turtles, and animals killing one another. Prominent in this art are mythical creatures of fishlike origin, small human figures engaged in rituals, and large men wearing rayed head-dresses. Occasional figures of a man and woman in coitus appear; but, again, sex is not a dominant theme.

Across on the mainland, human and animal tracks become the commonest pecked motifs at Port Hedland, where a very limited range of human figures, snakes, goannas, fish, and other animals, boomerangs, and other artifacts and designs appears in this technique. Reports of similar naturalistic figures in unrecorded sites in various parts of north-west Australia reveal that most of them are hammered into the thickly or thinly patinated surface of granite, dolerite, and basaltic rocks on pyramid-shaped hills, cliffs, and on limestone and sandstone ridges. Similar sites in western New South Wales display pecked figures of human beings, kangaroos bandicoots, emus and their eggs, goannas and other lizards, as well as the hunting of these animals. (See Plate 46.) In the Flinders Range, owls, lizards, human and animal tracks occur in this technique (see Plate 47), which was not highly developed in this particular area.

From north-west Australia to western New South Wales, little pecked men armed with spears or boomerangs are shown fighting, hunting, dancing, or performing ceremonies. They are probably part of the same aesthetic movement as we find in the Mimi paintings of western Arnhem Land (see Chapter Two), and those in central-western New South Wales and Victoria. It has been the custom in the past to speak of these sites where engravings are located as totemic centres, and since in many instances the local Aborigines do not know their meaning and usually assign them to the Dreaming or creative times (see Chapter One), we in turn are apt to regard them as prehistoric. We know now that many of them are, in fact, traditional sites that have been used from the abraded groove to the final, pecked phases of engraving, while others display the work of only one or two phases. The mythology of the prehistoric phases can, of course, never be known; but that of the pecked phase should be recorded wherever possible, because this art is the latest one, and belongs to the culture of Aborigines living at the time of European occupation.

A modern subphase of pecking of a highly imaginative kind occurs in the Gallery Hill and Wamerana galleries in north-west Australia where, apart from a few animals, extraordinary human figures of both sexes with greatly exaggerated genitals are depicted. These are gracefully posed figures, wearing head-dresses, and their significance is obviously of a sexual nature. Father Worms (1954), who recorded them, has called them the *Gurangara* engravings. According to him, this is the name of the female consort of Djanba, a cult hero. The *gurangara*, a term usually referring to a specific ritual, is associated with the Kunapipi (Gunabibi) of Arnhem Land and the Northern Territory. (See Berndt, 1951*a*.) A final subphase of pecking observed in the Northern Territory is one in which the living natives lightly hammer such subjects as motor-cars and trucks onto the surface of igneous boulders.

Paintings: Cave paintings are known in every State of Australia, including Tasmania. Like the engravings, they may be categorized as belonging to a number of phases, some of local and others of continent-wide significance; and here, also, it is only through careful scrutiny of the various superimpositions of colours, styles, and motifs, that an understanding of this problem and the separation of the prehistoric from the later series can be attained.

Such paintings are made most commonly on sandstone, but granite, limestone, quartzite, and other rock surfaces are utilized too. Up to 300 figures in one cave are not uncommon; and in the Black's Palace and the Carnarvon Ranges in central Queensland, friezes of abraded grooves and linear engravings, with stencils, run for 200 to 400 feet along the cliff-face. (See Plates 50 and 51.) Caves in Arnhem Land and on Groote Eylandt have their flat ceilings of 50 to 60 feet long by 20 to 50 feet wide covered with paintings. Many of these sites contain exceptionally fine examples of Aboriginal art, and every effort should be made to preserve and protect them from vandals. It is obvious that an environment which amply provides protected rock surfaces, a religion which inspires and demands visual symbols, and a strong aesthetic feeling among the local population, could well combine to find expression in an immense range of such art. This is the case as far as the Australian Aborigines are concerned. But, at the same time, the quality of production and the nature of the motifs vary considerably from one part of Australia to another. This may be ascribed to the remoteness of the southern tribes from those in the north, whose art and religious ideas were enriched by contact with Indonesians in Arnhem Land and Papuans from Torres Strait in Cape York. (See Thomson, 1933; R. and C. Berndt, 1954.) For this reason the art of the north is often technically superior. There is a greater range of colours and combinations of colour, more imaginative application of motifs, and more diversity in art styles. These features of cave art decrease in quality as we move toward the south-east and south-west of the continent.

The technical procedures of the artists are similar throughout the continent. The natural ochres of red and yellow, white clay, black manganese and charcoal, are in universal use. Human blood was occasionally used, and brown, purple, and blue have been recorded in the north. In some sites in South Australia up to nine shades of colour have been noted. The pigment is rubbed in water on a stone and the paint applied with the finger, a twig brush with a teased end, or a feather or hair brush. Extensive deposits of ochre like those at Yarrakinna in the Parachilna Ranges of South Australia, Wilgimia in Western Australia, in Arnhem Land and elsewhere, became centres of mythical and religious significance. These pigments were traded and sought hundreds of miles away from the quarries, because it was believed that they possessed a mystical power through their having been created by particular ancestral spirit beings. (See McCarthy, 1939: 86–8.) On the whole, red is the predominant colour in Australian cave art; white is widespread; black is common in some areas and uncommon in others; yellow appears to be the least favoured,

being most popular in Arnhem Land. These colour preferences are not due solely to the availability of pigment, because changes have taken place on Groote and Chasm islands and in eastern New South Wales, where all of the colours used occur naturally.

Stencilling was practised in the earliest period of painting in Australia. The human hand is the commonest subject (see Plates 3, 4 and 41) among others are kangaroo and human feet, lizards, fish, snakes, small mammals, coolamon, shield, boomerang, club, spearthrower, emu's leg and foot, emu's head and neck. The greatest number known is over twelve hundred in the Black's Palace frieze in central Queensland, and displays of a hundred or more are not uncommon. Stencils are the dominant motif in caves in south-west Australia; red stencils are favoured in northern Australia and in the interior, and white ones in eastern New South Wales. The Worora in the northern Kimberleys believe that the hand stencil is a link between the living people and the spirit world; the Djauan in southern Arnhem Land believe that it actually represents the person, and it is mourned over in the same way. The other stencilled motifs are never in mixed combinations, and appear to be simply reproductions of everyday objects.

In the central coastal region of New South Wales the first phase of cave art was stencilling, perhaps allied with simple outlines of animals and hunters. It was followed by a second phase consisting of drawings of ancestral spirits, human beings, animals, and weapons, in dry red, white, or both pigments. This was a true naturalistic phase. After it came a third phase of drawings in black or white, or black and white, of most of the common animals, the whale and dingo being notable, with a variety of birds. Hunting compositions of men and kangaroos or emus are numerous. The animals are slightly bigger than life-size; and smaller species, like the echidna, may be drawn as large as a kangaroo. The rock wallabies are gracefully posed. The art of the red and white, and black and white, phases is concerned primarily with food, with fish and animals hunted by men, drawn in rock shelters which have either been occupied for a long period, or not lived in at all. These animals were possibly totemic, and may have been associated with hunting magic, or with initiation ritual. Ancestral spirit beings are represented in very few sites. (See Plates 2, 3, and 4.)

The fourth phase is known from only one site in the Hawkesbury district. It consists of an ancestral spirit being eight feet high, with the head of a koala or other mammal, and holding in his left hand a huge, curved club. Drawn in red, yellow, black, and white stripes, this is the only four-colour polychrome known in south-eastern Australia. The striped body and limbs, of heroic proportions, resemble such figures in the local rock engravings, thus linking the two kinds of art in time. It also has characteristics which appear in the Wandjina of the Kimberleys. This type is a basic one, and an indication that the Wandjina heroes were not necessarily introduced into the Kimberleys—not unless this were long enough ago for their type to have diffused from the north-west to the south-east of the continent. But, of course, not too much emphasis can be placed on the matter of diffusion, without taking into account the possibility of independent development. With this hero is a forty-foot-long banded figure in solid red. The most plausible explanation of the composition is that it represents an All-Father hero or his emissary from the sky world, as mentioned previously, making his appearance on an initiation ground, or that he is pictured with a rainbow serpent of a variety not previously recorded.

The cave art of Victoria is confined to a dozen or so sites of red-ochre drawings of animals, a bichrome of an ancestral being, and scenes depicting little men. Its affinities are with the paintings of central western New South Wales. Here, in the ranges of low hills, about forty rock shelters display an art of stick-man style. The figures are from a few to eighteen inches high. Some sets of them are seen dancing and hunting emus and kangaroos, and these seem to be the principal inspirations of this joyful, living art.

Frequently, a figure resembling a native doctor is drawn, beating a pair of clapping-sticks. (See Plate 3.) Usually he is part of a hunting composition, and his function may be to render the game sought more easy to kill. Each set is in only one colour, not in mixed pigments. Among them are some remarkable compositions: men and animals linked together with lines, and men drawn in fine red lines standing in three-tiered series upon one another's shoulders. The few animals include the dingo, echidna, and lizard. Here and there are some concentric circles, line images, nets, and other motifs from the linear-design phase of rock art, and stencils also appear throughout the painting period in this area. Some of the human figures are equally as fine, aesthetically, as the Mimi of western Arnhem Land.

In Queensland many fine series of naturalistic paintings have been reported from Cape York and farther south, but few have been recorded. At Laura there is a remarkable assortment of human spirit figures, kangaroos, emus, bats, and other animals; these are featured in a polychrome art, whose inspiration again appears to be totemic or magical (as an aid in hunting), with ancestral spirit beings who represent the source of life. This zoomorphic art is dominant again in the early phase of painting found in the numerous rock shelters of Arnhem Land and its offshore islands. It is part of a widespread mantle of large and colourful paintings of the animals upon which the people lived, an art that survived throughout the Aborigines' occupation of the country, apart from local changes and variations as in eastern New South Wales. It was not influenced by the linear-design art which spread through the interior of the continent. Developing as it did through the more intensive use of colour from monochromes to four-colour polychromes, it is the basic representative art of Aboriginal Australia.

The cave art of Arnhem Land did not stagnate, nor become restricted, any more than did the traditional beliefs directly or indirectly associated with it: changes did take place. Stimulating these to some extent were the contacts of Indonesian traders with these north-coast Aborigines. To what extent they inspired the quite radical changes and developments in cave art, apparent in this region, is not known. However, on Groote and Chasm islands there is the first phase of outlines, striped and barred, with monochrome silhouettes in dark red, white and yellow, illustrating fish, dolphins, dugongs, turtles, and crocodiles, in fishing compositions which include bark canoes; goannas and a few other animals; weapons, such as returning boomerangs (no longer used), stone axes, clubs of now unknown types; and a few sets of little dancing men. Very few ancestral spirit figures are to be seen in this art. (See McCarthy, 1960: 297–401.) With the coming of the Indonesians, the Aborigines added to their material culture the dugout canoe, the detachable-headed harpoon, the metal axe, and many other objects. In the cave paintings these newer traits were superimposed on the old, and bright-red paint superimposed on the older dark-red variety. Attractive line patterns in white and yellow were added to the assortment of sea creatures, and Macassan praus appear in polychrome styles. The artists, although still interested at this time in the marine animals which provided the bulk of their flesh food, and which were in many cases totemic and thus a part of their religious view of life, nevertheless took full advantage of the new ideas and objects which served as a source of inspiration in their art motifs. It was probably in a ritual trade context that Indonesian motifs were introduced into the cave art. When these visits began is not yet established, but the evidence suggests that some centuries are involved. (See R. and C. Berndt, 1954.) The history of non-Aboriginal contacts is further recorded among the cave paintings: there are figures of Japanese pearlers, missionaries, aeroplanes, luggers and ships, water buffaloes, and other motifs of modern times. (See McCarthy, 1958: 64–6.)

In western Arnhem Land, in the inland sites between Tor Rock and El Sharana, the basic naturalistic art was apparently abandoned quite abruptly: there is an intrusion (of unknown origin) of a great variety of paintings relating to malignant and beneficent spirits, reported by the local Aborigines to live in the rocky escarpment or in the bush near waterholes. (See Plates 39, 40 and 42.) These spirits, shown sitting, bending, standing and running, from the side and front, have large genitalia and an amazing variety of head shapes: they are said to be visible only to native doctors and sorcerers.

The Mimi specimens (see, for example, Plates 36, 37 and 67) are the most gracefully drawn and posed human figures yet found in Australian cave art. They are small, sticklike people, spirits so delicately made that they can hunt only in calm weather; on the approach of living Aborigines, they escape to safety by blowing on a crevice to open the rock-face, which closes after they enter. These sometimes harmless spirits live and hunt in the same way as the Aborigines do. Static drawings of men carrying spear and spearthrower, basket and fan (or fly whisk), are just as aesthetically attractive as are those depicted in action, rushing with giant strides, fighting with spears, dancing and performing rituals. As some of them carry hafted stone axes, they are probably of no greater age than the introduction of this artifact.

The Mormo or Namandi make up a further series of malignant spirits, and some paintings of these are up to eight feet tall. (See, for example, Plates 39, 40 and 42.) They attack lone wanderers in the bush, or steal their spirit-stuff through the solar plexus. Adungun (or Aranga) is one who ate whole camps of people, but who was himself struck with so many spears that his stomach fell out of his body and he died. The Nabibi have stingray spines on their knees, elbows, and elsewhere, with which they shoot people as they drink from a waterhole. The Mali use their elbows as pointing-bones to kill human beings, and the Madjiba catch people with a hooked stick. Warlug lives high above the clouds, but comes down to steal food from the camps at night. The Namaragain women play string figures (or cat's-cradles), and use the string to move from one place to another. Barunbarun taught native doctors how to make stone spearheads. Some Mormo are hairy-bodied, their hair rustling as they move, and human-bone ornaments hang like pendants from their legs. The plain-surfaced Mormo painted in the caves differ to some extent from the highly decorated ones of greater variety painted on bark. (See Spencer, 1914, 1928; Mountford, 1956; Elkin and R. and C. Berndt, 1950.)

In the more recent phase of cave art in western Arnhem Land, X-ray figures (see Plates 33 and 60) are painted of various creatures, usually life-size or larger, and in bark paintings the small stick-men are shown hunting them. The barramundi, a large fish abounding in local waters, is a common subject, with geese, pelicans, emus, native companions, kangaroos, crocodiles, snakes, lizards, and other animals. On a white or yellow background, internal details like the backbone, alimentary tract, gills, heart, liver, pelvic girdle, and sometimes a young bird or fish, are painted in panels of fine parallel lines with a feather brush. Friezes up to a hundred feet long of this colourful art cover ceilings and walls of shelters. The natives remember the painting of some of these figures.

The meaning of the Arnhem Land paintings has not been clarified to a very satisfactory degree. The Mimi and other spirits illustrate mythology and folklore still extant. R. Berndt has said that some of the figures (in the late to recent phase) were painted to illustrate a myth or other story as it was told. (See R. and C. Berndt, 1951: 206–10.) The Mormo spirit figures, with their enormous genitals, more often shown in an aggressive manner, are the most heavily emphasized erotic subjects (comparable with the *Gurangara* engravings at Abydos), but they are not obviously so when compared with many which have been drawn on sheets of bark. These latter figures (see Plates 20, 39, 42 and 56) were used in imitative love magic designed to attract the attention of a specific woman, or to induce pregnancy. Some are concerned with sorcery, designed to punish a woman who has refused the approaches of a man. When a woman has committed adultery, and her husband hears

about it, he may perform sorcery: in this case, he paints her image and calls her name; as a result, or so local belief has it, she becomes ill and possibly dies within a few days. Enemies are punished in the same way. An important function of some of the paintings is that of a medium, to spread around the countryside, or in the water, the life essence of the mythical ancestor whose body such a painting represents, and thus increase the supply of food. There is as yet no comprehensive statement about the function of the X-ray cave paintings, which are apparently associated with hunting and fishing magic, and with totemic increase rites.

In the caves at Beswick and Tandanjal, on the fringe of south-western Arnhem Land, where many animals are painted, together with men and women in coitus, the emphasis is upon the continuance of male potency, as part of a fertility cult which embraces the rainbow serpent and Malindji spirits. One cave is a rock-wallaby totemic sanctuary, another a native-companion totemic site. (See Macintosh, 1951; Elkin, 1952.)

Equally outstanding as a region of cave painting are the Kimberleys, where two kinds of art are found. (See Worms, 1954, 1955.) The earlier one consists of graceful, life-size figures with rounded limbs and bodies, wearing unusually shaped head-dresses, and armed with spears and boomerangs. It may be possible to draw a parallel between this style and that associated with the Mormo spirits of western Arnhem Land. Not much of it has as yet been recorded, but it has a beauty of form and poise rarely seen in Aboriginal art. One remarkable painting is of a child drinking from its mother's breast.

The later Kimberley phase of the Wandjina ancestral spirit beings (see Chapters One and Two) is well known, but its origin has been the source of much speculation since its discovery by Sir George Grey. The Wandjina anthropomorphs, up to sixteen feet long, are painted in a thick-line design on a white ground. (See Plates 43 and 44.) On the head is a red and white or yellow oval band, which encircles the face, and from its outer edge radiates a fringe of red lines

41

tipped with black. This headband represents a strip of red ochre and fat, such as is commonly applied to the head and face of Aborigines today. The eyes and nose form one unit, usually in red, with long eyelashes encircling both eyes. Body and limbs have a thick red or black outline, covered with red stripes which represent falling rain. The hands and feet are large, and the latter lie on top of each other to expose the soles. Toes and fingers vary in number from three to seven. The genital organ is indicated in the female Wandjina, but not in the male. The mouth is never shown. The general effect of Wandjina is one of great mystical power vested in a kindly spirit possessing no dangerous attributes.

Wandjina are the named ancestral spirit beings of local clans—creator-heroes, each of whom made portion of the landscape, its fauna and flora, its rivers and caves. They were the first people, whose journeys are marked by pools rocks, bottle-trees, stone arrangements, and other sacred landmarks. Each one went into a cave, lay down and died, and his spirit entered the sacred Ungud pool. Another surviving Wandjina traced the outline and painted the dead one lying on his side, as many of the figures are posed. The Wandjina are asked or requested by the clan leaders to increase the spirits of babies, totem animals, and plants, and especially to make rain at the end of the dry season. Wandjina is 'a regenerative and reproductive power in nature and man'. (Elkin, 1930, 1948.) The belief and cult is fused with that of the rainbow serpent, called Galeru (or Galaru by Elkin, Káluru by Petri, and Kaleru by Kaberry) and Ungud in the northern Kimberleys. This huge serpent, frequently depicted in the caves, occurs also among the engravings of eastern Australia. Galeru serpents live in sacred pools, which they stock with the spirits of babies, near the Wandjina caves. (See, for example, Elkin, 1948,

1938/56; Petri, 1954; Worms, 1955: 548–52; McCarthy, 1958: 53–8.)

The Wandjina may be portrayed as a cluster of mouthless heads or busts, complete figures either upright or lying down, groups of males and females, and in haphazard series on a large wall. With them is shown an unusual range of the local totems, including kangaroo, wallaby, echidna, eagle, dingo, goanna, frilled lizard, crocodile, duck, cockatoo, wedge-tailed eagle, native companion, rainbird, snake, tortoise, barramundi and other fish, bats, bees and wild honey, and a wider range of plant motifs than elsewhere, including blossoms frequented by bees, macrozamia seed, black plums, yams, lily roots, and sprays of leaves and fruit. The animals are drawn in broad, simple style, their bodies covered with a dotted, broken line, striped or maze patterns. Malignant spirits, some said to be cannibalistic, are also portrayed. Clouds are represented by line designs, or by the loose boulders on the floors of the shelters. Series of figures of rainbow serpents and frilled lizards are also worthy of special mention.

The Lightning Brothers' caves at Delamere, in the Northern Territory, illustrate the difficulty of securing accurate interpretations of such motifs from the local Aborigines. (See Plate 38.) Davidson (1936) was told in 1930 that the two mythical brothers visit these rain and lightning totem centres, separated by a few hundred feet, during the rainy season. They are painted in four colours over an extensive series of animal and other figures. These beings are also said to have introduced subincision to the local Wadaman as part of their initiation ritual. The elder brother, Tjabuinji, carries his wife in the form of a forked stick under his arm. W. Arndt (see Arndt, 1962) was told more recently that the tableau was painted for rain-making purposes by an Aboriginal named Emu Jack, who did not complete it until 1956. (What is no doubt

9 A Maroota engraving of a male ancestral, or creative being
10 Engravings at the Devil's Rock group at Maroota, upper Hawkesbury River, New South Wales 11 Engraving at Maroota, depicting a life-sized figure of an emu with eggs, and some engraved tracks beside a natural sandstone rockhole

meant here is that the original paintings were retouched, so that rain would be magically induced to fall.) In this instance the striped body is said to be derived from a goanna, the black and white head-dress to represent storm-clouds, and the forked stick to be a stone axe used by Tjabuinji to split trees as his lightning strikes, while the so-called vulva is but a groove for sharpening this axe. W. E. Harney (for example, 1943) was told that a similar painting in the Victoria River gorge represents a fight between the two brothers over a woman, named Cananda (or Gananda), of the black cockatoo totem, shown as a non-human figure. The heads of the brothers are geckos, to symbolize rain because they can walk upside-down, and the body stripes are falling rain. As rain-providing heroes, the Lightning Brothers have the same function and significance as the Wandjina, and possibly represent an eastward extension of this art.

Study of the various strains of motifs and their superimpositions all over the continent represents a vital project, which must be carried out if we are to understand the development of Aboriginal art through time. The linear-design motifs in paintings and engravings occur in a band from north-west Australia, where they were possibly introduced, across Central Australia to the Great Dividing Range in eastern Australia. The great corpus of naturalistic rock art in the Kimberleys, Arnhem Land, Northern Territory, north Queensland, and eastern New South Wales appears, from its distribution, to have spread from the north-east. To this representative art belong the large ancestral spirit beings and rainbow serpents shown among paintings and engravings from the Kimberleys to eastern New South Wales. Sticklike human figures, from the small Mimi to the tall Mormo, occur throughout Australia, with the finest Mimi in the north.

In western Arnhem Land across to north-western Australia, the *Gurangara*-Kunapipi engravings and paintings, with erotic emphasis and huge genitals, form a more recent art movement. The correct interpretation of motifs, the linking of art phases with prehistoric cultures, and the separation of motifs belonging to each of the art phases—these are major problems for future research work on Australian Aboriginal rock art.

CHAPTER FOUR

The Art of Circle, Line, and Square

T. G. H. STREHLOW

The Aboriginal pictorial art of inland Australia appears to have been linked almost everywhere to a greater or lesser degree with the religious beliefs of the native population. In this respect it resembled the other art forms of this region— song, dance, and verse. In the case of the art patterns associated with sacred drama and ritual these links were naturally strong, and their nature obvious. But, even in the purely decorative designs that were applied to weapons, tools, and utensils in everyday use, there was little interest, traditionally at least, in introducing new patterns. For it was maintained that the local supernatural personages who had first fashioned these weapons, tools, and utensils, had determined their form, their shape, and their decorative patterns at the beginning of time. Hence the native artists seem to have made few attempts in recent times to change the decorative patterns, even when ornamenting non-sacred objects.

The best-documented designs of this vast inland region are those of Central Australia; and because of the intimate connection between Central Australian Aboriginal art and religion, I shall preface this account with a brief outline of the old religious beliefs of the Central Australian tribes.

Religious Belief and Ritual: The earth, so the Aranda and other inland tribes used to say, was uncreated and eternal. In the beginning it had been a bare plain, devoid of all physical features and of all forms of life. Then came the time when the great multitude of supernatural beings known as totemic ancestors emerged from their eternal sleep under the surface of this plain. The sacred sites where they emerged turned into soaks, waterholes, claypans, caves, and so forth. Each of these supernatural beings was normally, though not invariably, linked indivisibly with one particular animal or plant. Thus a native cat ancestor generally moved about in human form, but could turn at will into a native cat; and from him the native cats of his original district were believed to have descended, as well as the human beings conceived there. The latter were regarded as reincarnations of this ancestor, or of his supernatural children. Similarly, from a honey-ant, a kangaroo, or a carpet snake ancestor in any district the local honey-ants, kangaroos, or carpet snakes were believed to have descended, together with the human beings whose conception sites lay in this area. Hence any native belonging, say, to the kangaroo totem would not, except as a last resort, kill or eat kangaroos, since he believed that both he and they were descended from the same supernatural being. This, then, was the link between any man and the animal or plant that he regarded as his totem: he shared the same life with this animal or plant.

These totemic ancestors were also believed to have created all the prominent physical features of the present-day landscape—its ranges, hills, rocks, plains, sandhills, rivers, springs, and so on. At the end of their labours and their wanderings these supernatural personages either returned to the earth whence they had first sprung, or changed into sacred rocks, trees, or *tjurunga* slabs. They slept again in eternal sleep, as they had done at the beginning of time. But they retained their power to send down rain, and to fill the earth with the plants and animals of their own totems, whenever they were summoned by magic increase rites, in which their human reincarnations intoned the secret verses that they themselves had first sung during their own labours of creation. (See C. Strehlow, 1907–20; T. G. H. Strehlow, 1947; Spencer and Gillen, 1899/1938; 1904.)

One of the main functions of artistic endeavour in the Central Australian tribes was to honour the supernatural personages that were celebrated in the sacred myths and songs, and to introduce them—and the cult objects they were believed to have created—visually before the eyes of those fully initiated adult males who were entitled to witness this revelation. The audience included, in the first instance, men regarded as the reincarnations of the supernatural personages thus revealed. Secondly, the nearest male kinsmen and descendants by blood were eligible for this honour; these could inherit also the myths, songs, ritual, and *tjurunga* of dead men who had been regarded as such reincarnated persons. Thirdly, men from sites linked by sacred myths with the totemic centre, from which the owners of a ritual cycle came, had to be invited by these owners to witness at least some of the acts of that cycle, whenever it was being performed, and to help with the preparations of any cult objects used in them, and also with the decoration of actors in any of the individual rites constituting the cycle. Finally, it was open to the owners (called *ingkata* in Aranda, and *atanari* in Kukatja, or Gugadja) of the sacred traditions and ritual objects—that is, to the initiated males in the first two categories —to invite outsiders as their assistants during the performances. These could be related or unrelated persons. They are known as *kutungula* in the Aranda-speaking area. The *kutungula* could carry out only the tasks allotted by the *ingkata*. They were not allowed to reveal, on pain of death, what they had heard and seen, or to perform elsewhere the ritual in which they had taken part.

Women, since they were also believed to be reincarnations of local totemic ancestors, conventionally shared in the ownership of the sacred traditions and performances. In practice, however, they were not permitted to take part in any of their own totemic ceremonies, or to know the sacred songs and myths associated with their own centres. These were held in permanent trust for them by their fathers, brothers, or other male kinsmen. In any case, most women in the old days—because of the principle of exogamous marriage—lived most of their years after puberty in the territory of their husbands, not in that of their fathers and brothers. Women, however, had a role to play at the initiation festivals, and older women assisted the men in certain other secret rites as well. Moreover, there was a body of special women's lore, which was kept a close secret from men.

All breaches of the rules regulating the transmission of the sacred traditions, the performance of the ritual acts, the ownership of the sacred objects, and the artistic use of the decorative patterns and combinations of totemic motifs, were punishable by death in Central Australia. Consequently, sacred art was approached with an attitude of reverence. All incising of designs on the *tjurunga*, all work on cult objects, totem-poles, *waningga*, and ground paintings, all decorating of the ceremonial actors (see Plates 12, 13, and 16), and all sacred performances and ritual, took place to the singing of the appropriate song verses, believed to have been composed by the supernatural personages themselves. There was, in the old days, a complete ban on speech on all these occasions. If any man present had to make some personal communication, he used sign language. In the case of the sacred dramatic performances, any *kutungula* who had been permitted to act in one had to be freed from his ban of silence by having his mouth brushed by the *ingkata* with a cult object used in the act.

From these general observations on the religious concepts permeating the sacred art of Central Australia, we may pass to a discussion of totemic emblems and their art motifs.

The Totemic Emblems and Their Motifs: The commonest art motifs in Central Australia are curvilinear designs, which have often been labelled geometric figures. The most frequent of these are concentric circles, U-figures, spirals, straight and curved lines (also dots). To these may be added the simple bird footprints and stylized animal tracks engraved on many *tjurunga* associated with bird and animal totems. (See Plate 70).

While these figures are found in their artistic perfection only in the sacred decorative patterns, they are used in their simple forms also for ordinary story-telling purposes by men, women, and children throughout Central Australia. In my own boyhood days among the Western Aranda, for instance, children used to make drawings in the sand when telling stories, which were closely parallel to our own nursery tales. Thus, a girl telling the story of the *njunju* (or *njibantibanta*) women who had chased, killed, and eaten a boy who had wandered away too far from his parents' camp, would first smooth out the sand in front of her. She would then make a slight circular depression with the side or back of her hand to denote the *njunju's* camp or camp-fire, and then mark out a U-figure open toward the circular depression to indicate the *njunju* herself, sitting cross-legged and facing her fire. Next the boy would be shown approaching: the story-teller would walk her fingers

across the sand, leaving behind a series of dots. The U-figure would now be rubbed out, to show that the *njunju* had got up to chase the boy. The story-telling fingers would stride rapidly from the fire across the sand to the point where the boy's tracks had ended. The chase would begin —round and round the camp-fire; and the index finger would indicate the trail and the pace of pursuer and pursued by drawing a narrowing spiral more and more rapidly around the central circle that stood for the camp-fire. Suddenly the finger would stop: the boy had been clubbed and killed by the *njunju* woman. The dead boy was depicted, lying dead on the ground, by a slightly curved line marked into the sand near the fire. It would now be rubbed out and marked across the fire itself, after which the sand from the edge of the depressed fire-circle would be heaped into the centre, to show that the hot ashes from the *njunju's* fire were being heaped upon the body of the boy in order to cook it. Throughout the story the smoothed sand in front of the story-teller became covered with marks showing what was happening to the personages of the tale. The girl would, of course, relate the story while her fingers were telling the details in the sand. Finally, the whole sand story would be wiped out, and some new tale would begin to take shape on the ground.

Because of the practice they had gained as children in making running illustrations for their secular stories, the older men were fond of using sand drawings also when passing on the sacred myths to the younger initiated males. They frequently used the flat side of a boomerang for the preliminary smoothing-out of the sand, and the rounded tip for delineating the circles, U-figures, and curved lines required by their story. It is an easy step from these simple sand figures to the similarly shaped, but highly elaborated, incised figures on the sacred *tjurunga*, especially if we remember that the artists working on these stone or hardwood mulga objects (see also Plate 70) had only the sharp incisor tooth of the possum as their engraving tool. (The jaw in which this tooth was set was used as a natural handle.) Since it was impossible to scrape out a large circular area, or a broad U-figure, or a similar broad mark of any kind with the sharp point of a possum tooth, the engraver resorted to drawing a large number of concentric circles, a series of U-figures, a number of close and parallel straight or curved lines, and so on. The meanings of these elaborated figures, on the other hand, remained unchanged. Many of these elaborated figures were used also on the sacred ground paintings, totem-poles, *waningga*, and persons of the ritual actors, even though the Aboriginal artists—who were here working in down and painted stripes (see Plate 12)—could in these cases have used the broad and simple figures found in the sand drawings.

The basic figures themselves were undoubtedly stylized representations of the actual marks of persons, animals, and objects left behind on the surface of the ground. The ashes of a camp-fire *are* roughly circular in shape when viewed from above; the marks left behind in the sand by a person who has been sitting cross-legged are roughly U-shaped; a large camping-ground pitted by hundreds of footprints does look from above as though its surface has been sprinkled with dots; and sticks lying on the ground leave behind imprints like broad, straight lines; and so on.

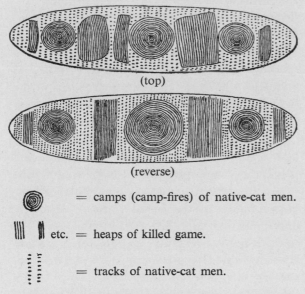

(top)

(reverse)

⊚ = camps (camp-fires) of native-cat men.

‖‖ ‖ etc. = heaps of killed game.

⫶ = tracks of native-cat men.

Fig. 5. Tjilpa (native cat) tjurunga from Kataka (western Aranda)

It has already been remarked that, on some stone and wooden *tjurunga* associated with bird and animal totems, stylized imitations of actual bird and animal tracks are found—a further proof that their makers had here incised marks symbolical of those which the mythical beings had left behind them. As I have written elsewhere (in Battarbee, 1951: 3):

A central Australian native used to read the ground like a book. If he came upon a deserted camp site, he could tell from looking at the earth how many men, women, and children had left their marks behind, where they had slept, where and what they had eaten, when they had last been there, and so on. The position of windbreaks and fires indicated to him facts about the presence of married couples and the number of husbandless women. Centuries of acute observation had similarly taught him to tell from tracks not only what kind of birds and animals were in his neighbourhood, but also what they had been doing before his arrival and what they were likely to be doing at the moment. As a result the Aranda people had, naturally enough, developed in their pictorial art the habit of looking down upon a landscape from above and not from the side, as we do.*

In Central Australian sacred art the figures that had originally been free representations of tracks and marks on the ground were not only elaborate and stylized; they were also combined into artistic patterns so as to achieve balance and symmetry of design, and often great elegance, rhythm, and vigour in their total effect. Just as in the Central Australian dramatic performances the actors tended to avoid completely realistic gestures, and used stylized and highly rhythmic movements in their miming techniques, so the native artist avoided fully representational figures in his patterns. He also avoided the normal everyday arrangements of persons and objects in his combinations of the figures representing them. Two persons sitting at a common fire would be shown as two U-figures facing each other across a common central circle. This would correspond to the arrange-

*During the writer's camel travels over thousands of miles through the trackless interior years ago, his Aboriginal companion, who was riding on the leading camel many yards in front, never ceased reading the ground for tracks, marks, or footprints, and kept on pointing out by means of sign language anything of more than usual interest that the ground had revealed to him. The writer himself still enjoys reading the ground on his own visits to the Centre.

ment of two actors in the sacred dramatic ceremonies: these, if they shared a common ceremonial object, such as a totem-pole or a ground painting, would sit facing each other (or one behind the other, facing in the same direction), but *never* side by side—which would have been the normal position in actual life.

The Materials: The fine talents of the best Central Australian artists may be gauged also from the skill with which they used the four vivid colours available to them for their body decorations, ground paintings, and painted and down-covered cult objects. Their media were the natural pigments of yellow ochre, red ochre, and pipeclay (or other soft white rock, like gypsum), plus charcoal. Yellow ochre was used only in a small number of the inland totems. In the remaining totems the often amazingly varied colour effects had to be achieved purely by the use of three colours—black, white, or red; and in most designs only two colours were used. Occasionally white would be used on its own. Some of the most strikingly decorated actors in the Ilbalintja Bandicoot Cycle were men who wore patterns made in white down on upper bodies painted with white pipeclay: these men were wearing what was called 'the ghost-gum pattern', ghost-gums being among the prominent trees in the Ilbalintja landscape.

Red and yellow ochre were readily obtainable throughout the greater part of the Aranda-speaking area, also in the hilly country of other inland tribes. The sandhill and plain dwellers, however, had to obtain them by trading from their more fortunate neighbours. Since yellow ochre, while used much less frequently than red ochre in the artistic patterns, was to be found much more plentifully in the interior, it was often burnt until it took on various shades of orange-red, and then used in place of the natural red ochre, which tended to be of a rather darker colour. Red and yellow ochre and pipeclay (or gypsum) were ground into powder on flat stones. They were then mixed with water, and applied direct to persons or objects. If the decorative scheme called for the use of coloured birds' down or vegetable matter, the birds'

down and vegetable matter were placed on top of the flat stone, covered with some of the ground pigment, and rubbed by hand or ground with a smaller stone until they had turned colour. The best soft black was obtained by burning pieces of the thick bark cut from corkwood or honeysuckle trees: this yielded a rich, soft, sooty-black pigment.

Extensive use was made of birds' down in the Central Australian sacred patterns. (See Plates 12, 13 and 14.) The down normally came from eagle nestlings, which had been killed in their nests when they were almost ready to fly. Such a nestling is a surprisingly big bird, and yields a large amount of white down. One killed near Alice Springs in 1955 supplied most of the down in the eighteen three-inch-wide bands that ringed the black totem-pole of Urumuna. In a great part of the MacDonnell Range country, where eagles are common, down was put on profusely in many acts, and the whole head and upper body of actors were sometimes completely covered with it. In the western and eastern desert areas, on the other hand, the use of down was often confined to thin strips and curved lines only. The tops of a certain plant (apparently a portulaca) were sometimes ground up and used as a substitute for down; this, of course, was possible only in good seasons—the only times when full ceremonial festivals could be held. On other occasions, further north, wild cotton was used. In pre-European days all hunters pursuing game in mountainous districts of the Centre kept their eyes open for eagles' nests in the appropriate seasons, and killed and plucked the young fledglings. The fully grown eagles yielded the bold plumes used as decorative bunches in many ritual and ceremonial acts. Red-and-white cockatoo crest feathers, red-and-black cockatoo tail feathers, and plumes taken from hawks and owls, were also used in different contexts. So were the rabbit bandicoot tails known in Aranda as *albetja*. All these articles— red and yellow ochre, gypsum or pipeclay, birds' down and vegetable matter, balls of hair-string and furstring, and bunches of bird plumes —were stored, along with the sacred *tjurunga*,

48

in the sacred caves or the storehouse trees. It may be added that down (or its substitute) was stuck to both human bodies and ceremonial objects with blood donated by some of the men present—generally by the *kutungula* (ceremonial assistants). Since no sight of this blood was permitted to the women and children, even the decoration of men and objects in the semi-sacred acts (or in the non-sacred ceremonial dances) had to be done secretly; and the performers had to wash off all signs of blood before returning to the main camp. (This was not the case, however, among the people of the Western Desert). *The Sacred Patterns:* Each totemic centre in Central Australia was associated with one or several sets of traditional patterns; and none of these could be copied and used by men of other centres, on pain of death. This was one of the reasons why, at all ritual and ceremonial festivals, the men revealing the complete cycle of the local totemic centre were careful to invite representatives from all other sites linked by myths with their own centre. For these vistors would, upon returning to their own homes, bear witness that no 'stolen' patterns had been surreptitiously revealed at the festival.

The total number of totemic patterns in Central Australia must have run into many thousands. Their multiplicity is a tribute to the skill with which both the four colours and a few simple figures available were combined, so as to avoid duplication of any design.

These sacred patterns were applied to persons and to cult objects during the singing of the appropriate song verses. No verses from other totems, or even from other centres of the same totem, could be used during the actual decoration. When the initial ground painting of the Aranda honey-ant centre of Ljaba was being prepared in 1950, the work of making it began at nine in the morning, and continued without a break until three in the afternoon. During the whole of this period only three verses from the long Ljaba Song were permitted to be sung; and these were repeated time and time again, until the ground painting had been completed. All three related to the original honey-ant nest at Ljaba, from which the superantural honey-ants had emerged at the beginning of time:

From the crest-top they (i.e., the honey-ants)
   fling the soil,
From the crest-top they scatter afar the soil.

Far-flung it spreads out,
In scatterèd rings it spreads out.

Here in the hard, blood-soaked clay soil
Cells upon cells open their mouths.

The different colours used in the concentric ring bands of the Ljaba ground painting had symbolic significance. The charcoal bands signified the nectar of the honey-ants. The red-down bands stood for the red nectar-filled bodies of the storage ants. The white-down rings stood for the mulga sugar. The yellow-ochre bands symbolized the yellow blossoms of the mulga trees. In nature, when the mulga trees are in blossom, the honey-ants emerge from their underground cells in order to gather their nectar. Hence the yellow bands on the initial ground painting showed that this was 'mulga blossom time' for the honey-ant totemic ancestors: it was time for them to reveal themselves once more to their human honey-ant clansmen. Accordingly, in the redecorated second Ljaba ground painting which was revealed at the end of the festival the yellow-ochre bands were eliminated—a sign that 'mulga blossom time' was over, and that the moment had come for the honey-ant totemic ancestors to sink back to sleep once more.

As far as we know, there were in Central Australia no totemic patterns which ranged unchanged over the whole area. All complete colour and figure arrangements were associated not only with totems, but also with definite centres, as was the case with the myths, songs, and sacred acts themselves. There were, then, no general honey-ant patterns in Central Australia—there were only sets of distinctive patterns for definite local honey-ant centres, such as Ljaba, Alkala, Lukaria, Popanji, and so on; and the right to reveal any of these was jealously guarded by the local owners.

The restrictions under which the Central

Australian Aboriginal artists laboured were indeed formidable. They had to confine themselves to a small number of figures, most of which had been stylized into geometrical shapes —circles, U-figures, straight and curved lines, dots, rudimentary footprints, and so on. (See Basedow, 1925: 334–55). They could not depart from the figure combinations traditionally associated with the totemic centres and their ceremonial cycles. They could not—since these figures and patterns were believed to have been provided by the local supernatural beings— adopt into their own sacred art, at least within recent historic times, any new styles (for instance, X-ray designs, naturalistic, and anthropomorphic figures from the northern and northwestern Australian areas). Even their use of colour was strictly limited to red, black, white, and yellow. Yet these artists managed to produce hundreds of highly decorative patterns, capable of impressing even alien observers, most of whom were completely ignorant of their sacred significance. Again, in the incised designs on stone and board the manifold repetition and elaboration of each motif were aesthetically pleasing. On an engraved *tjurunga*, for instance, the plain circle found in the sand drawings was normally elaborated into a figure of ten, twenty, or even more concentric circles, or into a cleverly executed spiral containing the same number of convolutions. (See Plates 14 and 70.) Similarly, single lines or U-figures were rarely found: they were generally doubled, trebled, or repeated still more often. The best artists showed a keen feeling for the beauty of line and contour; and some of their freehand concentric circles were remarkable not merely for their elaboration, but for sheer beauty.

The circles shown in the larger ground paintings were executed not by one, but by several men, sitting opposite each other on different edges of the same hardened circular piece of ground. The central circle would be made first. After that, the additional concentric rings would be etched out by several men, working outward; and each man would do only that part of each circle which curved immediately before him.

In most cases these circles were beautifully regular in their shape. In contrast, when some years ago the sound-tracking of one of the writer's ceremonial colour films required that a man's hand be shown drawing a series of simple concentric circles and duplicated U-figures during the telling of an abridged native myth, it took days for the film producer to find even one 'white' commercial artist in Sydney who could draw freehand circles with the sureness and speed that characterized the Aboriginal artists.

The best Central Australian works show that the Aboriginal artists who created them had developed considerable skill in mastering the basic problems of composition, drawing, and colour, and their best work was notable for its fine feeling for balance and rhythm. (See Davidson, 1937; McCarthy, 1938/58, 1957a.) The most serious defect—if we can call it that— of Central Australian sacred art was its inability to achieve its full emotional effect independently of verbal explanations. The artists, and the audiences which viewed their efforts depended for their understanding of all completed works on the secret words of the sacred songs that referred to them. Hence Central Australian pictorial art was never able to achieve its full emotional appeal without the help of a different medium—the medium of sacred verse. Because of this, the pictorial art of Central Australia will probably alway rank, at least in the eyes of alien observers, lower than the anthropomorphic and X-ray designs of northern and western coastal Australia. But in one sense, because of their integral connection with poetic songs and ritual action, they are infinitely more subtle; and they should be evaluated in these terms.

The various categories of Central Australia art forms may now be considered in more detail.

Ground Paintings: Ground paintings were produced only within a limited area. The writer has seen over thirty of these designs so far among the northern and western Aranda, the Unmatjera, the Pintubi, the Kukatja, the Pitjantjara (or Bidjandjara), and the Iliaura. Spencer and

50

Gillen (1899/1938, 1904) and others (for example, McCarthy, 1938/58, 1957a) have illustrated some of these beautiful ground paintings, mainly from the Waramunga. They were not made among the groups of the Eastern or Southern Aranda, or of the Western Desert, but were relatively general farther north, as far as the Victoria River country. To produce a good surface for a ground painting, the artists normally spread broken-up termite mound on the selected piece of ground, softened it with water into a thick paste, and patted its surface into the required shape. In many areas it was then hardened by blood from the arm veins of the totemites before receiving its decorations of coloured ochres and feather down. (An example may be seen in Plate 14.) The designs ranged from the simple circular ground paintings of certain Western Aranda and Kukatja kangaroo centres, done wholly in white down, to the elaborate colour and down patterns of the long series of interconnected honey-ant sites that stretched from the Pintubi (Bindubi) into the Iliaura area. Not all of these designs used birds' down in their decorations: the five Iliaura plum-tree and honey-ant ground paintings witnessed by the writer used rings and ornamental figures done in colour only.

The most beautiful of these Iliaura designs was the honey-ant ground paintings of Unggwalala-nama. This consisted of seven large U-figures, grouped like the petals of a flower around a cluster of yellow and black concentric rings, in the midst of which was a hole holding a slim totem-pole covered with red down and broken by three bands of white down at its top, middle, and bottom. The black U-figures enclosed white areas, which had been dotted plentifully with yellow ochre and charcoal spots. The spots within the U-figures represented the honey-ants resting in their subterranean cells. The central concentric circles depicted the honey-ant nest, with its central pipe-throat leading from the surface down to the cells below. This ground painting was revealed to postulants as a verse from the relevant myth-cycle was sung. This compared the honey-filled storage ants with

their reddish bodies in the underground cells to sleeping men, their bodies gleaming red in the glow of camp-fires burning behind their wind-breaks:

> *Where far-flung their hollows stretch*
> *With firelight aflame they dwell, ever dwell.*

Among the most elaborate artistic designs ever recorded in Central Australia are the ground paintings associated with the Wollunqua (mythical water-serpent) and Thalaualla (black snake) totems of the Waramunga tribe. These were shown to Spencer and Gillen (1904).

In general, ground paintings were symbolic representations of certain major totemic sites, especially those associated with the emergence and disappearance of important supernatural beings. Consequently, they were constructed at the beginning of the ritual cycles concerned with those particular beings; and all subsequent dramatic acts were staged near them until, at the end of the festival, the ground paintings were ritually destroyed.

In many areas where ground paintings were not made (for instance, in the Southern and Eastern Aranda areas), painted shields were used for the same purpose—that of representing the major totemic centres figuring in the dramatic performances. (See Plate 13.) In the *utnurungita* (green caterpillar) rites of Alice Springs, Emily Gap, and other associated centres, the performers, who mimed the fluttering actions of the butterflies which spring from these green caterpillars, made their way slowly towards shields bearing the totemic marks of the appropriate centre. In the kangaroo ceremonies of Krantji and Ulamba, painted shields bearing the patterns of these sites were placed on top of the pure-white ground paintings. These shields were then left on the ground paintings for the duration of the kangaroo increase cycles—a period of several weeks. In areas where painted shields were used by themselves, they were normally decorated for use in one act only, and stripped of their patterns immediately afterward.

Decorated Human Performers: The mythical supernatural beings, who emerged from the sacred sites indicated in the ground paintings and painted shields, were brought before the eyes of the totemites in sacred dramatic performances by actors masked and disguised by traditional designs executed in the four ritual colours and in down. (See Plates 13 and 16.) Such patterns served to hide the human identity of the actor, just as face masks and costumes were once used in performances in other parts of the world, to indicate to the audience that the human personages, representing superhuman beings, had temporarily assumed superhuman likenesses and superhuman personalities.

Most of the great Central Australian ritual centres had their dramatic acts grouped into cycles. Every cycle included *all* the acts which revealed the supernatural beings mentioned in the myth associated with the centre. These mythical figures were presented in a kind of living portrait gallery. The acts in which they appeared were graded according to their sacredness. In the initial acts the least important supernatural beings were revealed. The more important figures delayed their appearance until the middle or end of a cycle. If the important mythical personages were revealed several times, they appeared at various points in the cycle—at first with plain patterns only, then wearing more elaborate designs, and finally bearing the most sacred symbols of their power, such as ornamented *tjurunga* and other pieces of headgear, *waningga*, or totem-poles. In many Central Australian cycles the main 'earthborn' totem-pole was revealed in the final act.

For acts requiring the wearing of head-dresses, the performers wore special head coverings of tree or shrub tips. Those made from mulga tips were deemed to be the best, since they were the least likely to slip during performances: such an accident would have been regarded as foreshadowing the death of the performer. To make such a covering, short branches were laid, tips downward, against the forehead, sides, and back of the performer's head, after which hairstring was wound around them tightly until a helmet-shaped top had been formed. After the actor had been decorated, the ritual headgear was either stuck directly into this helmet, or fastened to it with long skewers.

Waningga: The *waningga* (also known as the 'thread cross') was a sacred object made by tying two sticks into a cross, or three sticks into a double cross, and then stringing parallel bands of hairstring or furstring across the resulting frame. (See Plate 14.) A spear was sometimes used for the upright pole. The string base was then decorated with feather-down patterns. *Waningga* were used particularly in the southern and western areas of Central Australia, and their use extended westward over most, perhaps all, of the desert areas of Western Australia. Among the Aranda the *waningga* was used only by the western and southern groups: the other Aranda groups used the decorated *tjurunga* and the totem-pole instead.

Waningga varied in size from small hairstring crosses, stuck into the hair of the performers, to much larger objects that were either carried on the backs of the performers (like the Southern Aranda rain *waningga* of Idracowra), or stuck into the ground close to them. The rain *waningga* just referred to represented a storm-cloud, with flashes of lightning and streaks of falling rain emanating from it. Frequently, however, the *waningga*—like the ground paintings and the painted shield—symbolized the local ceremonial centre. Thus the Pintubi honey-ant *waningga* of Tatata (like the Western Aranda honey-ant *waningga* of Alkala) represented the honey-ant nest, from which the local supernatural beings had emerged.

Totem-poles: The totem-pole (*tnatantja*—and sometimes *kauaua*—in Aranda, *anatantji* in Kukatja and many of the western languages; Spencer's spelling was *nurtunja*) was a cult object of many forms and sizes. It could be a short stick ornamented with bands and stripes of colour or down; it could be a long stick or spear (several spears were sometimes tied together to give extra length and thickness), covered with grass or shrub tips (generally mulga), wound round with hairstring, and ornamented in the same way; or it could be a tall, slim gum sapling, up to twenty-three feet in height, which bore similar decorations. It could also be, especially among the Aranda people living along the Lower Finke and Hale rivers, a long, flat slab of mulga, perhaps twelve feet in length and often provided with a horizontal cross-piece, which was covered with bands and rings of down. All forms of *tnatantja* pole could have cross-pieces attached to them, if the local ceremonial centre traditionally demanded this. In many, perhaps most, cases bullroarers were suspended from the smaller totem-poles and their cross-pieces, and larger *tjurunga* from the large poles and cross-pieces. In some ceremonial centres totem-poles with cross-pieces had a *waningga*-like square of hairstring bands strung across them.

Just as the ground painting was essentially a female symbol, so the totem-pole was essentially a male symbol.

The tops and the ends of the arms of all *waningga* and totem-poles were decorated with feather tips. Eagle, black cockatoo, white cockatoo, hawk, and owl plumes were used for this purpose, the use of any particular feathers being governed by tradition at each centre. In the old days bandicoot-tail tips were also frequently used to ornament *waningga*, totem-poles, and the sacred actors. But these animals became virtually extinct over Central Australia about fifty years ago, and their tail tips are rarely seen today.

Perhaps the most common sacred verses in the whole of Central Australia were the two ubiquitous couplets referring to the totem-pole. They occurred in the songs of most Aranda and Unmatjera centres, and also at many Loritja sites. These were the couplets:

> *Lo, the tnatantja pole,*
> *Covered with rings and stripes!*

> *Lo, the kauaua pole,*
> *Covered with rings and stripes!*

Some other ceremonial objects, especially various pieces of headgear (for instance, objects symbolizing the sun disc, or soakages), were found in some totems of this area; but space

will not permit any discussion of them.

Tjurunga: We now come to the sacred objects (see Plate 70) called *tjurunga* in the Aranda-speaking area (*kuntangka* was the common Loritja form). These were slabs of stone or wood, which, in most cases, had the totemic patterns of the appropriate sacred sites incised into them with possum teeth. They varied in size from about a foot to six feet. Both sides were decorated, but not necessarily with identical patterns. Not all *tjurunga*, however, bore these incised designs. Everywhere in Central Australia *tjurunga* stones and slabs could be found that were completely devoid of ornamentation; and these sometimes were the oldest and most prized objects in the *tjurunga* storehouse. Again, the Southern Aranda used mainly plain wooden sticks that had been liberally coated with fat and red ochre. The *tjurunga* storehouse was generally a cave; but in many areas *tjurunga* were stored on platforms of branches and leaves set up on storage trees. Such storehouse trees were a necessity for ceremonial centres situated on plains and among sandhills, but they were by no means limited to them. In the cave-rich eastern MacDonnells, for instance, all Hale River rain *tjurunga* used to be stored on gidyea-tree platforms.

These *tjurunga* were intimately associated with the supernatural beings. (See T. G. H. Strehlow, 1947.) It was believed that, when the totemic ancestors sank back into eternal sleep, some changed into rocks or boulders, others into sacred trees, still others into *tjurunga* (especially into plain, unmarked stone *tjurunga*). Their weapons and implements generally turned into wooden *tjurunga:* for these objects also contained the same 'life' as the supernatural beings who had made and used them. Every human being in Central Australia was represented by a *tjurunga:* this was regarded as a person's immortal body, in which his spirit had been encapsulated since the period when the supernatural beings themselves were still roaming the land. Hence, if a child was 'reincarnated' at a centre for which no *tjurunga* slab could be found in the storehouse, an elderly male relative was authorized to fashion a new mulga *tjurunga* for the child, and to ornament it with the child's totemic pattern. Such a man-made *tjurunga* was regarded as a replica of the child's mysterious immortal body, which could not be found, because it had gone into the ground at the child's conception site at the beginning of time. In addition to the normal *tjurunga* here described, there were special small wooden objects known as bullroarers. These had holes at one end, and could be swung by an attached hairstring. They varied from about six to eighteen inches in length, and were used at the initiation ceremonies and in love magic.

In Central Australia each *tjurunga* had its personal 'name', which had to be sung whenever it was being inspected or handled. This name was one of the verses from the sacred song cycle associated with the appropriate totemic centre. Similarly the individual figures, constituting the complete designs incised on the *tjurunga* and the bullroarers of this area, were authenticated or substantiated by verses occurring in the relevant songs.

In my volume on Aranda religion (1947) I endeavoured to describe in some detail the major concepts underlying traditional beliefs concerning the *tjurunga*, along with the rules governing the ownership of these objects.

Only initiated adult males were permitted to view their *tjurunga*. Women's *tjurunga*, like their own personal ritual acts, were kept and performed for them by their fathers and brothers.

All *tjurunga* storehouses, since they were believed to contain objects still imbued with the life and the power of supernatural beings, normally had to be avoided on pain of death: even initiated men could approach them only on ritual occasions under the leadership of the local headmen. At such times all weapons had to be left outside the sacred area: even animals were safe from the spears of hunters within the precincts of the storehouse. Such a game sanctuary generally comprised an area of at least one or two square miles around the cave, or storage tree.

Since the men who visited such a sacred area had to do so before they had eaten anything for the day, some of them would hunt some game in the morning and leave this meat on the branches of the same trees beneath which they put their spears. Upon arrival at the storehouse, the men would take out the *tjurunga* with great reverence, and rub them with fat and red ochre, singing at the same time the verses that contained their secret names. Only after performing these rites could the party return to the place where their spears and the meat had been left; and here they had their first meal for the day.

Sacred and Semi-sacred Art: Only the sacred art of the inland tribes has been considered so far. It constituted by far the largest and most interesting part of the men's artistic endeavours, but was kept secret from the women and children. The latter could, however, witness the patterns worn by the men in their semi-sacred acts and in their secular dances.

In some Aranda totems semi-sacred acts were performed in which the actors even wore sacred *tjurunga* veiled with strips of down on their heads, and down patterns of the normal sacred type on their bodies. Had these acts been classed as sacred, no uninitiated person could have witnessed them; but during semi-sacred performances the women and children of the area were not only permitted, but actually obliged, to be present. As an instance here, in the Northern Aranda fire ceremonies of Urubuntja (or Rubuntja) the performers, wearing sacred *tjurunga* on their heads, moved up the fire-furrows to the women who sat at the far end of the ceremonial ground. (See Plate 16.)

Again, some of the most pleasing designs among the Aranda were the semi-sacred patterns painted wholly in colour on the backs and chests of men who had participated in a ceremonial festival and were about to return to their everyday way of life. (See Plate 12.) The paints were applied either by finger, or by means of little sticks around which hairstring had been wound. These patterns were still associated with the sacred totems, but could be applied generally to all male participants (that is, without regard for their personal totems). They were intended to be viewed by women and children: in fact, the women put the decorated men through the rite of ceremonial smoking—a rite which marked the close of each festival.

Among the 'settled' Central Australian tribes (see below) only secular art forms were vulnerable to the imitator and innovator. There were no restrictions on ornamental patterns worn by performers in the non-sacred 'folk' dances, which have been commonly called, by Europeans, corroborees. These could be traded from tribe to tribe: and their decorative patterns, songs, and dance-steps were copied in much the same way as, for example, American jazz and modern dance forms have been adopted and adapted over wide areas of the European world and elsewhere. The corroboree decorations were, of course, diffused over large areas, along with the relevant songs and dances.

How widely these ceremonies travelled in historical times may be learnt from some old gramophone cylinders of Aboriginal songs made by Baldwin Spencer at the Stevenson River, in the lower Southern Aranda area, in 1901, and kept among the records of the Royal Geographical Society, Adelaide, for about half a century. These cylinders contain a number of sacred verses, taken from lower Southern Aranda songs. But they contain also a number of non-sacred verses, not only from that area, but also from the Wailbri (or Walbiri), Unmatjera, and Waramunga. Of these, the Ltata Molunga (that is, the Molunga ceremony: see Roth, 1897; McCarthy, 1939: 83–5) had first been introduced from the Tennant Creek area into Queensland, had travelled from there south through the Channel Country to Port Augusta, and had moved back north from there along the western side of Lake Eyre into the southern Aranda area. One of my informants, who helped to identify this Molunga verse for me in 1960, had first heard it at Peake Station in 1901. Some time afterward it came north to Horseshoe Bend, and by 1950 it had reached as far as Maryvale Station, on the Hugh River in Central Australia.

Passing reference must be made also to the variously shaped *toa*, or wooden direction signs, of the Dieri and other Lake Eyre tribes. These *toa* were often beautifully decorated in the usual four colours, with figures similar to those found in the sacred art of the inland tribes. Although it seems (from the little that is known about them) that the *toa* were not sacred objects, their shapes, colours, and patterns appear to have referred commonly to episodes in the wanderings of the supernatural beings of the Dieri, the Muramura. To quote from Stirling and Waite, (1919: 112) who first recorded them:

When a native is about to break camp and move to some other place he makes a Toa representing the locality to which he is moving and sticks its pointed end into the earth at the camp about to be left; signs are also made on the ground to call attention to its presence. In this way the friends of the departing native, who recognize the significance of the Toa, are made aware of the place to which he has gone.

The rock paintings and rock carvings of inland Australia may be mentioned only in passing (see Chapter Three). For instance, the cave drawings at Ayers Rock—many of which are secular, and some of which add human and animal forms to the usual footmarks, circles, and similar geometric figures—are widely known now to European tourists. There are also many other places in the Centre where simple, painted designs occur, and a number of sites which show simple figures engraved into rocky surfaces; but in point of artistic interest none of the works at these inland sites can compare with the rock paintings and carvings found in certain other parts of the continent, especially in northern and north-western Australia. (See Chapters Two and Three.)

Diffusion of Central Australian Art Style, and Comparison with Other Areas: I have emphasized that, generally speaking, severe penalties were once imposed on those who copied the sacred art patterns and designs of Central Australia. In pre-European times death was the supreme sanction for all forms of sacrilege: and this included copying and using in a different context the sacred patterning relevant to 'other men's' centres and cult objects. There are a number of records relating to the killing of persons, and even whole groups, for offences of this nature from 1860 onward. The death penalty in this respect was undoubtedly a powerful factor influencing the relative stability of sacred art forms in this part of Central Australia for a very long period, and militated against the introduction of new forms. However, two qualifications must be made. Many of the religious myths themselves describe the wanderings of supernatural beings through the territories of several other tribes: and clansmen from these other tribes, living along these mythical routes of travel, used to meet at one another's ceremonial festivals. There can be little doubt that totemic art patterns and cult objects were diffused along such mythical tracks: for what would have been more natural for the heroes of these myths—whose travels may well have had a firm historical basis in actual wanderings undertaken in far-off times by real individuals or groups of totemic clansmen—than to spread the art forms of their ritual at the totemic centres they established on those journeys?

An undoubted instance of diffusion of this kind may be seen in the honey-ant songs, acts, and ground paintings of the Kukatja and Pintubi tribes. Their myths relate how an Iliaura honey-ant ancestor came from the Sandover River, through the territories of the Iliaura, the Unmatjera, the Northern Aranda, the Western Aranda, and the Kukatja, to a Pintubi honey-ant site not very far from the Ehrenberg Ranges —a distance of about four hundred miles. The ancestor then took a party of the local honey-ant people back with him to the Sandover River. This myth undoubtedly had a historical basis; for practically all verses in the Kukatja and Pintubi honey-ant songs were composed or rendered in Aranda, while the ground paintings, despite minor differences, also showed the usual Aranda honey-ant patterns.

Secondly, my contention that sacred art and ritual had become static (or rigidly formalized) in Central Australia well before the arrival of the first European settlers is intended to apply only to that very extensive, well-watered area,

 = long furstring bands hanging down from heads of *mala* men, with *tjurunga* tips pushed under them.

 = homes (nests) of *mala* rat-kangaroos.

 = tracks linking nests.

Fig. 6. Time-beating stick, mala totem, Maurunga (Kukatja).

which was occupied by 'settled' Aboriginal groups able to live within tribal territories cut up into numerous small hunting-grounds—that is, into the *njinanga* section areas mentioned in my *Aranda Traditions* (1947: 128, 139–50). These were the tribes occupying the MacDonnell and James ranges, the Burt Plain, the valleys of the great dry river systems (the Finke, Palmer, Sandover, Lander, Todd, Hale, Hugh, and Alberga), and the areas immediately adjoining these regions. This area stretched from Oodnadatta in the south to at least Tennant Creek in the north, and from Mt. Liebig and King's Creek in the west toward and across the Queensland-Northern Territory border in the east. West of Mt. Liebig and King's Creek the situation changed completely. Here began the great desert areas, which swept on through the greater part of the interior of Western Australia toward Kalgoorlie, Meekatharra, Marble Bar, Anna Plains, and the Fitzroy River. The so-called Western Desert tribes which lived in them were forced by their relatively inhospitable country, and the frequent droughts that ravaged it, to spend most of their lives in wandering over relatively large areas; for not many of their waters—which consisted mainly of limestone soaks, rockholes, and the like, but included few river systems—could be depended on for any length of time. (See Berndt, 1959.) It is, therefore, not surprising to find recorded in anthropological literature some instances of cults and art symbols which have spread from the interior into the north-western and northern coastal areas in quite recent times, and of art patterns that have come into the Western Desert area from some of the coastal tribes of north-western Australia. (See Lommel, 1952, 1959.) While the usual circles, U-figures, and other ornamental figures so far listed kept on recurring also in the Western Desert art patterns, they were here often arranged into patterns unmistakably different from those found among the Aranda-speaking and other more eastern inland tribes. These differences may be seen in figures 6 and 7.

The first (Fig. 6) shows the design on a time-beating or clapping stick associated with the *mala* (sandhill rat-kangaroo) totem of Maurunga, a centre situated on the Kukatja-Pintubi border. The second (Fig. 7) reproduces a *jala* (desert yam) pattern on a stone *tjurunga* from Watikinbiri (Ngalia tribe). Farther west new figures, such as zigzag patterns, herring-bone patterns, concentric squares, angular meanders, and other non-rounded, angular figures make their appearance. In the Pintubi and Pitjantjara areas concentric squares begin to be combined with the concentric circles and curvilinear figures discussed earlier. The angular western figures belong, however, to a different world of artistic design.*

The Central Australian curved and circular figures were stylized representations of marks or tracks on the ground. They were accordingly —as in nature—painted or incised as elaborated, but always individual figures, on a single base, with empty spaces left between them. The Western Australian angular and straight-line figures, on the other hand, were combined into patterns that covered practically every inch of the surface on which they had been incised. They do not seem to represent any marks or

*An instance of the combination of concentric circles with concentric squares may be found in the 'churinga of the bell-bird totem', illustrated in Spencer and Gillen (1904: 735). This *tjurunga* is, however, not an Aranda but, like the '*mulla churinga*' associated with it, almost certainly a Pitjantjara *tjurunga*: for *mala* (Spencer's spelling *mulla*) is the Loritja word for the sandhill rat-kangaroo, and the *mala* myths link up with Ayers Rock. So does the Pitjantjara bell-bird tradition. A *mala kuntangka* (that is, a sandhill rat-kangaroo *tjurunga*), which I collected in 1933, shows on one side a single concentric square figure among some concentric circles. It came from Inintitjara, a rockhole on the northern side of Uluru (Ayers Rock).

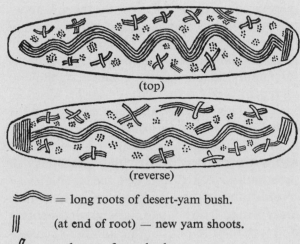

(top)

(reverse)

〜〜〜 = long roots of desert-yam bush.

||| (at end of root) — new yam shoots.

✦ = leaves of yam bush.

❃ = small yam bulbs.

Fig. 7. Jala (desert yam) stone tjurunga from Watikinbiri.

tracks on the ground, but appear to be heavily stylized drawings of the actual objects themselves. The two designs reproduced from spear-throwers (page 59) that I obtained from Pintubi men in 1933 will illustrate this point.

The first design (Fig. 8) is intended to show how rain falling from a storm-cloud turns into a flood, which lifts up the leaves and driftwood in a creek-bed. The second (Fig. 9) is intended to depict a twisting whirlwind column of dust and debris rising to the sky.

There is a strong resemblance between some of these angular western art figures and certain Aboriginal string figures. Thus the incised concentric square figure strongly resembles the squares of parallel hairstring strands that formed the body of many *waningga*; and *waningga* were common cult objects in the western region. Again the zigzag and some of the other angular, incised figures of the western art recall some of the string figures produced in games of cat's-cradle: this was once a popular form of Aboriginal entertainment throughout the inland.

The bullroarers and sacred boards found among the desert tribes living in Western Australia proper also showed these straight-line, angular patterns of ornamentation; and these patterns were incised on one surface only. Davidson (1937: 78–9) notes:

Incised decoration on one surface apparently is typical for the remainder of Western Australia. All bullroarers, churinga and 'dancing boards' in this tremendous area, except specimens intrusive from the central regions or emulations thereof, are decorated in designs of varying character derived from a few basic motifs such as the longitudinal zigzag, herring-bone, concentric squares and rhomboids, and angular meanders.

Regarded purely as designs, the patterns found on the Western Australian sacred boards are strongly reminiscent of the incised herring-bone, concentric square, and concentric rhomboid patterns found in south-eastern Australia, that is, in eastern South Australia, Victoria, New South Wales, and southern Queensland. (See Davidson, 1937: 137; McCarthy, 1938/58, 1957a; also Plate 70.)

In yet another form the sacred boards in the coastal regions of Western Australia appeared as plain, unincised pieces of boards (sometimes called *kurangara*), which were on occasion ornamented with simple painted designs, and stuck into the ceremonial ground as a kind of background for sacred dramatic performances. (Lommel, 1952, 1959.)

In the Kimberleys and the adjacent coastal areas, pearlshells with incised, angular meander patterns were in common use. (See Plate 70.) These were also traded inland for considerable distances. The farthest eastern point of penetration of these Western Australian pearlshells seems to have been the Wailbri (or Walbiri) area in northern Central Australia. Pearlshells were also used in sacred ritual in the lower Southern Aranda areas; but the Southern Aranda shells seem to have come from Queens-land waters, and had probably been traded into Central Australia from tribes living to the east of Lake Eyre.

The artistic devices and sacred emblems of the northern Australian regions, including Arnhem Land, are sufficiently different in pattern, design, and intention to warrant independent treatment (see Chapters Two and Three).

The close ties between Aboriginal art and religion throughout inland Australia—ties which constituted the great source of its inner strength and deep emotional appeal in pre-European days—inevitably led toward its rapid eclipse when alien settlement began in the interior. Cattlemen with their stock desecrated the sacred sites, if they were close to permanent waters (as they frequently were), and drove out the guardians of the sacred storehouses. Many missionaries, especially in the earlier days, refused to allow their converts to take any part whatever in any ritual. In our own days many Government officials are adopting, in the name of assimilation, an equally hostile attitude toward Aboriginal culture, religion, and art. In the face of so much active European antagonism, Aboriginal religion, art, and culture are rapidly dying in inland Australia. In my view, this is nothing less than a national tragedy. For various reasons Australia is, in the opinion of many competent critics, a cultural desert with a modest sprinkling of oases growing mainly imported trees. For the present generation of European-Australians—a generation which has not yet learnt to appreciate the fine heritage of the country in which it is living—to destroy wilfully and deliberately an indigenous form of

12
13 14 15 16

12 Three male actors resting during a semi-sacred ceremony. Their decorations refer to the fire totemic ancestors of Rubundja (Mount Hay), on the western boundary of Aranda territory, Central Australia 13 A ritual actor of the snake totem of Hale River, decorated with feather down and wearing an elaborate head-dress 14 A *waningga* of the Western Aranda, standing within a ground painting on a sacred dancing-place. It refers to an important waterhole on the Finke, named Ntarea, which is also the native name of the Hermannsburg mission site 15 Snake-tracks made by an actor in the snake totem ritual of Hale River, in Aranda territory 16 Fire totemic actors of Rubundja, wearing ritual headgear of *tjurunga*, covered with down and tipped with feathers

art, thousands of years old, which has aroused world-wide interest among educated critics, would be an act of vandalism that our descendants would find difficult to live down.

Already in Central Australia few trees now support any *tjurunga*; and the old sacred caves in the MacDonnells and other inland ranges today are open and empty, with gaping mouths. Rarely do the feet of ceremonial dancers thud the ground in the glow of the camp-fires. Over most of the inland there are few men left who know the complete song cycle of even one of the sacred centres, or who remember the full sets of ceremonial and ritual patterns associated with them. Only where Europeans remain ignorant of their existence can the old sacred sites today hope to avoid desecration and looting.

Most of the *tjurunga* have been sold by the younger natives to the aliens, and considerable numbers have also been stolen by unscrupulous 'white' and 'dark' intruders. But some of the most sacred *tjurunga* will never be found: in many districts their aged guardians, despairing of the irreverence of their own disobedient young men, hid them away in wild country before their deaths, or buried them in the ground, so that no sacrilegious hands might touch them.

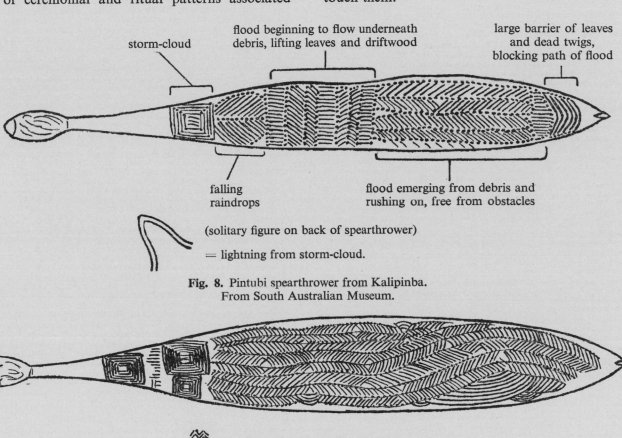

storm-cloud

flood beginning to flow underneath debris, lifting leaves and driftwood

large barrier of leaves and dead twigs, blocking path of flood

falling raindrops

flood emerging from debris and rushing on, free from obstacles

 (solitary figure on back of spearthrower)

= lightning from storm-cloud.

Fig. 8. Pintubi spearthrower from Kalipinba.
From South Australian Museum.

 = columns of dust raised by winds.

= spiral of passing whirlwinds.

 (solitary figure on back of spearthrower)

= wind pattern.

Fig. 9. Pintubi spearthrower.
From South Australian Museum.

CHAPTER FIVE

Aboriginal Art and the Western World

J. A. TUCKSON

Interest in the visual arts has grown steadily over the first part of this century, and particularly since the last world war. No doubt this is due partly to the general spread of knowledge in this direction. Increasing numbers of people from all walks of life have visited art galleries and museums, where original works of art from different cultures and periods may be seen under one roof. Exhibitions, too, have played their part—including those of a temporary nature, which have toured regions where people would not normally have the opportunity to see a comprehensive collection of different works. There have also been art publications, with their beautifully produced photographs and colour reproductions of works from all over the world—and, of course, there is television.

These various channels of communication have brought to the attention of the public not only the works of art themselves, but also something of the research and interest of art historians, critics, and collectors. All, in different ways, have contributed toward a greater understanding of art.

The Growth of Appreciation of the Art of Non-literate Peoples: Even so, there is still a strong tendency today to think of the arts of painting, sculpture, and drawing, as being primarily concerned with representation, if not imitation, of the natural world. This view has inhibited our enjoyment and appreciation of Australian Aboriginal art. This art is, I believe, conceptual, subjective, and symbolic, reflecting the Aborigines' spiritual, as well as everyday life. This is not always the opinion of the anthropologist, but here I am considering primarily the belief and attitudes of the artist and art critic.

Man, generally speaking, when he expresses himself through visual form does so in relation to his environment. Environment involves not only time and place, but also the society in which the artist works, as well as his training and knowledge and whatever he absorbs through perception of the outer world. René Huyghe (1959: 405) explains the relationship between the individual, outer world and a work of art in these words:

This duality between inner and outer that man perceives and that he experiences as a split is present in the work of art . . . makes of it a link between those two realities. This link moreover is polyvalent for it connects not only the I and the universe by giving rise to the image in which the two are jointly and inseparably embodied . . . it also connects the artist and his fellow men for it enables him to communicate himself to them, and enables them to perceive and to experience him as a part of themselves.

The duality of the inner and outer worlds, the

subjective and objective, gives rise—through an emphasis in one way or another—to two distinct forms of visual art. The first is based on 'knowing', on tactile as well as visual sensations of enduring form, of a 'thing in itself'; this is a conceptual or linear art. The other is based on visual appearances, where the momentary and changing aspects of the outer world are seen and expressed in a permanent form, as in the painterly world of the Impressionists.

Impressionism was an art of momentary effects of light, a harmony of beautiful colour transitions pictured by boating-parties and pleasurable pursuits, by landscapes and urban scenes. It was extroverted and visual. The artist painted from nature, transposing his delight in optical sensations directly onto the canvas. It was Cézanne, however, who at that time first felt the need to give a greater sense of permanence to his visual sensations from nature, by searching for its inner structure. He achieved this by a simplification of form, and organization of space by colour and line. From the mid eighties of the last century, in the works of the younger and more perceptive artists, Gauguin and Van Gogh for instance, there were further simplifications. There was a greater dependence on line and colour used in an expressive, emotional, and symbolic manner.

Du Jardin (Rewald, 1956: 157) wrote in 1888 of symbolist art:

An outline is sufficient to represent a face. Scorning photography, the painter will set out to retain with the smallest possible number of characteristic lines and colours, the intimate reality, the essence of the object he selects. Primitive art and folklore are symbolic in this fashion ... And so is Japanese art ... Line expresses what is permanent, colour what is momentary ...

It was not unnatural, then, that the painters of the early twentieth century, the inheritors of this new outlook, should be attracted and excited by the expressive and structural qualities, the simplicity of form, of African Negro sculpture. These were qualities which they sought in their own work.

In 1906 Picasso started the preparatory sketches for one of his most important early paintings, the 'Demoiselles d'Avignon'. John Golding, in his detailed analysis of this painting and its sources, first shows the important influence of Cézanne, then demonstrates Picasso's use of forms derived from Iberian and Negro sculpture. Discussing Picasso's attitude to Negro art, Golding (1959: 59) writes:

Salmon quotes Picasso as saying that he admired Negro sculptures because he found them *raisonnables*. In stressing the more 'reasonable' or rational character of African art, Picasso was underlining the quality that distinguishes it most fundamentally from Western art. As opposed to Western art, Negro art is more conceptual, much less conditioned by visual appearances. The Negro sculptor tends to depict what he knows about his subject rather than what he sees ... Or to put it differently, he tends to express his *idea* of it. This leads inevitably to great simplification or stylization, and, at the same time, to a clarification and accentuation of what are felt to be the significant features or details of the object depicted.

European artists have often sought inspiration in a particular master, or in the art of the past. In the nineteenth century, for instance, there are several examples of revivals. Artists have also been influenced by work outside their own tradition. The impressionist painters gained much from Japanese colour (wood block) prints. From Picasso onward, however, artists, as well as finding inspiration in their own art traditions, have turned more and more to the work of tribal and so-called primitive peoples, and to the artistic productions of prehistory. This particular interest seems to be associated, in part, with man's search for fundamental values. In doing this, the artist is returning, as it were, to the genesis of art—its means and meaning. Emphasis on the means has within the last fifty years brought about an abstract, non-figurative art based on the aesthetic and plastic values of colour, line, and shape; on movement, muscular action, and rhythm; on a combination of materials that might ordinarily be considered inartistic. Megaliths, totem-poles, and burial posts influenced sculptural form quite considerably. The twentieth-century artist rediscovered the essence and magic of art through what were believed to be primordial images and symbols. Artists such as Picasso, Klee, Miro, Moore, and many others, have incorporated elements from extra-European sources into their work. These have now been absorbed into the main stream of Western-European art tradition.

Some contemporary artists who have responded to these trends have used a simple imagery and form in their work—which, in consequence, has often been described as childlike. Comparisons have been made between modern art, primitive art, and child art. However, the charm of children's drawing, especially in the earlier years, can be attributed in part to their lack of muscular control, and therefore to an underdeveloped technique, although one which is possibly adequate for their purpose. On the other hand the adult artist, to whatever civilization he may belong, has in the course of training acquired mature techniques, through which his ideas may find expression. Viktor Löwenfeld (1939: 135) considers that it is possible to make comparisons where:

. . . the creative impulses are determined by subjective relationship to reality. In this field we find the most far reaching parallelism both in the representation of space and in the manner by which expressions are symbolized by means of shape. We find over-emphasis employed to symbolize the importance or significance of that which is represented as well as over-emphasis determined by bodily experiences.

He makes other comparisons of this sort, too, in reference to X-ray drawings, the treatment of temporally separated events in one composition, and the use of plan and elevation within the same picture.

The part played by the artist of the nineteenth and twentieth centuries in shaping our taste, and our appreciation of the tribal arts of Africa, Oceania and the Americas, has been considerable. But to this must be added the contributions of explorers, travellers, missionaries and, later, museum curators, who with ethnologists and anthropologists have assembled large collections of 'native' works of art and craft for the museums and universities of the world. Among these men—these collectors—were many of discernment and taste; but there were also many who had no such appreciation, and took little account of the aesthetic qualities of so-called primitive art. It was left to the ethnologists and anthropologists, however, to study the

tribal arts of non-literate peoples: and they have remained, up to the present day, the main contributors in this field.

The Development of Interest in Aboriginal Art, as Art: From the time of first European settlement in this country, at Sydney in 1788, there was some appreciation of the rock engravings of the Sydney-Hawkesbury district. Navigators and explorers in the first half of the nineteenth century had also made important discoveries of rock paintings and engravings and other art forms in various parts of the continent and had recorded their impressions. (See Chapter One.) But it was not until much later, in the eighties, that non-professional anthropologists, and others, became interested in making a more detailed study of the Australian Aborigines. (See Elkin, 1961.) The most important figure here was Sir Baldwin Spencer, who has been mentioned several times in this volume; appropriately enough, before taking up biology at the University of Melbourne, he had studied art at Manchester for a year. The bark paintings now in the National Museum of Victoria, which he collected at Oenpelli in 1912, undoubtedly laid a foundation for our present interest in this form of Aboriginal art. (See Chapter Two.) It is probably no more than a coincidence that in recent years painting on bark from Arnhem Land has proved such a popular field of study, and such a profitable business commercially. In 1929 the National Museum of Victoria held its first exhibition of Australian Aboriginal Art. This was gathered from various sources and a booklet, with articles by Charles Barrett and A. S. Kenyon, was published to celebrate the occasion.

If we can take as our guide *Art in Australia*, which was the main art periodical published between 1916 and 1942, and possibly the arbiter of artistic taste between the two world wars, it is in retrospect surprising to find only six articles on Aboriginal art: four by Margaret Preston, a painter (in 1925, 1930, 1940, and 1941), and two by anthropologists—Ursula McConnel and F. D. McCarthy (in 1935 and 1939). This apathy on the part of the Australian art world was probably due to the fact that art movements and ideas from overseas were slow in coming here, and when they did arrive were expressed in a diffused form. With the possible exception of a short period around 1919, when Roland Wakelin and Roy de Maistre were painting their colour music pictures, Australian painting generally was more visual than conceptual—and this continued until the late thirties. However, Aboriginal art was given official sanction, as it were, when eleven bark drawings (paintings) and three pen drawings were included in an exhibition of 'Art of Australia' shown in the United States in 1941. Margaret Preston wrote the introduction to the section on Aboriginal art. Two years later the National Gallery and National Museum of Victoria organized an exhibition of 'Primitive Art'. In the catalogue associated with it Daryl Lindsay, then (1943) Director of the Gallery, wrote, 'Personally I rate very highly the bark drawings of our own Australian natives, who seem to possess a certain delicacy of line all of their own.' Leonhard Adam, writing in the same catalogue, pointed out that while 'the scientific study of primitive arts, art techniques and styles, the investigation of their historical developments and their religious and social functions is an important subdivision of Ethnology . . . at the same time it is part of the History of Art.'

It was perhaps this, more than anything else, which attracted the interest of artists and art critics, and it was only a matter of time before the art galleries in Australia began to form collections of Aboriginal art. Admittedly this was done, at first, in rather a negative way by gift from various sources. In 1956 each State gallery received from the Commonwealth Government twenty-four paintings from Arnhem Land, either on bark or on card: these had been collected by the American-Australian Scientific Expedition to Arnhem Land in 1948. Later, in 1959, when the Art Gallery of New South Wales accepted from Dr. Stuart Scougall a gift of Melville Island grave-posts (see Plate 5), there was still doubt as to whether Aboriginal art should in fact be shown there. Douglas

Stewart, writing in the *Bulletin* (1st July, 1959), took this negative stand:

 . . . the 17 grave-posts . . . make a somewhat bizarre display . . . and most people, admitting that the poles are delightful in themselves, will wonder if the proper place for them is not the museum . . . These Mclville Island posts, though they have definite artistic merit of an elementary kind, are really more in the nature of ethnological curiosities than works of art.

James Gleeson, writing for *The Sun* (18th July, 1959), reacted differently:

Whatever their symbolic significance might be they represent an ensemble of abstract shapes of considerable aesthetic appeal. The very limitations of the technique and the restrictions imposed by the media produce a fine unity of design despite the fact that no two posts are identical in shape or decoration. Even in the artificial atmosphere of an art gallery they are impressive, for the painted posts stand about the grave in a protective ring, forming as it were, a barrier between the world of living reality and the shadowy world of the spirit.

The State art galleries focused further attention on Australian Aboriginal art when, in 1960, they organized an exhibition, mainly of bark paintings, which was shown in the six State capitals.

Aesthetic Interpretation of Aboriginal Art: There is no doubt that appreciation of Aboriginal art has widened immeasurably because the general public and artist have been given a greater opportunity to see it *as art*, not as part of an ethnological collection. Moreover, works of art exhibited in an art gallery can be contemplated in some form of isolation. They can be compared with other works of their period, and furthermore, differences between productions of various cultures can be quite easily observed. Yet there is a unifying quality over and above the different styles. There is the question not only of visual sense of balance and proportion, but of the underlying spirit of their imagery. These two factors make it possible for us to appreciate visual art without any knowledge of its particular meaning and original purpose. Our enjoyment of a Chinese tomb figure of the T'ang Dynasty is not necessarily dependent on a knowledge of its significance as a guardian, or companion, or servant, of the dead. Nor would lack of recognition of the many symbols and their meaning greatly alter our first appreciation of mediaeval European art. Notwithstanding this view, many writers on, for example, the art of non-literate peoples insist that, without knowledge of the purpose and meaning of the symbols in such art, the outsider is left only with a sense of pleasing design without meaning. In the words of Linton (in Elisofon, 1958), appreciation is then only 'an intellectual exercise which helps to clarify his understanding of aesthetics.'

It may perhaps help us to recognize the varying levels of appreciation, if we consider the several components manifested in a work of art.

Foremost is man himself, the artist. There is also his particular social and cultural environment: he is a member of his society, influenced by his training, his knowledge, his self-awareness. But equally important, in my view, in the act of creating is the use of his intuitive faculties—the influence of the unconscious. Eric Neumann (1955) writes, 'the symbolic imagery of the unconscious is the creative source of the human spirit in all its realizations. Not only have consciousness and concepts of its philosophical understanding of the world arisen from the symbol but also, religion, rite and cult, art and customs.' The intention of the artist presupposes the purpose of the work of art, along with the symbols, images, representations, subject-matter; its content, its meaning; the materials and technique; and its resultant style and form. We cannot dissociate one from the other, and meaning is not possible without the means. Content and form are fused by the intuitive processes of the artist. And to appreciate fully any work of art, we must use the same sense of intuition as the artist, together with our conscious knowledge of other works of art, in order to judge quality.

The first reaction of most people to a work of art is a response to its representational features, to its subject-matter: here there is the question of meaning and association. A landscape painting may give pleasure to a spectator because of its particular location: and the picture is judged according to whether the observer feels that the artist has depicted the scene correctly. Similarly with a portrait—a likeness to the sitter is expected, if it has been commissioned with that in mind. It may be that such a portrait is intended to serve as a memorial, to retain an image of a person who has devoted his life to good works in his community. However, if this painting is removed from its particular context, away from the community to a place where these associations, its purpose and meaning, are unknown, other values, and other criteria, must be found if appreciation is desired. The rapport between the artist and his subject must be inferred from the way he intuitively interprets his subject, and from the way he forms his subject into a visual unity by technique.

Strehlow (in Battarbee, 1951) has pointed out that a very old and crudely decorated *tjurunga* will have more significance to an Aranda man than a beautifully engraved new object. In the same way the image of a Madonna and Child, irrespective of any artistic merit, might evoke an emotional response in a devout Christian. In other words an object may have value and meaning without having any intrinsic quality of form. Meaning in this sense is restricted and literal. But when a work of art has a life of its own, it also has a universal, or potentially universal, appeal. The false assumption that the aim of the artist should be based on the classic norm of the Renaissance has in the past, and even today, led to misunderstanding, disparagement, and underrating of other art styles.

An Aboriginal artist's attitude is related to his totemic spiritual life, and his conception of the world around him. His art is subjective, symbolic, based on knowledge rather than visual appearances. This, of course, is not to say that the Aboriginal artist's optical sensations are different from ours, but simply that he perceives his world differently. As has been shown in other chapters, the Aboriginal is acutely observant, and has an intimate knowledge of his physical environment. In his traditional art he is not necessarily concerned with depicting the landscape in a visual, representational sense. (See Preface.) For him a waterhole is not a place to admire the reflection of a blue sky: it is a place from which to drink, and may also be a totemic site made by a mythical ancestor, and linked with fertility. In his art an Aboriginal artist may depict it by a symbol, such as a circle, or series of concentric circles. But variations are numerous. There is, in fact, a fairly wide range of representation, including the naturalistic as well as the highly stylized, and these may be used separately or in combination. Let us consider some of them.

Evaluation of Specific Examples of Aboriginal Art: Generally speaking, certain views are preferred at the expense of others, and emphasis is placed on particular features of the subject-matter that may be important. In the bark painting of 'Two Spirits of the Geimbio Country' (see Plate 30), from Oenpelli, the female figure on the left has the head drawn in profile, but with two eyes (since the artist *knows* she has two eyes, even if only a single one can be seen from that position). Both arms are drawn coming from the same part of the neck, as the artist has possibly had difficulty in fitting them in and, at the same time, retaining the position of the breasts; these are attached to each side of the figure, but probably seen in side-view. The feet are shown in plan, not because we are looking down on them, but because normal footprints are seen in this way. In the male figure both the body and head are frontally placed; no mouth is drawn, and the basket, arms, and penis (which is greatly exaggerated) are shown from the side. Again, the feet are in plan. The subjective and consistent logic of the artist's depiction of his figures should not inhibit our appreciation of the work, especially the subtle movement of the vertical lines of the body and legs. The decorative 'Male Kangaroo' (see Plate 60) from Goulburn Island has a similar schema, with the addition of X-ray treatment showing the caul and body fats. X-ray art is not the result of seeing through, but of knowing what lies within. (See Preface, and Chapters Two and Three.)

Comparison between two areas in Arnhem Land, Oenpelli on the west, and Milingimbi and Yirrkalla on the north-east coast, will show differences in the way a figure is represented. (See Preface.) At Oenpelli, figures are often given a more natural and organic shape, while at Milingimbi and Yirrkalla they are schematically represented either by outline, or by an oval body shape. This image is used for humans, animals, and insects alike, and the particular character of the figure is attained by the addition of head, arms, or tail as required. There is at Yirrkalla quite a distinctive way of showing a person squatting with the legs tucked underneath, as in the 'Big Feast' (see Plate 67). This representation gives a sense of foreshortening, which was probably not intended. It should be compared with the 'Ubar Ritual' from Oenpelli (Plate 32). Figures in north-eastern Arnhem Land coastal art are normally quite small, and are used together with areas of cross-hatching. In relation to the over-all size of a painting they do not always have the same importance as the figures in Oenpelli and Groote Eylandt painting. In some, for instance, the whole surface of the sheet of bark is covered with a seemingly geometric motif. These designs of lines, triangles, circles, and other shapes, used in a strict or free way, are symbols for the expression of subject-matter in a number of regions.

On the northern coast of Arnhem Land the diamond-shaped patterning used by various clans and linguistic units of the *jiridja* moiety was in all probability introduced, in the past, from what is now called Indonesia. (See Chapters Two and Three.) In the Milingimbi area such designs are often associated with myths and rituals relating to honey-bees; around Yirrkalla they are connected with the mythical being Laindjung, who distributed these patterns among the *jiridja* clans and linguistic units. (See Plates 35 and 68.) In the first example the design is painted in a careful, all-over fashion, while the second is much freer and more varied. (See Warner, 1937/1958; R. and C. Berndt, 1948: 317–23; Elkin and R. and C. Berndt, 1950.) Both these areas belong to the same cultural bloc.

It is through his materials, his skill in using them, and his technique, that an artist gives style and form to his conception of his subject. Choice of materials is critical, and this is governed mainly by what is available in a particular region. Some pigments are traded; some materials, even if they are available, are not used. But the inherent qualities of the natural stone, wood, bark, pearlshell, feathers, down, string, paint, and so on, when used, are generally retained in the finished product. The texture of cleaned bark, the lustre of pearlshell, and the softness of down or the colour of feathers and paint, have a direct impact on our senses. And this directness is an important characteristic of Aboriginal art. There is actually no room for mistakes or for alterations. Each stage of the technical process can be seen and appreciated. As we have seen in earlier chapters, the artist must prepare his sheet of bark, make his own brushes, and apply a ground colour before starting on his main design. He has a choice of four primary colours—yellow, red, black, and white. These are not normally mixed, but are used directly so that their natural colour is retained, and with it a simple harmony. There is both craftsmanship and skill here.

Although, as we have seen, Aboriginal artists do not form a specialized group, we must not lose sight of the particular ability of individual artists. It is possible to identify this individuality in the work of artists of certain areas; but, generally speaking, further insight into Aboriginal art as a whole is more easily gained by the study of regional differences in technique and form. For instance, in Groote Eylandt painting the bark is covered with a black pigment; at Yirrkalla a red pigment is mostly used; at Melville Island the bark is blackened by scorching. In these same three areas the tools used are related to different qualities of form. Mountford, in Chapter Two, has mentioned this. At Groote Eylandt, for instance, the brushes used produce a more sensitive line than that made in similar circumstances at Yirrkalla. In turn, the Yirrkalla line is finer than that appearing in Melville Island art, where much thicker, tougher, twig brushes are employed. The art forms of this last area are larger and more vigorous. They are bound by lines of a different colour, and of a suitable thickness and boldness to contain them and to make an impact independently. The cross-hatching and dots over the background colour have a commensurate open breadth. The most constant element is line. It is apparent in nearly all of the art, and whatever tendency toward mass is found in the north of Australia may very well be a result of outside contact. Drawing is line, and we can well understand the tendency in the past to speak of bark paintings as bark drawings.

Another general characteristic is a sense of scale, of proportion, which must be felt intuitively by the artist. I believe this is apparent, to a greater or lesser extent, in all Aboriginal art forms—in body decoration, in ceremonial paraphernalia, in engravings on weapons even when simply fluted, in the large rock engravings and in rock painting. (See Chapter Three.) Two particular cases may further exemplify this quality of proportion. There are cylindrical and conical stones, some possibly of phallic significance, which are found in the western region of New South Wales. Some of these vary between six and twenty inches in height, and many of them are engraved with simple sets of transverse vertical and oblique lines, with an occasional curve and symbol. These surface lines, through their sameness and variety and different spacing, create a visual rhythm of varying proportions, and in so doing enhance the elemental shape of the stone. The same feeling is achieved on a different scale in the rock engravings illustrated in Plate 49. When the artist paints and engraves, or makes his objects and weapons, he does so with an innate sense of balance. His natural ability for design, which gives variety to his shapes and spaces, however repetitive, ensures vitality in the finished work. When there are no containing boundaries, as is the case in rock painting and engraving, he relates the various symbols and figures through composition.

In this inward-looking art, events separated in time can be incorporated in a single composition, as in the 'Djanggawul' (see Plate 25). This is possible because of the non-visual attitude of the artist in his depiction of space. Space is realized in a subjective, not in a visual, fashion; and, paradoxically, the visual elements of the art, its lines, rhythms, and patterns are clear and direct. Further, there is no perspective. Only rarely are figures overlapped to indicate space. The use of a baseline with all figures 'standing up' on a bark, as in 'The Mimi Corroboree' (see Plate 66), is possibly modern in conception. There is also, in some paintings, a gradual building-up from ground to surface by super-imposition of lines, which itself creates a real, if minute space in the picture.

In the north of Australia, where in the past external influences have been strongest, we find the only important sculpture. (See Preface and Chapter Two.) The subjective perception of space is built on tactile sensations; it does not preclude sculpture. The sense of touch is manifest in many objects made by Aborigines, but most of these are two-dimensional. Sculpture is three-dimensional, and inherently an art form of mass. Apart from the outstanding carved human figures of north-eastern Arnhem Land (see Plates 68 and 69), the most impressive of these sculptural forms are the grave posts of Melville and Bathurst islands. (See Plates 5, 6, 7, and 8.) It is a wonderful experience to see them in their setting, either as a single group freshly painted, or massed together, sombre brown and black, their paint weathered and gone. Despite their massiveness when grouped, and the great variety of axe-cutting, the individual posts are essentially linear in their conception.

Line permeates all Aboriginal art. It is the essence of the various styles from different cultural regions. In all its forms their linear art reflects the image, the spirit of Aboriginal society as a whole.

Our Heritage of Aboriginal Art: Margaret Preston (1925) suggested some years ago that Aboriginal art might form a foundation for the development of a national art. She noted the precedents provided in the influence of African art on European art, and 'the need of fresh stimulus and a return to simple symbols.' She emphasized, too, the feeling of rhythm in Aboriginal art, and advocated that its decorative elements should be used in homes, cafés, and theatre, but '*no* realism'. Its simplifications were also recommended for landscape and figure painting. In the late twenties Mrs. Preston was painting pictures of decorative simplicity, which were essentially European in character. In 1940, after a visit to Arnhem Land, she again urged the study and use of Aboriginal art, and for a time the influence of Aboriginal art was clearly apparent in her work. But her painting never became pseudo-Aboriginal, and never lost its individual character. She has not been alone in this, however. Two other painters of distinction in Australia have in recent years had their work linked with Aboriginal art. One is Ian Fairweather, who, when he came to this country, already had a finely developed linear calligraphic style, which he has expressed at times in a format rather like that of some bark painting. The other is John Olsen, a much younger painter, whose direct linear forms and use of symbols show an affinity to some of the rock paintings of Oenpelli.

Artists since the first European settlement of this continent have portrayed the Aborigines. In recent years, however, this interest in Aboriginal life generally, and in the art particularly, has been increasing. Melville Island grave-posts and their associated ceremonies inspired two Sydney artists, Russell Drysdale and Sali Herman, who have made them the motif of a number of paintings. The most regrettable aspect of the influence of Aboriginal art is its use by Australians, with little understanding of its qualities, for decorative purposes and for the souvenir trade. All forms of visual horror have been perpetrated in the name of the Aborigines by, one can only assume, insensitive or commercially minded people. The sale of all kinds of objects with superficially imitative designs gives an impression of Aboriginal art which is completely false.

Interaction between members of our own Australian-European type of society and the Aborigines has meant an inevitable encroachment on their living areas, and their traditional way of life and beliefs are slowly disappearing. When this occurs, their art also is likely to dwindle and die. The beauty of their dance, poetic song, painting and engraving, the externalization of their life and ideas, will undoubtedly be lost not only to them, but also to us. Some artists are still working, today, through traditional media: but there are not so many of them, and such things are made less frequently now for ritual purposes. In these circumstances they will most certainly have a diminished meaning for the younger generation, who are bearing the full brunt of European-Australian influences.

The demand from the tourist trade has also been met partially by Aboriginal artists themselves, especially through the agency of mission distribution centres. In a minor way this has modified traditional style. Missions sometimes price the artists' work on the basis of size (of an object, or a bark painting), and of quality—but this is often quality based simply on apparent skill, or on a refinement in technique. And to meet the current demand, the artist has now taken to shaping his bark as rectangularly as possible, so that it may be packed and transported conveniently together with others. Over-encouragement of such art has tended to produce quantity rather than quality.

The name of the late Albert Namatjira is probably better known in Australia than that of any other artist. How he and others of the Aranda Tribe of Central Australia came to achieve fame as water-colour landscape painters is sympathetically told by Rex Battarbee (1951). It was Battarbee who guided them through their first technical difficulties in a foreign medium. These Aranda artists had first become absorbed in the work of Australian painters, who depicted the Central Australian environment in a visual, representational way, in direct contrast to their own linear, symbolic style. Namatjira gained greater recognition than any of the others, because in Western eyes his work was the least Aboriginal. In the technique of representation he acquired a skill far above the other members of his School. But, in doing this, he lost the pattern and rhythm which have been retained by some of his younger followers. The example of the Hermannsburg group, with its attendant financial success, may well become a symbol for younger Aborigines wishing to take up 'art' and dissociate themselves from what was once their own traditional background.

Although much has been achieved in the study of traditional Aboriginal art by the ethnologist, archaeologist, and anthropologist, there is (as Leonhard Adam noted in 1943) a need for such study on the part of art historians. There is an immense amount of work to be done in this respect. For instance, it is necessary to record, photographically, as much as possible of the rock art, a great deal of which is not easily accessible. Of course, photographs are poor substitutes for the originals, but they are better than verbal descriptions alone, or poor copies and fragmentary diagrams. Wherever possible, Aboriginal art objects of various kinds should be collected and preserved, and exhibited, in order to foster a greater awareness and appreciation of this form of art among members of the general public, as well as among artists. We have a rich heritage, the greater part of which remains neglected. And even if this is not specifically our own heritage, there is no question at all that it will come to have a much greater bearing on our own Australian art in the years to come.

CHAPTER SIX

Epilogue

R. M. BERNDT

The preceding chapter is, primarily, an assessment of Aboriginal art from the viewpoint of an art critic considering its significance to contemporary Australian artists. It makes use of a framework of basic assumptions which often maintain a dominant place in discussions of art —*all* art, irrespective of cultural origin. One is that art, as art, is universal and that, because it contains a special inner essence, there is no real barrier to general appreciation and understanding. Another is that the art of non-literate peoples is more elemental, better able to cope with basic urges and attitudes, than the art of those whose social organization is much more complex. There is the claim that art is predominantly an individual rather than a social expression, even though style is obliquely recognized. In this connection, too, it is said to have something to do with the unconscious.

In one sense there is a fundamental cleavage between an anthropologist who writes about Aboriginal art, and an art historian, art critic, or artist. Often they are looking at different facets of the same spectrum. At times this appears as a contrast between the empirical and the non-empirical; or, to put it another way, between the social scientist who relies on a systematic approach to his subject, applying the rules of consistency and logical arrangements of facts, and an approach which draws most heavily on intuition. Rarely, there are attempts to combine both.

An anthropologist is interested in the living art, and in the artists themselves; in their position, as artists, in their own society; in the significance of the subject-matter they produce, its meaning to them and to others; in the use and function of art, in style, and in its underlying values. (See R. Firth, 1951: 155–82; E. Leach in E. E. Evans-Pritchard, *et al.*, 1956: 25–38; C. Lévi-Strauss, 1958: 269–94; R. Berndt, 1958: 26–43; C. Berndt, 1961.) An anthropologist who calls himself an ethnologist is usually more at home in a museum setting. He is interested in such material primarily in terms of its origin, a quest in which he is closely associated with the archaeologist, and also in its relationship to other art forms. He is certainly influenced considerably by other aspects of anthropology—but his central problem still remains.

An artist, or rather (to generalize) a European artist today, is interested mainly in design and form, and in interpreting these within his own particular universe of discourse. He is concerned with establishing a relationship between himself and a given work of art, in order to project his own feelings into its interpretation. He attempts to get into the mind of the artist who produced it, and in this procedure intuition plays an important part. To do this, as Mr. Tuckson has pointed out, one need have no specialized knowledge of its social and cultural environment.

An art historian asks the question, where does this fit into the schema of the historical development of world art? In answering it, he takes into account a number of criteria, relating on one hand to substance or content, mostly on the basis of Western European art, and on the other to the use made by an artist of available techniques and media—whether he draws representationally, abstractly, conventionally, realistically; what use he makes of space and perspective, of line and figure, and so on.

Because the canons of taste of the non-literate world seem in many cases to be in direct contrast to those of the Great Traditions of Western Europe and Asia, their works of art have been viewed as either primitive or advanced, according to the standpoint of the speaker. In classifying them as primitive, the art historian and others have followed the approach of the unilinear evolutionist who was, in the past, obsessed with staging cultures in a hierarchical fashion—which usually ensured that non-literate peoples appeared at the bottom of the rung and Western Europeans at the apex. It became customary to speak of the art of the Australian Aborigines, for example, as representing or reflecting an early stage in the development of our own art or in the art of man generally. And since it was viewed as primitive, by terminological extension it was also considered elemental and basic. As Mr. Tuckson has noted, the European post-Impressionists and others were influenced by a variety of alien art forms, including African. In fact, they went directly to these exotic examples for inspiration. In part this was a reaction against traditionalism, and the pervading and continuing influence of the Renaissance (or some features of it) and of realism, accentuated

by the spectacular improvement in photographic techniques for recording the external world. It was also an escape from the dictates of their own artistic conventions. It is tempting to read into this development an acknowledgement of their own inadequacy and lack of aesthetic imagination, their need to go beyond the confines of their own artistic tradition, their own culture. They saw primitive art as possessing an essential truth, as having a spirit of its own, and a vitality, lacking in their own art: and it was these which they attempted to capture and to reinterpret. Their pursuit of the elusive primitive entailed discarding, at least in some degree, their own aesthetic and traditional values; and the repercussions of this are felt today, in so-called abstract and fragmented art.

The break with European art tradition meant, further, a shift in emphasis from the realm of the social to that of the individual. In traditional European art, generally speaking, the artist's main intention was that his art should mean something to, and be appreciated by, the largest possible number of viewers. With the move in the opposite direction, the individual artist concerned himself not so much with producing a picture, or a piece of sculpture, which would conform reasonably well to some recognizable shape in the physical world. He became concerned with expressing its inner quality or essence, but, even more than this, with interpreting his subject as he himself saw it, projecting upon or into his work his own individual feelings. It is in this sense that the unconscious, or what passes for such, is said to be expressed there. Correspondingly the viewer as well, apart from being given a clue in the form of an attached title or label, was invited to identify and interpret it for himself and, particularly, to 'feel' it. In its extreme form this is an individual artist's conception of his subject, specifically intended to be appreciated at the individual level —each individual viewer making his own peculiarly personal interpretation, his own assessment. Such a work does not convey any agreed-upon meaning within the wider social context: it is enough if the appeal is at this individual level. We might speak here of a break-down in communication. In this view, an explicit language of art is not needed.

The search for inspiration beyond the confines of an artist's own cultural tradition, on the part of Western European artists particularly, has possibly been influenced indirectly by the spread of Europeanization throughout the world in recent years. It is also, perhaps, one response to a heightened awareness of other ways of living and thinking. More broadly, it is one indication of the increasing interaction between different peoples: of expanding cross-cultural horizons, resulting in a blending of certain elements and a blurring of cultural boundaries. The shift in stress from the social to the individual conception of art may represent a delayed reaction to the ideology of equality and of human rights, which began to make its appearance on the European scene as part of the Renaissance upsurge, and gained in momentum over the years. Freud and his colleagues, with the ego and the id, and the popularization of psychology, were also possibly responsible for this particular emphasis, far more than many artists would be ready to acknowledge.

No one, perhaps, and certainly not an anthropologist, would wish to speak against individual expression and interpretation. But it seems to me, having in mind the social significance of Aboriginal art and its general relevance to Aboriginal cultural life, that some sort of balance is essential. There is no question that an individual artist projects something of himself into every work he accomplishes; but, if it is to be a great work of art, his subject-matter and the symbolism he uses must be readily identifiable by the members of his own particular cultural group, and its aesthetic appeal must be on something more than a purely private basis. If not, then it is not art in the generally accepted meaning of the word. The problem of universal appeal is a different matter.

A major bar to *our* acceptance of Aboriginal art has been its divorcement from its own social and cultural context. To repeat, all art is symbolic in one way or another: and all great art speaks or communicates to its patrons and to its viewers. Living Aboriginal art has all this, and does all this, in its traditional setting. If it is to have the same kind of meaning for us, as Australians, we have no alternative but to learn its language. The simple realization that it *does* involve another language may help, up to a point, in so far as it leads to a more sensitive awareness of the existence of divergent frames of reference. It may hinder too, however, when it impedes communication between object and viewer, by making him conscious of a barrier which he is not equipped to surmount. In one instance known to me, a person standing in front of a bark painting claimed that he could not appreciate it fully, because he had been told (by anthropologists) that to do so he must know its meaning; in accepting the warning, he found himself unable to enjoy such a painting in the same way that he would others, which he saw as belonging frankly within his own cultural tradition.

But Mr. Tuckson has drawn our attention to another way in which such things can have meaning for us, and not necessarily in anthropological terms. His contention is based on the universality of *all* art, irrespective of provenance. It is important to us to know exactly what this means. The cultural background is not, here, taken seriously into account; the function or use of an object or a painting, even the identity of the artist, may be completely unknown. Mr. Tuckson mentioned, for instance, a T'ang mortuary figure. We can take an Arnhem Land bark painting. Its decorative qualities, its design, its treatment, its over-all appeal, are what matter: we *like* its lines, its curves, its colouring, its boldness, its sense of balance, and so forth. We are evaluating and interpreting it in our own idiom, within the climate of our own aesthetic traditions. There is no question of exploring its background. We do not ask, What is it for, and what does it mean to the people for whom it was produced? Instead, we simply interpret it in our own terms, and place it in our own perspective. It may be that this is as far as most of us can go. In this volume, however, we have attempted to

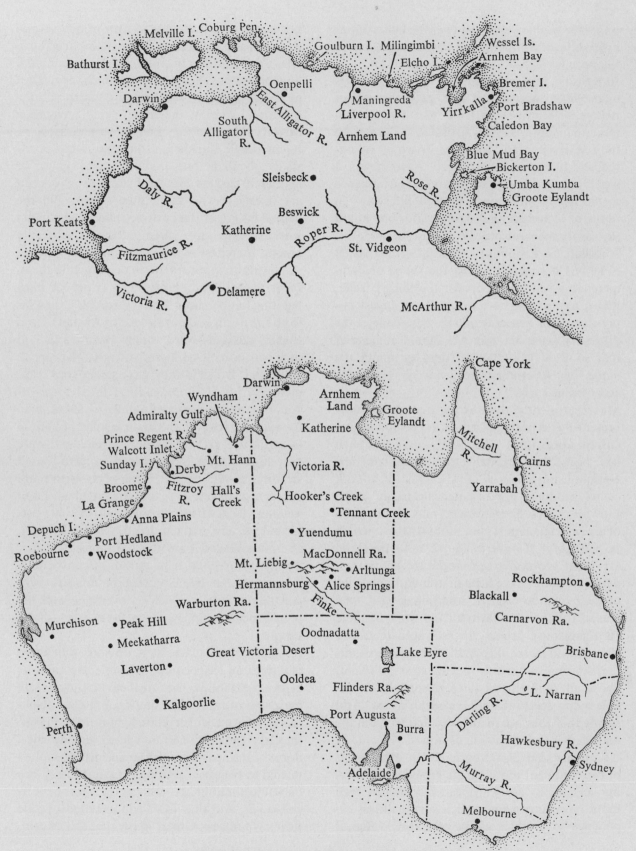

Fig.10. Sources of the works illustrated in the plates.

go a little farther—to cross over the limits of our own cultural frontiers, and to see something of the broader significance of Aboriginal art.

In the past, and even today, Aboriginal art has made little impact on the development of Australian-European art. As Mr. Tuckson reminds us, only a very few artists have done more than take a second look at it. It would be unrealistic to expect much more. Nevertheless, I would expect Aboriginal art to exert an influence in the future, in a much more subtle way—in terms of technique and design, and, one might say, in its inherent beauty. Pseudo or imitative Aboriginal art is *not* art: and, unfortunately, it is in this debased form, in the shape of commercially produced items for the tourist trade, that it appears to have made the strongest impression. This aspect is outside our scope in the present discussion, but we should remember that some of this material does go under the name of 'Aboriginal art', and is popularly accepted as such.

More pertinently, there is the question of how present-day Aboriginal artists are responding to current pressures; and one such approach has been the gradual establishment of the Hermannsburg School of Art. Most, if not all, of its products are oriented primarily along European lines. Some viewers may see the echo of an Aboriginal past; but, if it is there, it has to be hunted for. This is, of course, not Aboriginal art. It is European art produced by Aborigines, many of whom have little first-hand knowledge of their own Aboriginal traditional past. One reason for the popularity of the work of these Hermannsburg artists can be traced to astonishment and incredulity on the part of Europeans that Aborigines are able to paint so skilfully and, above all, so intelligibly, in a reasonably acceptable way—acceptable in European terms! And saying this does not in any way detract from the real merit of what they have done.

Aborigines and part-Aborigines in other parts of the continent too have attempted, with varying success, to use European media. But even more have drawn upon their own cultural experience to produce works of artistic value, if not works of art, for sale to Europeans. Several missions and settlements have encouraged local Aborigines to do this, and the European staff have themselves acted as middlemen, or at least as initial agents in subsequent commercial distribution. Among the main items have been carved and incised boards, spearthrowers, boomerangs, shields, and in some areas pearl-shells, boabab nuts, emu-feather shoes, or feathered baskets. Some of these are works of art; many are no more than curios. But the demand is great, and informed checks on shoddy workmanship are often lacking, especially among purchasers who do not know what standards are appropriate in dealing with them. In Arnhem Land, however, the art of bark painting has persisted, and flourished. Examples from the north and north-eastern Arnhem Land coastal missions were among the first to find their way into the hands of Australian-European collectors. By 1954 they were being sold commercially in art shops in the United States of America, and at about the same time I saw some for sale in London, in a shop which specialized in 'primitive art'. The prices, even then, were very high indeed. Since then they have soared steadily, as far as the better-class works are concerned. In recent years other Arnhem Land missions and settlements have followed suit, so that western Arnhem Land, Groote Eylandt, and other art styles are now becoming available. Today, fairly good bark paintings can be purchased on the open market in almost every Australian State, as well as overseas: and the present demand appears to be far in excess of the supply.

In such circumstances it is obvious that these paintings no longer fulfil the same functions as before. Although the Arnhem Landers still make use of traditional motifs, and even depict sacred subjects which relate to important myths, they paint mainly with an eye to outside sales. Some of the artists are still sufficiently unsophisticated to believe that a high standard in choice of subject-matter as well as in treatment is called for, and that this is appreciated outside their own region. Others know that any reasonably well-executed design or figure is acceptable —that it is not necessary for it to have meaning. On at least one occasion, north-eastern Arnhem Land artists interested in selling their barks on the commercial market have been told that repetitive designs (as in Plates 29, 35, 58, 61 and 65), an essential part of their sacred art, are not wholly acceptable there. They have been urged to produce instead such things as hunting scenes and drawings of human beings; to innovate, and not to work solely in their own traditional style; and to make sure that each bark is a separate, distinctive item, differing in some major, or at least minor, respect from all others. Conversely, the painting of figures with protuberant genitalia, or fertility scenes, or those of love magic and sorcery—all well within the range of acceptable traditional design (see Plates 20, 26, 30, 38, 56 and 64)—has been discouraged, as perhaps offending European taste.

Arnhem Land art, to which a large part of this volume refers, is still vital and, as yet, shows little real tendency toward deterioration. In a changing economy this outlet is important to the local people, when there are still so few avenues at their disposal that they can exploit in this way. But social and cultural life is changing radically on this coast, and it is only a matter of time before traditional Aboriginal forms of behaviour and belief must disappear. Much has already gone; much has already been modified. These changes must surely be reflected in their art. Today, any man who can paint does so, and not all are particular as to how or what they paint. But there are now recognized artists who, although not devoting their entire time to this, are closer to professional standing than was possible in traditional times. Although they innovate much more freely and more obviously than in the past, they are still following basically their own styles, and in many cases concentrating on the same motifs. This, in itself, poses a problem for the future. Once art becomes divorced from its social setting, as must happen and indeed is happening here, once the focus is on an external and not an internal market, there is a danger that it will become a 'survival'—that artists will continue to reproduce the designs of the past because they are encouraged to do so, and because these are acceptable to buyers. It is essential, if Arnhem Land is to maintain its place in the field of art, that the artists themselves express the changes that are taking place in their lives, not necessarily through a European medium, but in a manner and style consistent with their way of living and of viewing their social, cultural, and physical environment. And at this point we return to the statement that art is a social phenomenon, even though it be interpreted in individual terms, and the set of values and symbols it uses must have some currency among its viewers. It must have meaning which is communicable.

While Aboriginal art in its traditional form can never, in a personal way, become our own art, it can stimulate and perhaps even influence our own. It is also being increasingly recognized as part of our national heritage, and this is even more relevant as Government policies of assimilation for all Australian Aborigines gain in momentum. It is pertinent to remember, however, that our interest in Aboriginal art has increased in inverse proportion to the disappearance of traditional Aboriginal life!

17 Bark painting from Goulburn Island, western Arnhem Land, of a yam plant, said to form the staple diet of the Mimi spirits

18 Bark painting from Groote Eylandt, showing two swimming turtles, waves, and a catchment

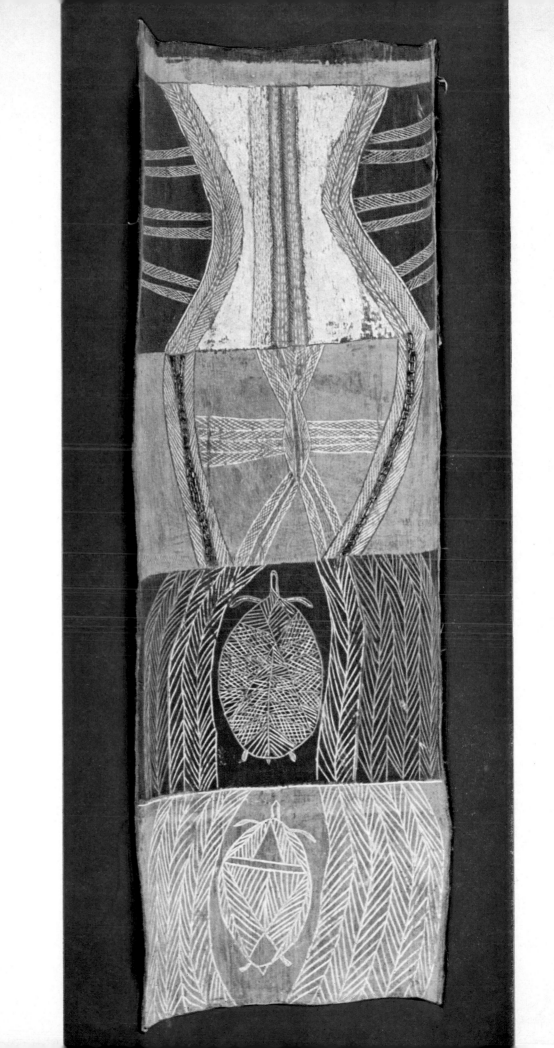

19 Wandjina painting on bark from Walcott Inlet, western Kimberleys

20 Bark painting from Oenpelli, western Arnhem Land, associated with love magic or sorcery. It shows a pseudo-historical woman named Manubi, wearing a headband, and feathered pendants at her elbows

22 An X-ray bark painting of a black kangaroo and a hunter, originally collected by Sir Baldwin Spencer at Oenpelli

23 Groote Eylandt bark painting, depicting a barracouta

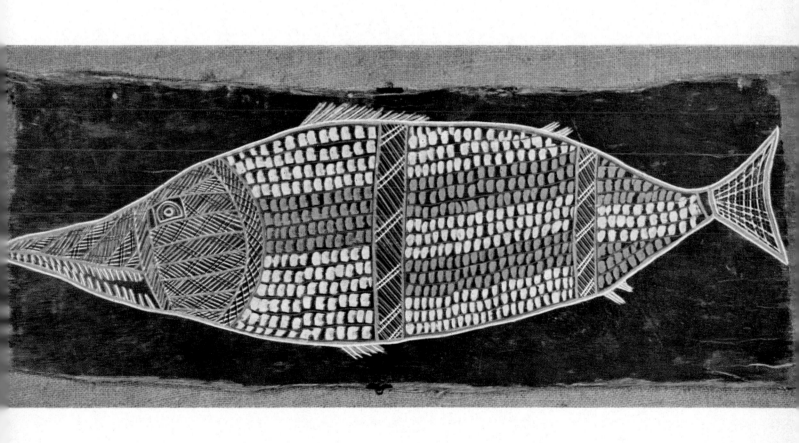

24 This Melville Island bark depicts various marine creatures, as well as boulders on the sea-bed, a creek, and a sandbank at Snake Bay

25 Bark painting from Yirrkalla, depicting scenes from the Djanggawul myth. In the bottom and third-from-bottom panel the two sisters are giving birth to the first Aborigines. The second panel from the bottom (*left*) shows sacred pole emblems and trees, which form a shade for the Djanggawul's children; on the right are the Djanggawul brother urinating, and his sisters. The two discs are the rising and setting sun, with its rays. In the top panel (*left*) the two sisters stand by a sacred spring: on the right is the artist himself, singing before his *rangga* emblem

26 In this bark painting from western Arnhem Land are the spirit-familiars of a songman: a male Dijalmung snake is dancing, while one owl man sings with his clapping-sticks, and another plays his didjeridu

27 Shield from Yarrabah, Queensland. The design represents two parent turtles and their young **28** Shield from the Roper River, Northern Territory. The patterning, referring to a snake and eggs, resembles the ground paintings of Central Australia

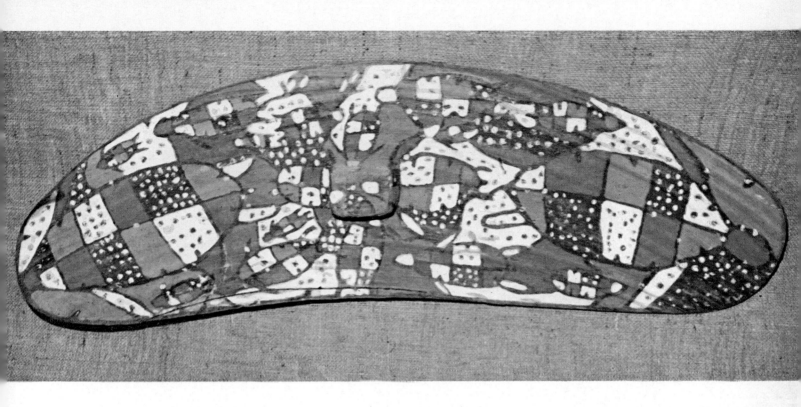

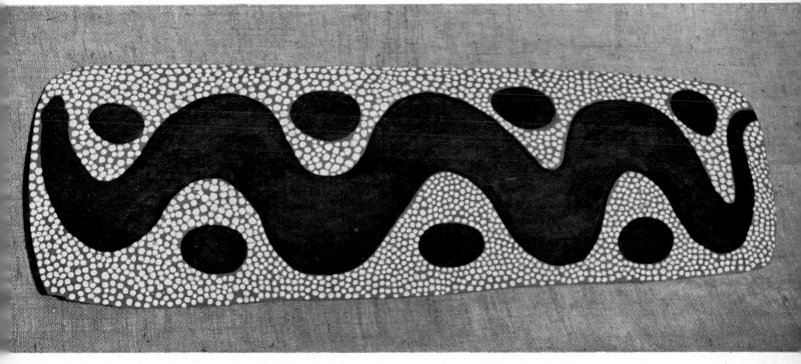

29 Sacred *maraiin* pattern from Cape Stewart, north-central Arnhem Land. It resembles the body designs painted on men participating in sacred ritual

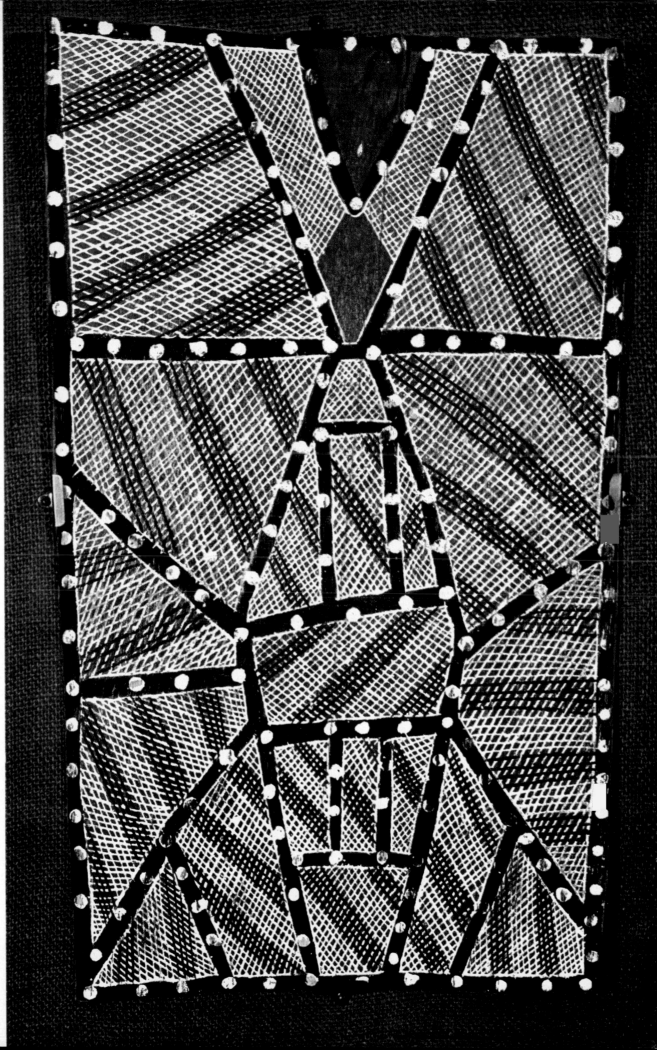

30 In this bark painting from Oenpelli are two Yerobeni spirits, who live in caves and holes in the ground, and dance around corpses which have been placed on tree platforms

31 In this bark painting from Yirrkalla, illustrating a myth of the Moon and the Dugong, are a crescent moon and a full moon with surrounding halo. The other designs have been interpreted as yams, but may be lily and lotus bulbs

33 An example of X-ray painting from Goulburn Island, showing a native companion, or jabiru, with three fish

35 Bark painting from Yirrkalla, dealing with a section of the Laindjung-Banaidja myth. In the bottom panel is a sacred totemic crocodile; in panel two, middle, a totemic bandicoot escapes from a fire by entering a hollow log. Immediately above is a design referring to a dream of one of the artists. The top panel is in two parts: on the left-hand side are ashes and smouldering fire; on the right, more ashes and fire with the bones of participants in a sacred ritual who were burnt to death. The figure is a spirit woman, Gurunga, who tried to put out the fire

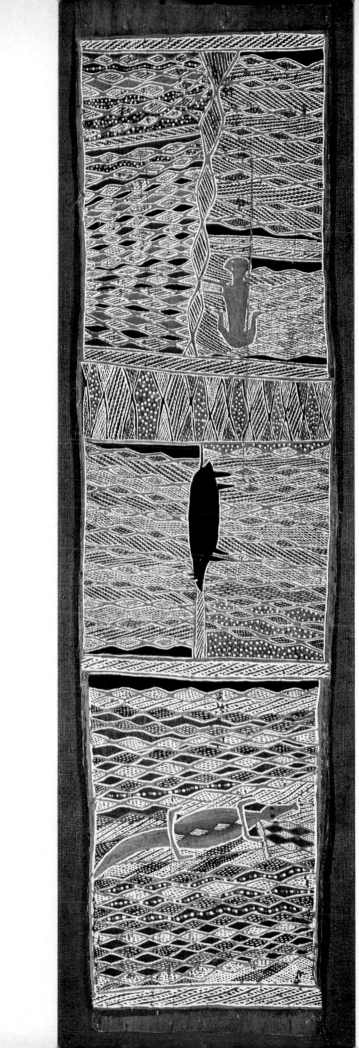

36 Bark painting from Goulburn Island, a sequel to Plate 37. Mimi are dancing. At the top left-hand corner is a yam (see Plate 17), and on the right the dismembered human corpse **37** Bark painting of Mimi spirits from Goulburn Island. A Gunwinggu man (*left*), taken into the country of the Mimi, refuses their hospitality and is captured by a Mimi headman (large central figure). His body is cut up. The figure on the right is holding his victim, cutting off flesh: other Mimi emerge from their caves and dance with pleasure

36

37

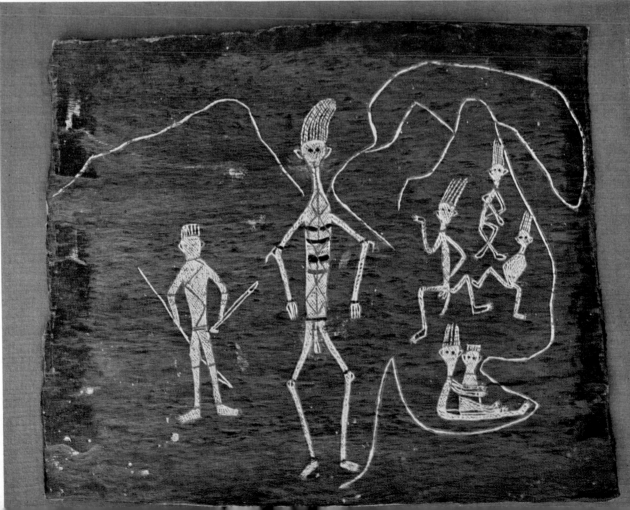

39 Two complex figures from a cave painting at Red Lily Lagoon, near
Oenpelli 40 A graceful cave painting of a woman. It comes from the
Sleisbeck Mine district, in the extreme south-west corner of Arnhem Land
41 A ritual postulant, or mythical figure, painted on a shelter facing at
St. Vidgeon, against a background of hand stencils and other small figures
42 Cave paintings at Oenpelli. Three fish and a Mimi hunter; superimposed
on these are two complex figures with contorted limbs, associated with magic

39	
	41
40	
	42

55 Bark painting from Milingimbi: the rock python, Julunggul, coiled around several eggs, rests at the bottom of the sacred waterhole associated with the mythical Wawalag sisters

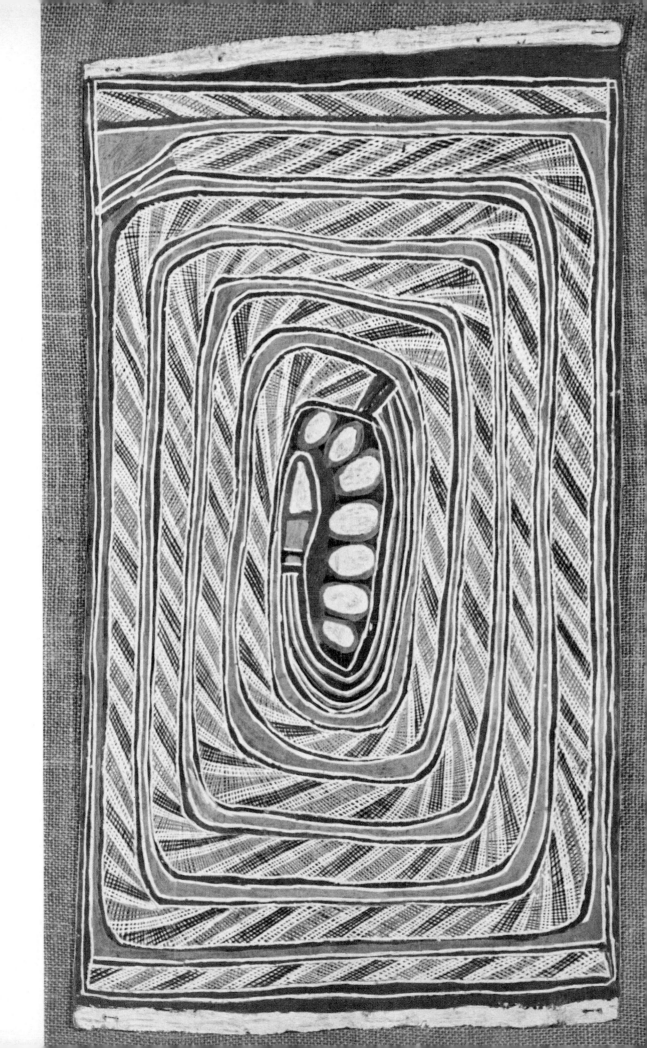

56 Sorcery painting from Oenpelli, of a man said to have seduced the wife of another. He has cockatoo feathers at the top of his head, and barbed stingray nails protrude from his body; two extra 'arms' have been added

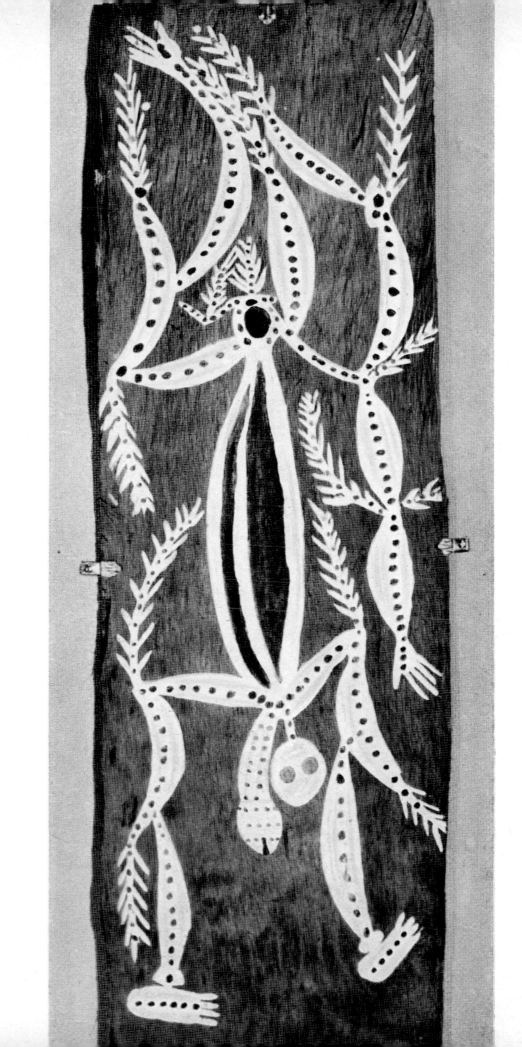

57 Bark painting from Melville Island, showing the totemic site of a spirit woman, Puruliangkala, associated with bush-fires. The central, enclosed white circle is Turiturina Island, and the smaller circles low rocks, fresh-water springs, and deposits of red and white ochre. Other designs refer to milkwood-trees, and the pin-point dots are fruit

58 Bark painting from Yirrkalla relating to the totemic centre of the Bremer Island Turtle Man. At top, a green-backed turtle; at bottom, a central figure of a whale, with a 'moon'-fish at each side, and a surrounding design of sea and waves

60 An X-ray painting of a male kangaroo, from Goulburn Island

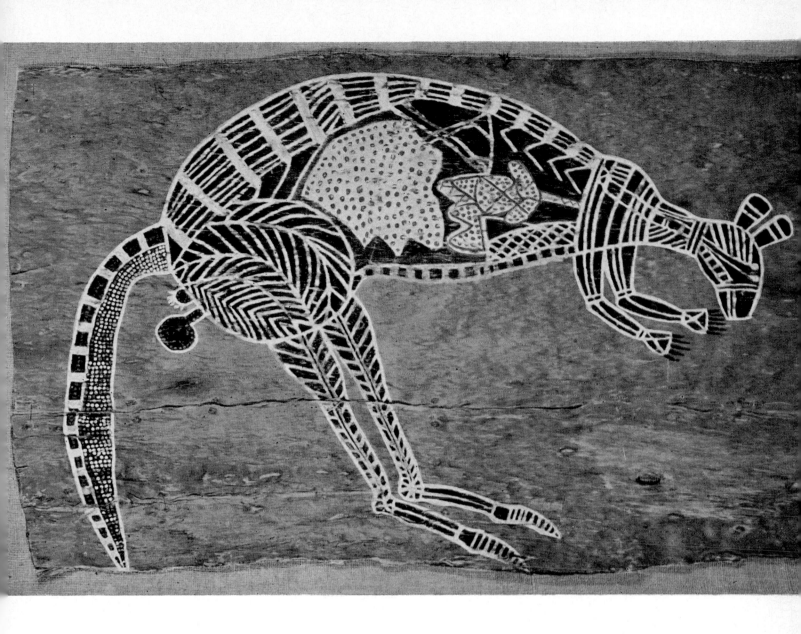

61 Bark painting from Milingimbi, relating to a myth. The central band of spots indicates reefs, and the rest of the painting fish-bones, symbolizing Daigurgur, or Deiwarur, clansfolk

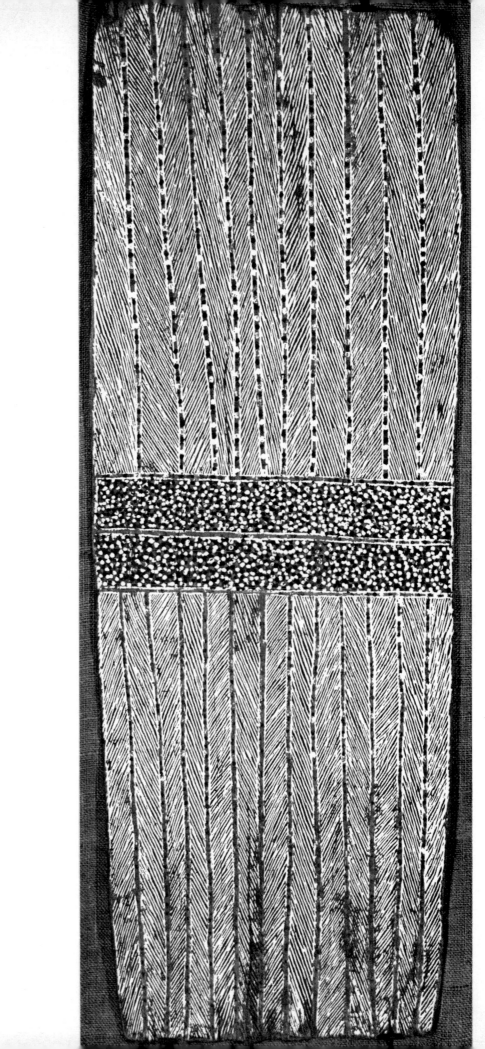

65 In this bark from Yirrkalla are human footprints, handprints, and (*right*) a row of stingray livers

66 Bark painting from Beswick Creek Government settlement, illustrating scenes from the life of Mimi spirits. At the top are a didjeridu player, a singing man with clapping-sticks, and four dancers. In the middle are a seated woman, a didjeridu player, and four women and a man dancing. In the bottom panel are more dancers, a songman, and a didjeridu player

67 Bark painting from Yirrkalla. It has been variously interpreted as, for example, a feast, but is more likely to represent a ritual scene

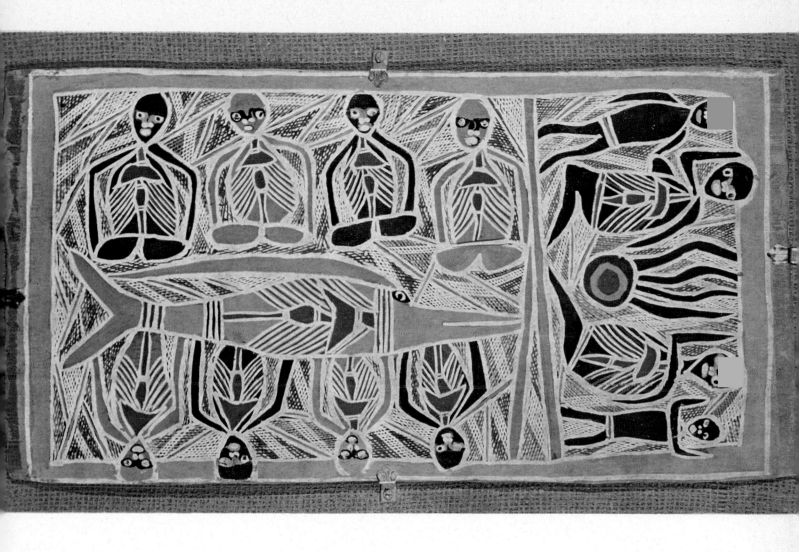

68 Carved wooden figures of sacred beings. *Left to right*: the younger Wawalag sister; the elder Wawalag sister; Laindjung, with foam-stained face after emerging from the sea

70 Incised objects. *Top*, shield from south-east Australia; *left*, ornate fighting boomerang from northern New South Wales; *middle left*, three engraved pearlshells from the northern Kimberleys, two with attached necklets or waistbands; *middle*, *third from right*, wooden sacred board from the Laverton area of Western Australia; hunting or fighting, fluted boomerang from Caledon Bay; *extreme right*, spearthrower from Western Australia; *bottom*, *left and right*, two stone *tjurunga*, both Aranda, from Central Australia

72 A collection of decorated spears, a fighting-club (*centre*), and four spear-throwers (*below*). The two spears on the outer left and right are from Melville Island: the other eight spears are from Yirrkalla. The flat-bladed club is from Milingimbi; and the four spearthrowers are from Arnhem Land, the first three from Groote Eylandt and the bottom one from Yirrkalla

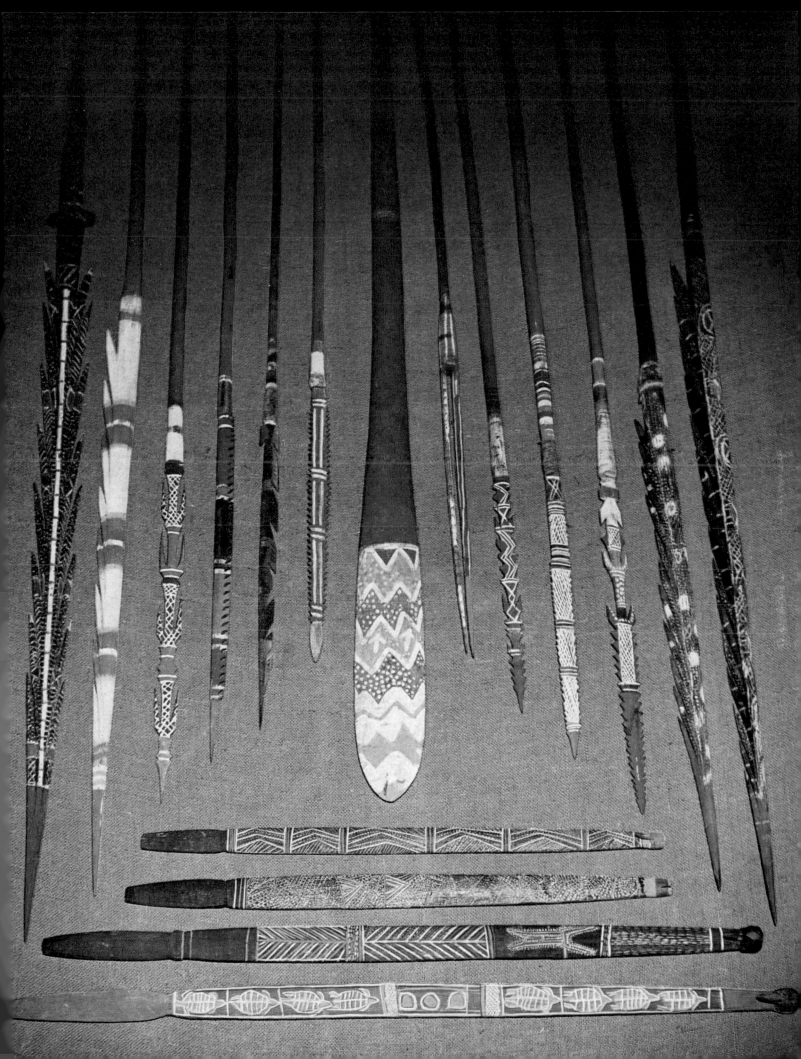

73 Painted objects from Arnhem Land. From left to right: **a** Sacred board used in the Arawaldja rituals at Groote Eylandt: the figure represents Aidja, a creative totemic being **b** Hollow log coffin from Yirrkalla, north-eastern Arnhem Land. Some time after the initial mortuary rites a dead person's bones are collected and placed in a long, hollow log, of which this example is a model. The design shows a Macassan prau **c** This is also a log coffin, but resembles a didjeridu, or drone-pipe, used in sacred ritual. The log, from the McArthur River, Northern Territory, has a stopper of bark protruding from the top; and on it is a feather-down pattern of a kangaroo's hind and front paws and tail **d** Hollow log coffin, or *uwar* gong used in sacred ritual: from Milingimbi, north-central Arnhem Land **e** Sacred *rangga* emblem representing Wunungu, the monstrous Lightning Snake. The top part of the design shows this snake surrounded by many younger snakes; and below is the waterhole from which they emerged, near Milingimbi **f** Two skulls from Yirrkalla, painted with the clan patterns of the deceased

Descriptive Annotations to the Plates*

R. M. BERNDT

Plate 1

A rock-pool with adjacent shelter, at Muly-areena Creek, western New South Wales. When the surface waters dried up, the Aborigines of this area (like those in many other parts of Australia) were obliged to rely on such perman-ent pools as the one illustrated here. Within its vicinity game and bush foods would be relatively plentiful, particularly the 'nardoo' grass (the seed of which was ground to make damper). Aborigines lived in such shelters, and there made their paintings.

Photograph by D. Milner; information from F. D. McCarthy.

Plate 2

Another section of a gallery on Mulyareena Creek. Four figures are painted, each holding a boomerang and shield, or two boomerangs. An incomplete female figure can just be seen on the right. It is possible that they are dancing.

Photograph by D. Milner; information from F. D. McCarthy.

Plate 3

This illustrates part of a cave or shelter at Mulyareena Creek (see Plate 1). Of the two central white figures, the one on the left is a songman, clapping sticks or boomerangs: the other, on the right, holds a boomerang and shield. According to McCarthy, the left-hand man represents a native doctor singing protec-tive magic into a warrior with a club and shield, or into a hunter to ensure his success in hunting. They could also be two men fighting.

The red figures show a set of men holding weapons, with a kangaroo or wallaby, which they could be hunting. Two stencils, made by blowing white clay around a hand placed on the rock surface, are also seen.

Photograph by D. Milner; information from F. D. McCarthy.

Plate 4

Typical of cave paintings in western New South Wales are those on Iona Station. This shows a section of a cave wall, on which sets of small human figures are painted in white ochre. In one scene, three armed men are hunting three kang-aroos: below is a set of linked men, who may be dancing. There are also some hand stencils.

Photograph by D. Milner; information from F. D. McCarthy.

Plate 5

Grave-posts from Snake Bay on Melville Island, now in the Art Gallery of New South Wales.

* All measurements are in inches.

(See Purchases and Acquisitions for 1959: 47–50.) They form part of a collection of seventeen posts, made and painted in 1958, and presented to the New South Wales Art Gallery by Dr. S. Scougall in 1959.

Plate 6

A collection of typical Melville and Bathurst islands grave-posts on a burial site. Spencer (1914: 228–39, various illustrations, for example, Figs. 51, 53, 54, 55, and Plate X; 1928: for example, Figs. 448, 457, 459, 462, 475, 476, 477 and Plate X) has recorded the mortuary rituals associated with these posts, as has Mountford (1958a: 60–121, with plates).

These unusual carved and painted structures, of sculptural dimensions, are part of the *bugamani* (*pukamuni*) mourning complex, which includes other smaller objects too. (See Plates 71 and 72.) They are erected on and around the grave in the culminating rites, which extend over a period of several months: the decorated participants wash off their designs, and men who have grown beards for the occasion cut them off; dancing takes place; and bark containers (as in Plate 71) are attached to some of the poles. Mountford (1958a: 109) speaks of such poles as gifts to the deceased. In general significance they have much in common with the post-figures of north-eastern Arnhem Land (see Plate 69), but the treatment and decoration are unique to Melville and Bathurst islands, and certainly in no other part of Aboriginal Australia are so many placed on and around a grave. In many cases they are human figures in highly stylized form—in some cases the deceased person himself; in others, his immediate relatives. Mountford notes that some sections of them represent forks or limbs of trees, women's breasts, rocks on the sea coast, as well as windows and doors (openings in poles); he mentions other meanings as well; and the ochre painting on the body of the poles is variously interpreted, as dealing with natural scenes and mythical incidents (Mountford, *ibid.*, 111–18). These designs closely resemble those illustrated in Plates 24 and 57.

Plate 7

A mortuary post of Bathurst and Melville islands

being painted. Mountford (1958a: 110, Plate 33) mentions that, after being shaped, the poles are scorched over a fire of blazing leaves to provide a black background for the designs; then they are moved close to the grave and set up ready for the application of ochres. The artist shown here is decorated for the *bugamani*; he wears a false beard and a head-dress of cockatoo feathers, and his face is decorated to represent the barn owl, of mythical significance. (Mountford, 1958a: Frontispiece, Plates 31C and 28J.)

Plate 8

A further collection of grave-posts from Bathurst and Melville islands. One (in the foreground) has an upturned bark basket at its apex. In this grouping, too, as in Plate 6, the wide assortment of shapes and designs is clearly visible.

Plate 9

This magnificent engraving from Maroota (see Plate 10) is just under fourteen feet in length. It is possibly a male ancestral or creative being (of Baiami type: see Chapter Three), with arms outstretched above the head; it wears a necklet and armlets, a waistband and thighbands. McCarthy notes that it has large ears and four eyes (which may represent two eyes, a nose, and a mouth); lines at the top of the head are hair or feathers, and pitted lines on the surface of the body may refer to cicatrization.

Photograph by D. Millen; information from F. D. McCarthy.

Plate 10

Petroglyphs, figures engraved or incised on rock, are to be found in many parts of Aboriginal Australia. In the Sydney-Hawkesbury district they are particularly extensive, and at least four thousand figures are known. (See Chapter Three, where McCarthy has discussed these; also McCarthy, 1941–56; 1957a: 183; 1958: 17–20, Figs. 1, 4, 5, 13; Elkin, 1949.)

The style of most of these engravings has few counterparts in other regions, especially in relation to size and freedom of conception, although there are stylistic affiliations with those at Port Hedland and elsewhere in Western Australia. McCarthy estimates that there are 'between 400 and 500 galleries ... within the area bounded by the coast and the Blue Mountains, extending from the southern side of the Hunter Valley in the north to National Park in the south'. Nearly all the figures refer to mythical and spirit beings, hunting scenes, and so on. Some of the sites are known to have been *bora* grounds, where initiations and sacred rituals were held. Many too possibly refer to mythical events, to the increase of the natural species, and to hunting magic. Such engravings were used, and added to, right up to the settlement of this region by Europeans: but some are undoubtedly quite ancient.

The photograph in this plate shows such a site, at what is called the Devil's Rock group of outline engravings at Maroota, upper Hawkesbury River, some forty miles from Sydney. Engraved sites in this district vary from small boulders to outcrops of several acres in extent. The outlines were made by a series of overlapping or conjoined pits hammered into the sandstone, up to three-quarters of an inch wide and up to three-eighths of an inch deep. The grooves of some of the more outstanding figures were deepened and widened by rubbing with an abrading stone. The design illustrated here could be a kangaroo.

Photographed by D. Millen; information from F. D. McCarthy.

Plate 11

Plate 11, from the same region, depicts a life-size figure of an emu with a clutch of eggs, and some engraved tracks. This is beside a small natural waterhole in the sandstone rock. It probably relates to the increase of this creature.

Photograph by D. Millen; information from F. D. McCarthy.

Plate 12

Three male actors rest during a semi-sacred ceremony among the Northern Aranda. The decorations on their backs refer to the fire totemic ancestors of Rubundja (Rubuntja), and Strehlow notes that these refer to the Simpson Desert 'final' (or concluding) patterns. The body decorations here (see Chapter Four) are virtually identical with those worn by postulants in the sacred rituals.

Rubundja (Mount Hay) is the most prominent point on the western boundary of Aranda territory—in Strehlow's words (1947: 48), its 'blue mass can be seen sixty miles away from the pass where the overland telegraph line leaves the MacDonnell Ranges'. Burt Plain lies before it, and within this area many myths are located. Spencer and Gillen (1938: 445–6) give a brief sketch of the myth associated with Rubundja (which they call Urapuncha). In the Dreaming period (see Chapter One) a spark of fire (*urinchitha*) ascended into the sky, and was blown by the north wind to the site now named Rubundja. A great fire sprang up; when it burnt out, the ancestors of the fire totem (*inapertwa* creatures) emerged from the ashes. These beings were found by two wild duck men, who made the fire creatures into men and women. As Spencer and Gillen say, 'The remains of the great fire still smoulders on the top of the mountain (Mount Hay) where the sacred storehouse of the totem is located, and at night time, especially if the night be dark and rainy, the fire can be seen from a long distance . . .' Comparison with photographs in Spencer and Gillen (1938), T. G. H. Strehlow (1947), and McCarthy (1938/58; 1957*a*), demonstrates how close the body designs illustrated here are to those used in sacred ritual. (Berndt, 1951*a*: Plate V, in a different setting, shows men putting feather down on their bodies for the performance of sacred ritual.) From left to right: painted white ochre design; bands of white and reddened feather down; central pattern, edged with feather down.

Photograph by T. G. H. Strehlow.

Plate 13

Plate 13 shows the ritual actor who made the snake tracks illustrated in Plate 15. He himself represents this totemic being. His body and face are patterned in reddened and white feather down, and he wears an elaborate head-dress. Beside him is a shield, decorated with feather down, which takes the place of a ground painting. (See Chapter Four.)

Photograph by T. G. H. Strehlow.

Plate 14

This is a particularly well constructed *waningga* (or *wonigi*) or 'thread cross' of the Western Aranda, standing within a ground painting on a sacred dancing-place protected by a windbreak of branches. (See Chapter Four.)

Ground painting and *waningga* are made of reddened and natural white down: on the ground, it is arranged in a series of lines within a circle of red and white down; on the *waningga*, it is superimposed on a basis of human hair, wound about the upright pole and two horizontal sticks, and the whole tipped with a bunch of feathers. (Examples of such workmanship can be seen in Spencer and Gillen, 1938; T. G. H. Strehlow, 1947; McCarthy 1938/58: 30–2, Plate 1, Fig. 19; 1957*a*.) In this particular case the ground painting refers to Ntarea, an important waterhole on the Finke, about one mile west of Hermannsburg mission station; this is the native name of this mission station site, in Western Aranda territory.

Photograph by T. G. H. Strehlow.

Plate 15

Snake tracks made by an actor in the snake-totem ritual of Hale River, Aranda territory. This is what can be called a ground drawing (see Chapter Four). Hale River is in the Harts Range area, near Arltunga, Eastern Aranda. Spencer and Gillen (1938: 444–5) give a myth concerning the snake of Imyunga: although this refers to a different site, the story itself is not unlike the one to which this design refers.

Photograph by T. G. H. Strehlow.

Plate 16

This illustration shows the fire totemic actors of Rubundja: see Plate 12. Stretching before the four main figures are symmetrically arranged mounds of earth, between which they move. They wear the ritual headgear commonly used in Northern Aranda totemic enactments of this nature, and called *tjurunga mburka*, or *tjurunga talkua* (see Strehlow, 1947: 56, 58, 85–6, 162, Plate 4; Spencer and Gillen, 1938). The upper part of the head-dress consists of *tjurunga* covered with down and tipped with a bunch of feathers. As Strehlow (*ibid.*, 56) notes, the

tjurunga is often covered with grass, then wrapped with hairstring, and finally feather down is superimposed. 'The actor always represents one of the totemic ancestors at a certain stage of his life's career . . .'

Photograph by T. G. H. Strehlow.

Plate 17

This yam plant from Goulburn Island is clearly within the western Arnhem Land art tradition. At the top is a flower or pod, with leaves; at the bottom is the yam or bulb itself, with fibres. Yams of this kind are associated with Mimi spirits, and said to form their staple diet. This bark painting belongs to a set of three, the other two being illustrated in Plates 36 and 37. (See Chapter Two.)

Size $21 \cdot 5 \times 18$; artist, Old Wurungulngul, Maung tribe. This specimen was collected in 1947 by R. Berndt, from whom it is on loan to the Department of Anthropology, University of Western Australia.

Plate 18

This bark, from Groote Eylandt, is not in the typical local style (see Adam, 1951; Mountford, 1956). Possibly it has been influenced by northeast Arnhem Land art.

The main figures are two swimming turtles. The designs on their back are the shell; at each side are waves, as they swim toward a turtle catchment or pot. No other information is available, although this painting was No. 12 of Teribus (Stuttgart, 1954/55). A search has been made through the catalogue of the Leonhard Adam Collection, part of which is now housed in the University of Melbourne, but no details about the painting can be found.

Size, unspecified; artist, unknown. In the Leonhard Adam Collection, Melbourne. Possibly obtained by Dr. Adam from either Mr. H. L. Perriman, or Mr. F. H. Gray. Originally in the University of Melbourne Ethnographical Collection (?).

Plate 19

Here a Wandjina (or Wondjina) creative being is painted on bark. (See Chapters One and Three.) Head, headband, typically linked eyes and nose, with shoulders and arms, are depicted against a background of white ochre.

This form of art, found in the northern Kimberleys among the Unambal, Worora, and Ungarinyin, has been discussed by a number of writers, most notably by Elkin (1930; 1938/56; 1948), Kaberry (1939); Lommel (1952), McCarthy (1957a; 1958), Petri (1954), and Worms (1955). This example is from Walcott Inlet, western Kimberleys.

The Wandjina, as noted in the main text, are creative beings who are closely associated with the rainbow serpent: they are concerned with the perpetuation of the seasons, and especially with bringing rain and supplying spirit children. According to Worora mythology, the Wandjina were the first people. They are said to have come from the wind, and to have wandered across the country creating all the physiographical features. Finally, they went to various caves and shelters and became paintings. But their spirits remain; and wherever a Wandjina painting is to be found, there too is its power—which is available to Aboriginal man through the performance of special ritual.

Size, 40 × 27; artist, unknown. Collected by Professor H. Petri, Frobenius Expedition to the northern Kimberleys in 1937–8, and presented in 1939 to the Western Australian Museum. It was exhibited in the Jubilee Exhibition of Australian Art, 1951, No. 16.

Plate 20

This is a pseudo-historical woman named Manubi. Feathered pendants hang from her elbows, and she wears a headband with protruding ends. Primary attention has been paid to the painting of the genitalia, which are enlarged, just as is done in the case of males. The body patterning is what might be called, superficially, a modified X-ray style; in typical X-ray style internal organs are at least partially identifiable, whereas here only the backbone and other skeletal material can be distinguished.

This example is from Oenpelli, western Arnhem Land, and belongs to a series of paintings (see, for example, Plate 56) associated with love magic and sorcery. They belong to the same cultural area as those in Plates 26, 30, 32, 33, 60, and 64, but differ somewhat in style. Plates 30, 33, 60, and 64 illustrate one style, Plates 20, 26 and 32 another, and Plate 56 a third. Some degree of stylistic merging has taken place, if only because within recent years, since Sir Baldwin Spencer's time, there has been a great deal of intertribal contact.

Stories about Manubi and her adventures relate mostly to sexual associations. This painting of her serves, as it were, as a model for men intent on reproducing the image of their beloved for magical purposes. Mountford (1956: Plate 56 D) has a poorer example of this kind of painting. R. and C. Berndt (1951: 206–10), and Elkin and R. and C. Berndt (1950: Chapter V), have discussed such paintings used in love magic and sorcery, as well as in illustrating a story. Also, paintings of this variety are to be found in local galleries of rock art, stretching from behind Oenpelli to the mainland opposite Goulburn Island and toward the Liverpool River. (See notes for Plate 56.)

Size, 22 × 21·5; artist, Midjaumidjau, one of the great artists of Western Arnhem Land, Gunwinggu tribe. Collected by R. Berndt in 1949. Originally in the collections of the Department of Anthropology, University of Sydney, and now on permanent loan to the University of Western Australia.

Plate 21

This bark, from Groote Eylandt, is illustrated and briefly discussed in L. Adam (1954:156–9, Plate 31; 1951: 172–3, Fig. 3). Arranged as two panels it represents a scene at Umba Kumba on Groote Eylandt—the site of a settlement previously occupied by Mr. F. H. Gray, but now a Government station.

The upper and lower horizontal lines are the Umba Kumba gardens cultivated by Mr. Gray, the central horizontal bands a recently constructed dam, from which a creek runs into a billabong (concentric circle). Three trees are shown in the upper panel and one in the lower. The dam, however, was made from sand excavated from a nearby sandhill, represented by an irregular encircling line (upper left). Fourteen men are working on the excavation: one holds a spade, another what appears to be an axe. In the course of this work a number of stone axe-blades were uncovered: two of these are drawn, one near the spade, and the other near the man holding an axe. Adam (1954: 158) notes that eighteen stone axe-heads, with ground cutting edges, were found here. The notes to the catalogue of objects in the University of Melbourne ethnographical collection (No. 5) mention eleven; these were subsequently hafted and painted. Three of the axe-heads are in the University of Melbourne collection; the whereabouts of the others is unknown. In the painting, the ten human figures in white within the circle of workers represent Umba Kumba people now long dead, who had originally camped in that area—presumably the former owners of the uncovered axe-blades.

Size, approximately 36 × 15; artist, Minimini of Groote. Collected by F. H. Gray and presented to L. Adam; it is now in the Leonhard Adam collection, University of Melbourne.

Plate 22

This bark painting was originally collected by Sir Baldwin Spencer, along with those illustrated in Plates 30 and 64, at Oenpelli in 1912. It should be compared with that shown in Plate 60. Initially illustrated in Spencer (1914: 437, Fig. 86; 1928: 809–10, Fig. 529) and later in McCarthy (1957a: 179), it was included in the *Jubilee Exhibition of Australian Art* (1951: No. 4) and in the *Australian Aboriginal Art Exhibition* (1960–61: No. 4). It is virtually a life-size painting of a black kangaroo (*Macropus woodwardi*), *madjiborla*, living among the ranges near Oenpelli. Spencer describes this X-ray-style figure in glowing words. The backbone is clearly visible, along with 'masses of flesh . . . The lung is seen in the thorax; immediately below this is the liver, and the abdomen is filled up with the intestines. The backbone is regarded as the main, strong support of the body, and to emphasize the strength of the hind limbs the femur is drawn in the same way as the backbone. The most striking feature, however, to anyone acquainted with the kangaroo in its natural state is the really wonderful way in which the

. . . artist has depicted the pose that is always assumed by the animal when alarmed—the erect position of the body, the head thrown well up and slightly back, and the two little fore limbs held forwards helplessly.' (Spencer, 1928: 809–10.)

Significant, too, is the relative size of the hunter. This stylistic device has been noted in Chapters Five and Six. His small figure is painted in the same way as the kangaroo: he is shown running, having just released from his thrower a spear which is about to enter its victim. In front of him hangs a dilly-bag. Spencer reports that the artist told him the man in this painting had been out searching for *mormo* (spirits), or wild honey, and had filled his bag with this. He was also carrying a stone (?) spearthrower, and saw this kangaroo on his way back to the camp.

Size, 51 × 32; artist, unknown. Obtained by Baldwin Spencer at Oenpelli in 1912, either from the artist, as he infers in his description of it, or from Mr. P. Cahill. It was presented by him to the National Museum of Victoria.

Plate 23

Plate 23 is an example of Groote Eylandt style, which is quite distinctively different to that of western and north-eastern Arnhem Land.

The fish depicted is a barracouta. Some similar paintings of fish are illustrated in Mountford (1956: 81–6), and in McCarthy (in Mountford, ed., 1960: 297–414).

Size, 36 × 13; artist, Minimini; collected by F. D. McCarthy, American-Australian Scientific Expedition to Arnhem Land, 1948, now in the Australian Museum, Sydney.

Plate 24

This Melville Island bark is similar in style to that illustrated in Plate 57. It has been discussed in Chapter Two, where a text figure (4) is also given. (See also Mountford, 1958a: 165, Plate 55 A and B.)

The painting, which is highly conventionalized, shows a shark, large sea-snakes, a smaller sea-snake, a mangrove-swamp snake, a sawfish, porpoise, sea-slug, shells, boulders on the sea-bed, a creek in a mangrove swamp, and a sand-bank at Snake Bay.

Size, 28 × 19; artist, unrecorded. Collected by C. P. Mountford, National Geographic Expedition, 1954, and presented by him to the South Australian Museum in 1955.

Plate 25

Plate 25 is an outstanding bark painting from Yirrkalla, depicting scenes from the sacred Djanggawul mythology. (See Warner, 1937/58: 335–56; R. Berndt, 1952.) Other refernces to the myth appear in Elkin and R. and C. Berndt (1950: Chapter III), where some sacred objects (*rangga*) used in the Djanggawul *dua* moiety *nara* ritual are illustrated; and in Mountford (1956: 267–75), who also includes some Djanggawul bark paintings and objects. (See also Chapter Two, Fig. 2.)

Like the majority of myths, this exists in a number of versions. Briefly, two sisters, an elder (Bildjiwuraroju) and a younger (Miralaidj), with their brother (Djanggawul), and in some accounts a companion, made landfall on the east coast of Arnhem Land after a long journey by bark canoe from the mythical island of Bralgu. The sacred site of their arrival on the mainland is Jelangbara (Yelangbara; Port Bradshaw). They were creative beings, and the main theme of the myth and the rituals it substantiates is fertility. They created part of the countryside, waterholes and springs, trees, and, most importantly, human beings.

This bark painting depicts certain sections of the myth. It is divided into four major panels, and should be compared with Aboriginal drawings illustrated in R. Berndt (1952).

In the bottom panel the two sisters are seen at Arnhem Bay giving birth to the first Aborigines, represented by clusters of red dots encircled by black or yellow rims: the children flow from these two Fertility Mothers. Male babies are placed in the grass (the three smaller, red-dotted circles), so that when they become adults they will grow beards, and be tough. Female babies are placed under conically shaped *ngainmara* mats (one at each side of both sisters), protected, so that they will grow up smooth-skinned, without body hair. In the Art Gallery of New South Wales Catalogue (1959, No. 189), apart from the four *ngainmara*, the enclosed circles of red dots are said to be menstrual and afterbirth blood, as well as water flowing from the two sisters.

In the second panel above this, on the left-hand side, are eight sacred *rangga* emblems named *djuda* (see R. Berndt, 1952), placed in the ground by the Djanggawul to become trees. (There are several varieties of these *rangga*, some of which were used by these creative beings as walking-sticks, or to make springs and waterholes, or left at various places to become trees.) In this particular case, the *rangga* are said to belong to Bildjiwuraroju, and to have been 'planted' in order to make a shade for the children removed from the sisters. Four trees, two at each side, have their branches facing one another; their roots are at each corner (these are *djuda rangga*, which have become trees). This relates to Ngeimil linguistic group territory. The right-hand panel shows the Djanggawul brother (centre) with his long penis, urinating, with a sister at each side. At the extreme right are two discs depicting the sun and its rays (at sunset and at sunrise). The Djanggawul came from the east, from Bralgu, on the rays of the rising sun; and finally, still travelling westward, they disappeared into the path of the setting sun. In some versions of this myth, the two sisters are said to be the Daughters of the Sun. The place shown in the painting is said to be Daduwo (Daramur, or Dararwoi), inland from Arnhem Bay. (See R. Berndt, 1952: 30, Plate 24.)

The third panel from the bottom repeats the theme of the two sisters giving birth to the first people. (According to the Art Gallery of New South Wales Catalogue, 1959, the dots and three yellow circles linked with the younger sister are said to represent afterbirth. However, in other examples which I have this design refers to multiple births.) The place is said to be Djiriliwuramaju (see R. Berndt, 1952: 48), not far from Milingimbi, on the mainland. The elder sister has bands across her hips; male children are yellow, and female children black.

In the top panel, at left, the two sisters are standing by a sacred spring with flowing spring-

81

water at each side. In the description of this scene given in the *Australian Aboriginal Art Catalogue* (1960–61, No. 71) and the Art Gallery Catalogue (1959, No. 189), the central circle is a swamp and the lines at each side lily leaves: this is not inconsistent with the above interpretation. But here the red-ochred area is said to be the grave of the two sisters, in which they are lying. After death they go to the spirit land and receive new names, Bangwoina and Gurugura: and the place is noted as Elcho Island.

No such mythical incident occurred at Elcho Island in the versions I have recorded; but at Damijagaju, on the mainland at Arnhem Bay, a Dreaming (or *wongar*) sorcerer killed Miralaidj when she was walking along by herself. She was buried at this place; the surviving Djanggawul erected a post over her grave, and hung upon it two special dilly-bags (similar to those illustrated in Plate 71). (See R. Berndt, 1952: 35.) However, Miralaidj miraculously reappears to join the others in their travels. And it is important to emphasize that these beings are immortal. They can be 'killed' (as in the case of the younger sister); but they do not die. They may be metamorphosed as stone at a certain place, so that part of their spirit or aura remains there, but they continue as they were before.

On the right-hand side of the top panel is a portrait of the artist, Mauwulan (Mawulan), sitting before his sacred goanna-tail *rangga* (in this case, named *djanda*), singing songs from the Djanggawul cycle. Suspended from the *rangga* are lengths of feathered string, which in some contexts symbolize the rays of the sun. (See R. Berndt, 1952: Plate 5, which shows an actual photograph of Mauwulan sitting by his *djanda rangga* at Yirrkalla.) The surrounding design of cross-hatching is earth and grass at Jelangbara. Size, 74 × 25·5; artist, Mauwulan (Mawulan), born c. 1908, Riradjingu linguistic unit, *dua* moiety. Other examples of this famous artist's work are to be seen in Elkin and R. and C. Berndt, 1950; Mountford, 1956. (See also New South Wales Art Gallery Catalogue, 1959, No. 189.) It was acquired in 1959 by Dr. S. Scougall,

who presented it to the Art Gallery of New South Wales.

Plate 26

This bark painting from Oenpelli is one of a series of three. Another, illustrated in Elkin and R. and C. Berndt (1950: 82–3, Plate 17), shows this special spirit-snake dancing around a grave on which is placed a European cross, holding a wand in its hand. The one illustrated here (in Plate 26) has appeared also in R. and C. Berndt (1951: 212–15, Plate 23); and the third (*ibid*, Plate 24) shows two of these snake spirits (male and female) dancing.

All three paintings, and this one in particular, refer to two Big-eyed Owls (*gwojuggwojug*), who are themselves spirits, and the Dijalmung snake spirits who live among the rocky hills on the mainland at Margulidjban, near the Liverpool River. These creatures are the spirit-familiars of the famous songman Balilbalil, a Margulidjban Gunwinggu of western Arnhem Land. At night they visit him in dreams and teach him new songs, which he learns and later sings, himself, in evening entertainments in the main camp. These so-called 'gossip songs' touch lightly on ordinary incidents which occur from day to day, but especially on the behaviour of sweethearts and extramarital lovers. Any item of gossip of this nature is brought to Balilbalil (he says) by the two Owls—and they compose the short song which he will later sing. Some of the songs are blunt and outspoken, others quite subtle, but most of them bring into the open private matters, which could not otherwise be made public without quarrelling and fighting. This is done in such a way that no offence is given; and the actual participants in a specific incident remain unnamed, although it may not be hard to identify them. In the dream-vision Balilbalil speaks to his spirit-familiars, and sees the spirit-snakes dancing. There are other accounts relating to the Owl performers. For instance, they are said to sing and play the didjeridu so well that the Dijalmung snakes are irresistibly drawn to them—the performance is so beautiful that the snakes cannot help weeping. And just as the Owls attract the Dijalmung, so Balilbalil attracts all the people who come to listen to him and dance.

In this bark painting one male Dijalmung is shown dancing with sinuous movement: he has legs and arms, a long tongue, beard, ears, and antennae. Below, left, one Owl man sits singing with his clapping-sticks: on the right is the other, playing his didjeridu.

Size, 25 × 15; artist, Balilbalil the songman, Gunwinggu. The painting, however, was obtained at Goulburn Island by R. Berndt in 1947, when Balilbalil was visiting there from Oenpelli. It was exhibited in the Arnhem Land Art Exhibition at David Jones' Art Gallery, Sydney, October 1949. Originally in the collections of the Department of Anthropology, University of Sydney, it is now on permanent loan to the University of Western Australia.

Plate 27

This very beautiful example of shield drawing comes from Yarrabah, Queensland. McCarthy (1938/58: 24–6, Figs. 13 and 14) speaks of these large oval shields as coming from the Cairns, Port Douglas, and Mitchell River area of north-eastern Queensland. McConnel (1935: 49–68, with coloured plates) has discussed them. Tindale and Birdsell (1941: 7, Plates II and IV) refer to the Cairns Rain Forest people as being of Tasmanoid-type, adding that their large fighting-shields made from the buttresses of *ficus* trees were used in conjunction with long single-handed, flat-bladed wooden swords, or clubs.

The particular example illustrated here comes from the Idindji tribe, and the design represents two parent turtles and their young. Each shield has in the middle a raised boss, which forms a focus for the patterning constructed around it. Two initiated artists using lawyer-cane brushes paint the design simultaneously, with the bulk of the shield resting on their knees. The motifs used in shield decoration are varied, and have direct totemic or mythical significance. Usually, each is associated with a particular totemic clan, the members of which perform the relevant rituals. The various things and creatures depicted in realistic or stylized form are all related to

Creative Beings, called *buleru*, who are responsible for them. The artists in representing them encapsulate also part of the power of these *buleru*. In one sense, the design signifies the clan associations of the bearer of such a shield and his links with the totemic world. In another, the representation itself provides him with extra power in fighting: he is aided by the *buleru*, who was originally responsible for creating whatever has been drawn on the shield.

Size of object, 46 × 14; artist, Dick of Mira Baki, Idindji (Yiddindye) tribe; collected by Miss Ursula McConnel prior to 1935; now in the South Australian Museum, having been presented by the collector in 1953.

Plate 28

In contrast to the shield in Plate 27 is this Northern Territory one from the Roper River. Its bold design, representing a snake and eggs, recalls the well-known ground paintings of Central Australia. (See Chapter Four.) Although there is no information on the significance of this shield, other than the meaning of its pattern, it is possibly associated with the mythical rock python and used in Kunapipi (Gunabibi) rituals. (See R. Berndt, 1951*a*: for example, Plate VIII; and McCarthy, 1938/58: Fig. 34.) It may represent the female counterpart of Lightning, husband of Kunapipi, the Great Mother, in his snake form. In other contexts it might refer to the rainbow snake, which has both male and female manifestations. Shields of this sort belonged to the Mara, Ngalagan, Mangarei, Alawa, Binbinga, Wadari, Galwa, and some other tribes in the vicinity of the Roper River. This particular shield is illustrated by McCarthy (1938/58: Fig. 15), who draws attention to the wide distribution of this form of art, marked by central curvilinear designs with small white dots on a background of red ochre. It can be found, he says, over most of the Northern Territory, including Arnhem Land, extending into Central Australia as well as into the Kimberleys, and exists alongside of varying art styles. This is partly because of the simple nature of the design, and because in most Aboriginal societies snakes are totemically and mythically significant.

83

Nevertheless, the way in which this snake is drawn, with the turn of its tail and the symmetrical arrangement of the eggs (or, alternatively, concentric circles, or U-shaped designs), is characteristic of Kunapipi ritual or its equivalents. In some cases such patterns are built up in feather down, using blood as an adhesive.

Size, 43 × 14; now in the South Australian Museum, which purchased it prior to 1915.

Plate 29

This bark painting from Cape Stewart, near the Liverpool River (central-north coast of Arnhem Land), reproduces a sacred *maraiin* pattern which is usually painted on a novice's or postulant's stomach, chest, and shoulders. The V-shaped design at the top indicates the space where a man's neck and chest should be: such patterning usually extends down the thighs to the knees. It is also typical of much of *maraiin* patterning in western Arnhem Land, and appears generally on a large range of worked and shaped *maraiin* objects representing various totemic creatures and parts of their bodies. Spencer (1914: 150–2, Plates III, IV, V, VI, VII), Elkin and R. and C. Berndt (1950: 47, Plate 5), and Mountford (1956: 460–6), have illustrated and discussed some of these. McCarthy (1957a: 124, 153) depicts men wearing body designs similar to this one.

The word *maraiin* (or *mareiin*, in north-eastern Arnhem Land) means, generally, 'sacred', and the religious rituals specifically known by this name extend throughout western Arnhem Land as far east as Cape Stewart. They were not traditionally associated with the Maung, but belong to the Gunwinggu, Gunbalang, Gunividji, Nagara, and Burera tribes. On the eastern side these rituals are equated with the *dua* and *jiridja* moiety *nara* (see annotations to Plates 25 and 35). There is a large body of mythology associated with the *maraiin* rituals, but the majority are concerned with totemic increase, and are sponsored by the Fertility Mother. (See R. and C. Berndt, 1951: 138–42.)

The actual patterning on this bark has not been interpreted; and, in fact, such designs, or designs very broadly similar, can mean a variety of things: the body of a particular creature, its internal organs, and so on. In some cases it is simply said to be a *maraiin* pattern, relevant to these rituals, with no special meaning attached to it.

Size, 20·25 x 11·75; artist, unknown. Painted 1959 (at Maningreda [?]), and presented by the Welfare Branch of the Northern Territory Administration in 1960 to the Art Gallery of New South Wales. (Art Gallery of New South Wales, Acquisitions, 1960, No. 153.)

Plate 30

Like the example in Plate 64, this bark from the Oenpelli region was collected by Sir Baldwin Spencer in 1912–13. A painting by a Gagadju (Kakadu) artist, it has been illustrated by Spencer (1914: 436, Fig. 82; 1928: Fig. 525), as well as in the *Jubilee Exhibition of Australian Art* (1951: No. 1, p. 50).

The figures are two spirits, or *mam*, male and female, belonging, Spencer says, to Geimbio country. The Geimbio have not been accurately identified. Spencer has placed them on his map (1914) where the Amurag, Ngamurag, and Dangbun had their tribal territories. Tindale (1940: 217) suggests that the name could possibly be a corruption of Gimbarlang, which in turn is equated with Walang, or Gunbalang, whose territory was originally around Gumader River, the source of which is behind Oenpelli (see R. and C. Berndt, 1951: 32–7); but this seems unlikely. These spirits, called Yerobeni by the Gagadju, live in caves and holes in the ground, or in banyan-trees in the jungles. During the day they leave their homes to dance under the tree platforms, on which corpses have been placed (one way of disposing of the dead in this region), but do not interfere with them. The female, on the left, is painted in profile, showing the long drawn-out mouth and nose: the male wears a dilly-bag or basket slung from his neck, and has an extended penis. He collects wild honey, which he puts into his bag; usually the woman carries a digging-stick (not shown), which she uses for collecting yams and turtles. Spencer says that toward daybreak they can be heard calling (in translation), 'Quick, it is daylight and it is cold!' They may be seen by a native doctor.

Size, 62 × 24; artist, unknown, Gagadju tribe. Obtained by Sir Baldwin Spencer at Oenpelli, 1912–13, either directly from the artist, or as a gift from Mr. P. Cahill, and later presented to the National Museum of Victoria.

Plate 31

This bark, which has been said to represent moon and yams, is from Yirrkalla.

In one variant of the myth a *wongar* (Dreaming), *jiridja* moiety man named Moon (Ngalindi) lived with his sister, Dugong (Bulungani), near Arnhem Bay. (See Chapter Two, for a slightly different version.) When they were digging out edible lily and lotus bulbs one day, the sister was bitten by leeches. The itching was so painful that she hurried down to the sea; but, before diving into the water, she told her brother, who asked what he himself should do. After some discussion she decided to 'make herself' into a dugong: when she died her bones would be found, but she herself would not return. Moon agreed to accompany his sister, but said that in his case he would not die. When he grew thin, he would throw away his bones into the sea, to be washed up as nautilus shells, but after three days he would revive, and gradually regain his strength and size by eating lily and lotus roots. They both went down to the sea, where she turned into a dugong, and he turned into the moon. Warner (1937/58: 523–4) has yet another version of the moon myth, in this case associated with a parrot-fish. The version given here in summary (there are several others, too) has been considered in some detail by R. Berndt (1948: 16–50), who also recorded the song cycle of the Moon-Bone.

The painting depicts a crescent moon, as well as the full moon, with a surrounding halo. Other designs have been interpreted as yams by Mountford (1956: 488–91, 493–6, Plate 156 C), who gives several versions of the moon myth: the cross-hatched ring around the moon disc is said to be the wet-weather camp of the Moon— the halo around the moon seen during misty weather. Certainly there is a close association between the Moon and a variety of long yam, which he is said to have with him in the sky. But in view of the emphasis on lily and lotus bulbs in the relevant song cycle, the elongated designs could equally well represent these. The background design of criss-crossing lines could be either the swamp where the lilies are growing, or the shine of the moon on the water, or (as in the song cycle) the light of the evening star shining on the sacred totemic place of the Dugong and the Moon.

Size, 36 × 16·75; artist, unrecorded, but most probably a Wonguri-Mandjigai man. Collected by Mr. C. P. Mountford on the American-Australian Scientific Expedition to Arnhem Land, 1948. Received by, and now in the possession of, the Australian Institute of Anatomy, Canberra, in 1954.

Plate 32

In this bark painting from Oenpelli, two men representing red-eyed *jawul* pigeons are decorated for the sacred *ubar* ritual. They wear cockatoo feathers on their heads, and their bodies are painted in pseudo-X-ray style (noted in Plate 20). Before them rests the wooden *ubar*. (The northeastern Arnhem Land variety has been mentioned in Plate 73 d; see Elkin and R. and C. Berndt, 1950: 39–40, Plate 4 A [b].)

This *ubar* gong or drum is one of the most important of the sacred objects used in this area. It was first described in part by Spencer (1914: 133–44), and later by R. and C. Berndt (1951: 114–38). There are several major versions of the *ubar* myth. In one from Oenpelli, Jurawadbad, a 'poison' snake, was the first to make such a drum when he was a man. To take revenge on two women, his wife and her mother, he placed his *ubar* in a spot some distance from the camp, and crawled inside it. The two women approached, put their hands inside, searching for possum, were bitten, and died. After this Jurawadbad went off to a sacred dancing-ground, where the *ubar* was used as a sacred drum. It was identified here as the Mother, a female rainbow snake, *ngaljod*. Jurawadbad introduced his own ritual, based on his experience with the two women: he also used his own *ubar*. Because of his experience he forbade women to perform or participate in men's ritual, and from this time onward a division of labour was maintained in the ritual sphere. In the beginning, however, women had possessed all sacred ritual. In the Goulburn Island *ubar* myth, this object was said to have originally belonged to women, and to have represented the uterus of the great Fertility Mother, Waramurunggoindju. The ritual, and the object itself, were taken over by Kandagi, a kangaroo man.

In present-day *ubar* rites the drum is placed in position on two forked sticks, and beaten with a pandanus stump: this must be done almost without ceasing during the whole ritual performance, which may contain several separate scenes. The sound of the *ubar* is the voice of the Mother; and it is answered by the women dancing in the main camp and calling, *Gaidba*! *Gaidba*! The bark painting illustrated here shows one of these, in which the two postulants move around the *ubar*, temporarily removed from its forked sticks. (See R. and C. Berndt, 1951: Plates 11, 12, 13, 14, and 15.) McCarthy (1938/58: Fig. 27) illustrates a bark painting of women dancing in the main camp during *ubar* ritual: this is in the Berndt collection, now in the University of Western Australia.

Size, 19·25 × 24·25; artist, Midjaumidjau, Gunwinggu tribe. Collected in 1950 by R. Berndt, from whom it is on loan to the Department of Anthropology, University of Western Australia.

Plate 33

A fine example of X-ray painting, in the tradition of some of those collected by Spencer at Oenpelli in 1912. (Spencer, 1914: Figs. 90 to 92.) Several of the same type are in the Berndt collection at the Department of Anthropology, University of Western Australia, and Mountford (1956: for example, Plate 76 A, 77) too has some.

The X-ray painting of western Arnhem Land and the Katherine River area is unique. (See Chapter Two; Preface, and Plate 60.) This specimen shows a native companion or jabiru, with three fish; the dashes on the bird's back represent feathers. It is said to have been painted by an unidentified Maung artist at Goulburn Island.

Although Maung is the local Goulburn Island tribe, covering part of the mainland as well, it is more likely that the artist was a visiting mainlander from the Gagadju, Jiwadja, or, even, Gunwinggu tribe, since the Maung did not traditionally paint X-ray figures.

X-ray painting of various animals, fish, birds, and other creatures is much more highly developed than in the case of human figures. In these last, a more obvious degree of stylization is apparent, while with natural species the internal organs are (within the framework of local conventions) more realistic. Mountford (1956) has published a large selection of X-ray paintings from the Oenpelli cave and rock-shelter galleries: McCarthy (1958), too, has some excellent examples. Mountford (1939*a*: 368, Plate XVI F) has previously illustrated this bark painting, but calls it a brolga.

Size, 40 × 21; artist, unknown, Maung (?) tribe. Collected by Miss M. Mathews, and presented by her in 1954 to the South Australian Museum.

Plate 34

This bark painting from Groote Eylandt records the travels of several ancestral beings. (See Chapter Two.) This particular painting and the story associated with it have been illustrated and discussed by McCarthy (1953: 101, 103, Plate VIII), and Mountford (1956: 33, 34, 62–3, Plate 10 B).

According to one version, it concerns Jundurana who, with his family, journeyed from the Arnhem Land mainland creating Bickerton and other islands on his way to Groote. Central Hill, called Jundurana, is his totemic site. From left to right, the smaller rectangle is a cave-painting site on the coast; the long rectangle represents his journey to Central Hill, and the oval a totemic centre; the central band is the channel of the Onguruka (Angoroko) River, which he made, in his sawfish manifestation—in this are two small sawfish and a stingray. The right-hand panel depicts Jundurana as a sawfish, and three stingray. Mountford (1956: 33, 34) calls the sawfish Ingurudungwa, and the stingray Imadoija, and gives much the same story. Finally, after making the Angoroko River (says Mountford), they came to Urulgurupa on the eastern coast of Groote, where they made their final camp. Their bodies were metamorphosed as rocks at this place.

In another myth, which Mountford (1956: 62–3) says is linked with that of the stingray and saw-fish, the travels of the man Junduruna (Jundu-rana, above) are presented. Although different place-names are mentioned, Junduruna is ob-viously the human manifestation of the sawfish: he was responsible for instituting circumcision in this area (McCarthy, 1953). Mountford in-terprets the three left-hand designs on this bark painting as referring to Junduruna. He notes, however, that McCarthy recorded cave paint-ings at Amaliba (where Junduruna had camped), and that one of these showed Junduruna with his wife under his arm. McCarthy (in Mount-ford, ed., 1960: 300–20) has discussed and illus-trated cave paintings at Junduruna (in this case a site near Winchelsea Island and not at Central Hill, as above): one of these is Junduruna, with his wife.

Size, 30 × 22·5; artist, Gulpidja. Collected by F. D. McCarthy, American-Australian Scienti-fic Expedition to Arnhem Land, 1948, and now in the Australian Museum, Sydney.

Plate 35

This bark painting is of the *jiridja* moiety, and concerns the Laindjung-Banaidja myth. Banaidja is sometimes said to be the son of Laindjung, but more often is one manifestation of him in his barramundi form. Laindjung, a sacred being (see Plate 68), emerged from the sea at Duwonmilingu, near Blue Mud Bay.

The bark shows clan and linguistic group pat-terns, painted on the bodies of participants in his rituals, the *jiridja* moiety *nara*. (See Warner, 1937/58: 356–70; R. and C. Berndt, 1948: 313, 318–23; Elkin and R. and C. Berndt, 1950; Mountford, 1956.) It is divided into three major panels. The bottom panel closely resembles one section of Plate 10 A depicted in Elkin and R.

and C. Berndt (1950: 66), painted by one of the same artists, Munggaraui. There, a sacred totemic crocodile (related to the Laindjung-Banaidja song cycle) lies on a bed of mud surrounded by seaweed: white dots represent flowers of the seaweed; black dots, bubbles rising to the surface of the mud and water; diamond shapes, the weed and leaves. This crocodile has short 'arms' as a result of being burnt. According to the myth, in the Dreaming era he made a sacred shelter, where he stored his *rangga* emblems (see Plate 25). During the dancing associated with these, a fire ignited the dry branches of the sacred shelter, destroyed the *rangga*, and burnt some of the ritual partici-pants. Crocodile had his 'arms' burnt, and escaped to Caledon Bay with some of the fire. The bottom panel refers to his Caledon Bay site.

In the annotation attached to this particular bark, in the Art Gallery of New South Wales, Purchases and Acquisitions Catalogue (1959: No. 195), the crocodile is in a billabong: the divisions at top and bottom of the panel are the banks of the billabong and water-marks. The area immediately surrounding the crocodile is its nest, and the remaining design represents lilies (foliage). The dots are bubbles from the crocodile, as it dives under the water.

In panel two, middle, a totemic bandicoot, escaping from the fire on the ritual ground, enters a hollow log (central vertical band). Mountford (1956: 365, Plate 116) has a com-parable painting of this section of the fire myth. The left-hand pattern refers to bush country, the right-hand pattern to swamp with an over-growth of weeds and white dots, and bubbles rising to the surface of the water. In the Art Gallery of New South Wales Catalogue (1959) the bandicoot is said to be surrounded by grass, and the dots are described as its footprints.

Immediately above is a band of diamond-shaped design referring to swamp and bubbles. The artist, Munggaraui, is said to have been worried because one of his sons, Garmali, had taken his canoe to Elcho Island: he feared that Garmali might sell it there. He dreamt about this, and later included this design in the sacred painting, because his canoe had been kept up on the beach in country associated with this myth; the design refers to that country, but no canoe is shown. The top panel is in two parts. On the left is a diamond-shaped design of ashes and smouldering fire, the dots being sparks. On the right are more ashes and fire, along with the bones of the participants on the ritual ground who were burnt to death. The figure is of a spirit woman, Gurunga (Gorrnga), who attempted to put out the fire. The Art Gallery of New South Wales Catalogue (1959) supplies the following information about the bark: a sacred *nara* ritual was held near Caledon Bay, by three brothers (Monaianggulnguru, Balangaridi, and Nereirei) and two sisters (Gurunga and Borgidj). When they called the name of Nereirei (which was the sacred 'inside' name for fire), a fire which was burning flared up, with the results already mentioned. Gurunga tried to put it out, but it spread. The vertical diamond pattern represents wood: on the left-hand side the black diamonds are ashes, the red the glow of the fire. The dots in the upper part of this section are sparks, and below a vertical band the dots are flames. On the right-hand part of the panel are the bones and ashes of the people who were burnt. Gurunga (below) has her head in the sacred shade or hut, while smoke swirls around her. Mountford (1956: 293–4) gives a brief version of this myth.

Size, 60·5 × 15; artists, Munggaraui (Mungarawoi), born c. 1907, and Bununggu, born c. 1917, who painted the crocodile panel. Both are of the *jiridja* moiety, Gumaidj linguistic unit. Other examples of the work of these outstanding artists are to be found in Elkin and R. and C. Berndt, 1950. (See New South Wales Art Gallery Catalogue, 1959, No. 195.) This bark was collected at Yirrkalla by Dr. S. Scougall in September, 1959, and presented to the Art Gallery of New South Wales in 1959.

Plate 36
The third of the Mimi trilogy. (See Plates 17 and 37.) Details as below.
In this bark painting, the Mimi story mentioned

below is continued. Six Mimi are dancing (three females and three males). At the top left-hand corner is a yam (see Plate 17), which they normally eat. On the right, alongside the Mimi headman (facing the dancers), is the dismembered human corpse.

Size, 21·75 × 18·5; artist, Old Wurungulngul, Maung tribe. Collected at Goulburn Island in 1947 by R. Berndt, from whom it is at present on loan to the Department of Anthropology, University of Western Australia.

Plate 37
The second of a trilogy of bark paintings, the first of which appears in Plate 17 and the third in Plate 36.

This example from Goulburn Island, in distinctive Maung style, shows perspective in the shape of a mountain outline, representing the rocky hills and gorges in which the spirits live. These are the Mimi, the sticklike spirits, mentioned by R. and C. Berndt (1951: 176–7). Mountford (1956: 112–27, 169, 182, 256, 258) has discussed and illustrated so-called Mimi cave paintings. The local people identify such sticklike figures as Mimi spirits. It seems fairly certain, however, that these cave paintings are not modern, and may indeed be quite early, and that the present-day Aborigines simply call them Mimi without really knowing to what they refer. On the other hand, the tradition that they are Mimi may have been handed down from one generation to the next. Mimi art, of beautifully drawn, small figures mostly with a lively sense of composition and movement (see Plates 39 and 42), differs noticeably in style from the Mimi represented in present-day bark paintings (as illustrated here). The Mimi in the rock galleries are nearly all executed in red ochre, blood, or red ochre mixed with blood, or in a single ochre. The nearest contemporary Mimi painting on bark comparable to these is one which was done for me in blood; it was displayed in the Australian Aboriginal Art, Arnhem Land Paintings on Bark and Carved Human Figures, 1957, exhibition in Perth (No. 29).

Spencer (1928: Fig. 540) first drew attention to Mimi cave painting, although he did not call it by that name. He does speak of *mormo*, of which the spirits illustrated in Plates 30 and 64 of this volume are examples: these are *mam*, and one variety which Spencer called Ingwalin (*ibid.*, 804–5, Fig. 521) is said to be tall and thin, with bushy heads of hair, but smooth and hairless bodies. These are possibly *mimi*. Spencer's bark paintings are closer in appearance to the cave paintings than those illustrated here, but quite obviously they are not in the same art style. Other small human figures he illustrates (for example, *ibid.*, Figs. 529 and 530) have only a passing resemblance. McCarthy (1957*a*; 1958: 50–3, Figs. 30, 31, 32) also discusses *mimi* cave art: he makes comparisons with other areas, and believes that this art tradition has a wide distribution in Australia.

It is clear, however, that the Mimi cave painting and bark painting differ radically in style, and should not necessarily be treated as one and the same thing. Mimi are often spoken of not as spirits, but as 'wild people': they live in rocky, inaccessible places, mainly in caves, and emerge only in still weather. Rock kangaroos are their 'watchdogs', which they tether by tying a leg with fibre and attaching the other end to a post or rock. They like their meat raw and bleeding, are occasionally cannibals when the opportunity offers, but usually live on yams. They keep away from human beings and are not always hostile to them, but if offended they are ready to kill. (See Chapter Two.)

In the bark illustrated here a Gunwinggu man has wandered into country occupied by Mimi, and has been invited by one to return to his cave home. The man is shown on the left, holding a spear, and 'thrower. He refuses the hospitality offered him and tries to escape, but is captured by a Mimi headman (large central figure, with long hair). This spirit cuts flesh from the face of the living man and shows it to other Mimi, who come out of their caves and dance with joy. (Three figures, one male and two females, are shown on the right, above.) In the meantime, the first Mimi has removed all flesh from the man's face and eaten it. The drawing on the right, below, shows him holding his victim while

doing this.

Size, 23 × 20·5; artist, Old Wurungulngul, Maung tribe. Collected at Goulburn Island in 1947 by R. Berndt, from whom it is at present on loan to the Department of Anthropology, University of Western Australia.

Plate 38

The Lightning Brothers at Delamere, Northern Territory, in Wadaman tribal country. This painting is considered in some detail in Chapter Three. It was first recorded by Davidson (1936), and later by McCarthy (1958: 57–8, Plate 1). Under the arm of the elder brother, the smaller figure, is a forked, sticklike design said to represent his wife. Their penes have been subincised, since these two were responsible for introducing this rite among the Wadaman people. One has an ornate head-dress built up on the head (as in Spencer and Gillen, 1938: Figs. 125, 126; Elkin 1938/56: plate opposite 159; and R. Berndt, 1951*a*: Plate XV), with a series of radiating, whittled sticks; the other wears feathers at the top of his head. The striped design on their bodies possibly represents falling rain. Another interpretation has been made, and this is referred to by McCarthy in Chapter Three. The myth tells how they fought over the elder's wife, a black-cockatoo woman. She is also represented beside the taller figure, in red, upside-down: each man, according to McCarthy (1958: 58), has the head of a gecko, 'which symbolizes lightning because it can walk upside-down'. If we accept this, then, the radiating lines from the head-dress of the larger figure could also symbolize lightning.

The brothers and the whole site, of which these paintings are part, are associated with rain-making; in fact, this is a sacred rain-totem site.

These two major paintings are superimposed over a series of human and animal figures, and may represent a later phase of painting in this area. They, as well as the totem centre itself, are associated with a long song cycle and ritual sequence, in some respects reminiscent of the Wandjina cult. McCarthy places them within the Wandjina art tradition; but there is no evidence to suggest any form of connection. The Wadaman did, in the past, have indirect trade relations with certain groups in the Kimberley, but not necessarily with those people who possessed the Wandjina beliefs and rituals. Wandjina-like figures do occur spasmodically in other regions—for instance, at Oenpelli, and in central-western Australia.

Photograph by G. Donkin.

Plate 39

Plate 39 is a further example of the outstanding art style noted in Plate 42. It is from the Inagurdurwil cave shelters or rock-faces adjacent to Red Lily Lagoon, not far from the East Alligator River in the Oenpelli region. In the illustration only two or three associated human figures may be seen. A line drawing and a coloured reproduction of these three have been given in Mountford (1954b: Plate X; 1956: 152–3, Fig. 40), the full length of the original being about 36 inches: they are red in colour, possibly blood mixed with ochre. Mountford mentions that they were identified by his informants as 'the work of the *Mimi* artists', depicting three Mamandi (Namandi) spirits. The first figure (the central figure in the present illustration) is a subincised male; the second (right-hand, upper corner), a circumcised male; and the third (not seen in our plate), a bisexual figure.

The complex figures with contorted limbs are unique; as suggested in the annotation to Plate 56 they are possibly of magical intent, and not specifically paintings of Namandi spirits. The local Aboriginal informants were undoubtedly interpreting on the basis of their experience, which may not have included any information about what they were originally meant to represent. Nevertheless, this is an excellent example of the so-called Mimi work.

In the painting illustrated, the head of the central figure is shown at the bottom, left; a distended belly, penis (top), legs distorted at each side; and arms from the back of head to the right corner. The head is probably non-human. The head of the other figure is at the top, right, with legs haunched, arms extending forward, penis, and testes (middle, right).

Photograph by C. P. Mountford.

Plate 40

This graceful example is from the Sleisbeck Mine district near the extreme south-west of Arnhem Land, on the Katherine River. Surrounded by several unidentified paintings, the main figure, in white (predominantly) with some use of red, is a striking one, beautifully balanced. She wears a nosebone, and across her breasts is a red dotted decoration. Unfortunately, no information is available concerning the significance of this painting. Mountford (1958b: 151, Plate XI B) has illustrated a tracing of this, and it is possible that it represents a mythical figure. Western Arnhem Land women did decorate themselves in this way for *ubar* rituals. (See Plate 32.)

Photograph by C. P. Mountford.

Plate 41

A remarkable figure superimposed on hand stencils and other smaller paintings from St. Vidgeon, near Hodgson River, south of the Roper River (South Leichhardt Crossing). Few paintings from this area have been recorded: McCarthy (1957a: 159) illustrates one example. The central figure in yellow, outlined in white, is of unusual character, and represents either a ritual postulant, or a mythical being. The face is decorated; and it wears armbands and an elaborate ceremonial head-dress. No information about its meaning is available.

Photograph by G. Donkin.

Plate 42

Cave paintings from Oenpelli, western Arnhem Land, near Gunbalanja billabong, which is now the site of a mission station. Mountford (1956) has discussed and illustrated some of the paintings to be found in this region. (See Chapters Two and Three.)

This particular example demonstrates quite clearly how designs have been superimposed on other, apparently earlier, ones. In this case, the basic figures are three fish painted in red ochre, with a small sticklike Mimi figure (see Plate 37) holding a dilly-bag (?) and a spear. Mountford (1956: 113–81) and McCarthy (1957a: 182;

1958: Figs. 28, 29, 30, 31, 32) illustrate some of these. Overlying the male hunter and one fish, however, is a complex painting in white ochre (left) of the variety mentioned in regard to Plates 20 and 56: limbs are contorted, with appendages, and this is possibly a female figure designed for the purpose of love magic or sorcery. The red-ochre 'line' figure (right), similarly complex, with limbs contorted, is possibly a male: the head is in the bottom right-hand corner, the penis at the top close to the fish. Comparable figures have also been illustrated by Mountford (1956: for example, in Fig. 45, Plate 57), who speaks of them as representing, in some cases, 'Mamandi' (Namandi) spirits. (See annotation to Plate 64.)

Photograph by G. Donkin.

Plate 43

Cave paintings of the northern Kimberleys: the particular gallery in which these are located is near the Prince Regent River, about fifty miles from its source, on the northern side and close to the Princess May Range. They refer to the great rainbow snake, usually seen in association with the Wandjina (see Plate 19). Elkin (1930; 1938/56; 1948), Love (1930), Schulz (1946), Petri (1954), Worms (1955), and McCarthy (1958: Fig. 34), have illustrated and discussed these paintings. Elkin considers their significance in Chapter One; and in his volume (1938/56: 220–1) he speaks of this rainbow snake, Galeru, who is specifically concerned with fertility. Kaberry (1939: 206–7) notes that its most important function was that of providing rain: 'The long coils of the snake are charged with the power that is the source of human life, of magic and of the fertility brought to the earth by the rains.'

Photograph by G. Donkin.

Plate 44

In this illustration are cave paintings of the famous Wandjina, already represented by a bark painting in Plate 19. For further references to the Wandjina see the annotation to that plate and to Plate 43, and Chapter One.

This beautiful example comes from one of the galleries in the vicinity of Mount Hann at the head of the Prince Regent River, northern Kimberleys. McCarthy (1957a: 155) has illustrated this photograph previously.

Photograph by G. Donkin.

Plate 45

Rock engravings from Woodstock, north-western Australia. (Compare with Worms, 1954: 1067–88; and McCarthy, 1958: 26.) These pecked engravings represent an open-mouthed and horned rainbow snake, with a male stick-like figure holding a weapon (?); on the left-hand side is a female figure, legs flexed, enlarged genitalia, and two lines, running from them (possibly representing semen?). The engravings have not been interpreted by Aborigines. (See Chapter Three.)

Photograph by F. D. McCarthy.

Plate 46

Plate 46 shows pecked rock engravings of male figures, boomerangs, kangaroo tracks, and emu eggs, among other motifs. The site is located at Mootwingee, western New South Wales. Similar pecked intaglios from the same area have been illustrated in McCarthy (1958: Figs. 7 and 8). No interpretation is available. (See Chapter Three.)

Photograph by D. Milner.

Plate 47

Pecked engravings from Red Gorge, Flinders Ranges, South Australia. (See McCarthy, 1958; and Chapter Three.) An owl and lizard are represented, together with linear figures of a bird track and a pubic apron. No interpretation is available.

Photograph by D. Milner.

Plate 48

Plate 48 depicts a linear engraving of unknown significance. It is from Panaramittee North, Flinders Ranges, South Australia.

Photograph by D. Milner.

Plate 49

This is part of the remarkable frieze of engravings in soft sandstone at Cathedral Cave in the Carnarvon Ranges, Queensland. Among the linear motifs are a chevron design, rows of short parallel grooves in various arrangements, a large bird track (upper left), a set of long parallel arcs (lower right), a radiate figure (middle left), and a number of long, straight and curved grooves. Interspersed throughout the frieze is a series of deep oval and circular holes enclosed by a groove. Close study of the frieze indicates that the latter are engraved over the linear figures. See also McCarthy (1958: Fig. 12) and Elkin (1949: 119–57), and Chapter Three. No interpretation of the meanings of these engravings is available.

Photograph by D. Milner; information from F. D. McCarthy.

Plate 50

Plate 50 depicts a painted frieze in the Black's Palace, Blackall, Queensland. The figures in red stand out strikingly against the almost white rock surface.

Photograph by D. Milner; information from F. D. McCarthy.

Plate 51

Part of a long frieze of paintings in the Black's Palace, Blackall, Queensland. (See Plate 50.) Netlike designs and rows of vertical strokes are painted over an older series of stencils of human hands, boomerangs, hafted axes, and other objects. McCarthy (1958: 35–9, Fig. 16) illustrates one example from this area, and discusses generally the question of stencilling.

Photograph by D. Milner; information from F. D. McCarthy.

Plate 52

In this bark painting from Groote Eylandt two men in a canoe, one smoking a pipe, are harpooning a dugong and a large, green-backed turtle. The dugong is attached to the canoe, but the turtle has just been harpooned: note the floats on the rope. The man with a pipe is paddling. The two long snakes (sea-snakes) have not been identified. Their size, however, suggests mythical significance, and they could refer to lightning (an approaching storm).

Size, 37.75×13.25; artist unknown. Acquired in 1955 by the Australian Museum, Sydney.

Plate 53

This bark painting from Groote Eylandt represents the south-east wind, a clan totem.

Paintings of this nature have been discussed by Adam (1951: 180–2), Mountford (1956: 94–7, Plate 24), and others. According to Mountford, the south-east wind is called *mamariga*, and its totemic centre is Aidjawalamadja in southeastern Groote. In a painting similar to the one illustrated here, Mountford interprets the corner projections as 'long pillars of rock which rise out of the ground' at the totemic centre. The central horizontal line, he says, refers to a waterhole at the site. A mythical snake, Aidja, is said to be associated with this locality.

It is possible, as Adam has remarked (following an earlier suggestion of F. G. G. Rose), that this design was directly inspired by the shape of the sails used by Macassan (Indonesian) traders visiting Groote and the north Arnhem Land coast. (See R. and C. Berndt, 1954.)

Size, 27.125×9.975; artist, unrecorded. The bark has been illustrated in McCarthy (1938/58: Fig. 28). Collected by F. D. McCarthy, American-Australian Scientific Expedition to Arnhem Land, 1948, and now in the Australian Museum, Sydney.

Plate 54

This bark painting is from Port Keats, on the Daly River Aboriginal Reserve between the Daly and Fitzmaurice rivers, Northern Territory.

Bark was not a traditional art medium in this region, where most painting was done on human bodies, on cave walls, and on carved boards. Other bark paintings, however, have been collected by Dr. W. E. H. Stanner and by Mr. R. Robinson, who has illustrated some (unfortunately redrawn) in his book (1956).

This particular design is taken from one on a sacred bullroarer, and refers to a totemic site named Ngagumada, associated (according to information supplied by Robinson, who collected it) with an ancestral being, Dimangi, who made the first boomerangs. The design itself is typical of much sacred art throughout the northwestern part of the Northern Territory and not unlike Central Australian *tjurunga* art. On the outer fringe of the design, the crescents are boomerangs thrown by a fighting man named Walagan, who is now a bird (his totemic form):

the main design represents a boomerang-shaped mountain, with streams leading down to the concentric circle, which is obviously the totemic site itself.

Size, $20 \cdot 75 \times 11 \cdot 75$; artist, 'Kianoo Tjeemairee' (Gianu would be his name, and *djimarei* or *djimara* possibly his subsection affiliation), of the Murinbada tribe. This bark has been mentioned in the New South Wales Art Gallery, Purchases and Acquisitions for 1959 (No. 210); collected by R. Robinson in 1954, it was purchased from him in 1959 by the Art Gallery of New South Wales.

Plate 55

This bark painting is from Milingimbi, north-central Arnhem Land coast. It represents the rock python, named Julunggul, who appears in the sacred Wawalag myth. (See Warner, 1937/58: 250–9; R. Berndt, 1951*a*.) The Wawalag are two sisters who, travelling from southern Arnhem Land, eventually reach a waterhole sacred to Julunggul. Not knowing that this powerful being lies within its depths, they begin to cook the food they have caught and collected; but each food, as they place it on the fire, jumps up and disappears into the waterhole: in this way it becomes totemic. Presently the elder sister gives birth to a baby, and Julunggul smells the afterbirth blood. Disturbed by this, and by all the creatures jumping into his water, the monstrous rock python emerges and swallows the two sisters and the child. This symbolizes the onset of the monsoonal season. Later, he vomits them. This particular myth, as noted below for Plate 73d, substantiates three major ritual sequences —the *djunggawon, gunabibi* and *ngurlmag*. (See Chapter Two.)

Virtually the complete surface of this sheet of bark is taken up with Julunggul, resting coiled, with eggs, at the bottom of the sacred waterhole of Muruwul (or Miraramina).

Size, $28 \cdot 5 \times 15$; artist, Dowdie (born 1921), *balang* subsection; clan and linguistic unit not recorded, but belonging to the north-eastern Arnhem Land cultural bloc. Acquired from the Methodist Overseas Mission, Darwin, 1959; presented to the Art Gallery of New South Wales by Dr. S. Scougall. New South Wales Art Gallery Catalogue, 1959, No. 182.)

Plate 56

This bark painting concerns magic and sorcery, and belongs to the same group as the one illustrated in Plate 20. It is from Oenpelli, in western Arnhem Land, and is—surprisingly enough— done by the same artist. In style, however, it differs considerably. According to my information, it is based upon the cave-painting art of this area, which includes male and female figures, highly stylized and curved, with misplaced limbs and appendages, combined with barbed designs; figures of both sexes are sometimes shown in combination (see Plates 39, 42). (See also Mountford, 1956: Plate 34; Figs. 28, 29, 32; Plate 42; Figs. 40, 44, 45, 49; Plates 46, 47, 57, 58 B.) The cave paintings are possibly quite old (age unknown), and although contemporary bark paintings do not exactly correspond with them, and are not necessarily imitations or copies, they do reflect the basic pattern of contour and curve. They correspond in another way too: cave paintings of this variety are said to have been made for purposes of magic, just as bark paintings of this kind are, or were.

Such paintings were first illustrated in Elkin and R. and C. Berndt (1950: 76–83, Plates 2, 15, 16); others appear in R. and C. Berndt (1951: 206–10, Plates 1, 8, 17, 18, 21, 22) and one was illustrated and several others included in the exhibition of Australian Aboriginal Art, Arnhem Land Paintings on Bark and Carved Human Figures, held in Perth in 1957. Among these paintings (those depicting coitus and involving imitative or sympathetic magic, and those of suggestive magic relating to pregnancy and so forth) is a series on sorcery. They serve as a substitute for arguments and fighting which might possibly arise from a husband's jealousy or a wife's infidelity. This is destructive magic, designed to bring about the death, or at least illness, of a victim. It may be used against a woman as well as her lover. The likeness of such a person is drawn by the artist-sorcerer. Usually he prepares a composite figure with an eagle-hawk or rainbow-snake head (or the head of some other creature—perhaps, even, a human head); several arms and/or legs may be painted, with stingray nails piercing the body.

The example shows a man (unnamed) who was said to have seduced another's wife. He has a human head, with cockatoo feathers at the top and side. Two legs and two arms end in hands, but two other arm-appendages are added; barbed stingray nails protrude from various parts of his body.

Size, 26 × 8·25; artist, Midjaumidjau, Gunwinggu tribe. This specimen was collected in 1947 by R. Berndt, from whom it is on loan to the Department of Anthropology collection in the University of Western Australia.

Plate 57

This bark painting from Melville Island depicts the totemic site of a spirit woman named Puruliangkala, who is associated with bush-fires. It has been discussed in Chapter Two, text Fig. 3, and in Mountford (1958: 51, Plate 16 D). The site itself is on Turiturina Island, in Port Hurd, western Bathurst Island, where in the mythical era a number of totemic and spirit beings performed the first initiation rites, called *kulama* (*gulama*). The *kulama*, which were concerned also with the increase and preparation of yams called by that name, have been discussed by Spencer (1914: 92–115; 1928: 658–76) and by Mountford (1958*a*: 122–43).

The central, enclosed white circle is Turiturina Island; smaller circles are low rocks now in the sea, but previously the camp-fires of the spirit woman, freshwater springs, deposits of red ochre and white ochre. With these ochres, so it is said, Puruliangkala and other totemic and spirit beings painted themselves for the *kulama*. Other designs refer to milkwood trees, the sap of which (like ochre) was used in body decoration. Small pin-point dots represent *mandikama* fruit.

The striking style and vivid colouring of this example of Melville and Bathurst islands art are typical of the region. It resembles closely the painted bark baskets which are traditionally used on these islands (see Spencer, 1914: Plates XXXIV and XXXV). In some respects this highly stylized form is reminiscent of Central Australian art (see Chapter Four), except that it is not ritually significant in the same way and that, especially in the symbolic representations used, the Bathurst and Melville islands design is more obtrusive and cruder. What is interesting in this respect is that traditionally these people, who have been called the Tiwi, differed markedly in their social and cultural arrangements from other Australian Aborigines: they were influenced by the mainlanders, but not to the extent of interfering with the over-all pattern of their life.

Size of bark, 31 × 20; artist, unrecorded; collected by C. P. Mountford, National Geographic Expedition, 1954; now in the South Australian Museum, having been presented by the collector in 1955.

Plate 58

A bark painting from Yirrkalla, in north-eastern Arnhem Land. It is executed in the complex criss-crossing patterning, with every part of the board filled, which is a feature of the art style of this area. (See Chapter Two, and Preface.)

This painting concerns the Dreaming or totemic centre of Murulma or Mururuma, the Bremer Island Turtle Man. Two carved wooden figures of this spirit being have been discussed and illustrated in R. and C. Berndt (1948: 324–6, Plate II, 3 and 4) and in McCarthy (1938/58: Fig. 22). Bremer Island was previously called Melville Island, but is not to be confused with the island of that name just north of Darwin. Bremer Island is near Yirrkalla.

Murulma and his wives and sons are immortalized in an elaborate song cycle. He is associated primarily with the Riradjingu linguistic unit, but also indirectly linked to the Djambadbingu. Among the wide range of topics dealt with in the song cycle and myth, turtle-hunting receives special notice. In the incised and painted designs on the bodies of the two carved wooden figures, his special rock (into which he was metamorphosed), 'moon'-fish, green-backed turtles, seaweed, waves, clouds, rain, shells, and so on, are shown. In Elkin and R. and C. Berndt (1950: 44, 95–6, Plate 18 B, [b], a log coffin (similar to that shown in Plate 73 *b* of this volume) has a design connected with the spirit (that is, Murulma) of the Muruwiri rocks. Mountford (1956: 299–305, Plate 96) also mentions Murulma (as Muruma); so does McCarthy (1938/58: Fig. 26). This spirit being is also associated with the Thunder Man.

The painting is divided into two panels. The top half shows a green-backed turtle eating seaweed; the surrounding design refers to seaweed and to waves.

The bottom, and larger, panel shows a central figure of a whale, the oval marks on its body representing barnacles (?). The parallel lines from the whale's head rising upward and falling to each side are said to represent hair (see Art Gallery of New South Wales, Purchases and Acquisitions for 1959 [No. 194]). They are more likely to be the spray of this creature, which is especially mentioned in the songs that focus on the whale. At each side of the whale are 'moon'-fish, and the surrounding design is sea and waves lapping against the whale.

According to the annotation in the Art Gallery of New South Wales Catalogue (1959), the painting relates to three hunters, one of which was swallowed by this particular whale. The remaining two unsuccessfully gave chase. Later the victim was vomited onto the beach, where he was found dead by the other two men who were looking for turtle eggs. The dead man was said to be white from head to navel. Wondjug, a Yirrkalla Riradjingu man, observed that the two surviving hunters were Djarungor and Badiri, one of whom was his father's father (Mauwulan's father: see Plate 25, concerning Mauwulan, Wondjug's father). Another man, Madaman, also Riradjingu, identified marks on a cliff-face north-west of Yirrkalla with the design of the painting. Mountford (1956: 360–2, Plate 115) mentions this story. He classifies it as a myth, but says that these three men were distant relatives of Mauwulan, who painted the bark he describes. However, in the version I obtained in 1946 at Yirrkalla, this was given as a historical (or quasi-historical) incident.

Several other bark paintings referring to the Turtle and Thunder Man have been noted in the Art Gallery of New South Wales, Acquisitions Catalogue (1960, Nos. 181, 187, 188): these have to do with the Thunder Man and the death and mortuary ritual of Murulma.

Size, 49·5 ×22; artist, Gungoilma or Gungujuma (Gunguyuma), born c. 1916, Djambadbingu linguistic unit, *dua* moiety. Painted at Yirrkalla in September 1959, it was presented by Dr. S. Scougall to the Art Gallery of New South Wales in 1959.

Plate 59

This Yirrkalla bark painting shows the rainmakers Wuluwaid, a man, and Bunbulama, a female, both *mogwoi* spirits, who soaked bundles of swamp-grass in water to bring clouds and rain. (See Chapter Two.) In local belief, rain can still be made in this way, but there is not the same need for it here as farther inland. (See Mountford, 1956: 296; Plate 49 C and facing 267, and Plate 133 A, B; Fig. 65 C, D.)

The large figure is Wuluwaid, holding a magic bundle; the woman holds another. Lines radiating from their heads are the water-grass used in making them: vertical lines are falling rain, coming from the bundles. Below, from left to right, are two rocks and three termite mounds associated with these spirits and with their totemic site. At the top, as a separate panel, is a rainbow with rain falling; the black central vertical band is a gap in the storm or, like the black background behind the rainbow, the darkness of approaching rain.

Size, 37·5 × 16·75; artist, unrecorded; collected by C. P. Mountford in 1948 during the American-Australian Scientific Expedition to Arnhem Land. Now in the possession of C. P. Mountford, Adelaide.

Plate 60

In this unusually good X-ray painting, of a male kangaroo, internal organs are indicated along with caul and other fat. In style it belongs, more or less, to the series collected by Sir Baldwin Spencer (1914: Fig. 86) and painted by Gagadju artists. (See Plate 22.) It is also very similar in style to the bark painting (Plate 33) collected by Miss M. Mathews at Goulburn Island, and may have been done by the same artist. In fact, what was said about the bark painting in Plate 33 could be said for this one too: it was almost certainly not prepared by a Maung artist, but by a mainlander working in the Gagadju-Oenpelli tradition. It has been illustrated in Mountford (1939a: Plate XVI B), and in Linton and Wingert (1946). Mountford (1956: Plates 53 E, 54 D, 67 E, 70 C, 71, 73 B, 74 D, 75) and McCarthy (1957a) illustrate others. An extremely beautiful example from the Berndt collection, Perth, serves as the cover of Lévi-Strauss (1962). In that case the bark painting depicts an ancestral being, Nadulmi, in his kangaroo manifestation. In mythical times he was the leader of the *ubar* ritual (see Plate 32). Size, 34 × 50; artist, unknown, Maung (?). Collected by Miss M. Mathews. Presented to the South Australian Museum by Mrs. W. A. Norman. It was exhibited in Arts of the South Seas, Museum of Modern Art, New York, 1946.

Plate 61

A bark painting from Milingimbi, with a particularly detailed repetitive pattern, such as appeals to the traditional artist of north-eastern and central coastal Arnhem Land. According to the Art Gallery of New South Wales, Purchases and Acquisitions Catalogue for 1959 (No. 176), and the *Australian Aboriginal Art Catalogue* (1960–61, No. 43), it represents, *in toto*, the catfish (*manbiri*) totem. The central band of spots indicates reefs, and the rest of the painting fish-bones, symbolizing Daigurgur clansfolk. Daigurgur possibly refers to the *jiridja* moiety Deiwarur clan, the word itself meaning catfish. A similar pattern, without the spotted band, is illustrated in Mountford (1956: 388, Plate 126 B): in his interpretation it represents spawn and the developing young of an unidentified fish living in the swamps south of Milingimbi.

The myth supplied with the bark painting tells how two water rats dived down and nibbled a catfish, which warned the others. Shark and stingray smelt the flesh of the catfish and swam around seeking prey. The catfish, however, were wary: they persuaded their two leaders, Mandjilidjili and Gururwirurwi, who were

brothers, to make two reefs to serve as safe hiding-places: they made these with their spears, Gunumba and Baminingu. The two reefs, now called Buguria and Baranudjbi, are in Ngunbulubulu Bay, within and on the west side of Arnhem Bay. When this was accomplished, all the catfish people danced in the same way as Deiwarur clansfolk do today. (In the mythical period many of the natural species resembled human beings.) The two leaders decided to eat some fish, so they cut some bark from a wild quince (*danggi*) tree, and used it for 'poisoning' the water. Soon many fish were floating on the surface: they collected these, cooked, and ate them. The bones, however, they threw to one side, and decided to make them the main part of the Deiwarur clan emblem. They gathered up some of the fish-meat for the women and children, and on the way to the main camp saw a hawk vainly seeking food among the discarded fish-bones. The leaders then gave further directions concerning the clan emblem: the two reefs were to be represented on it (tabu to all Deiwarur), and the diagonal pattern of fish-bones was to signify the many Deiwarur people.

This particular painting is not sacred, in the sense of being secret: it is used primarily for the decoration of the hollow log into which the bones of deceased female members of the Deiwarur clan are finally deposited, or for a grave post.

Size, 47·25 × 16; artist, Djawa, (Djalwar), Gubabingu linguistic unit, *jiridja* moiety. (Noted as being of the Deiwarur or Daigurgur clan.) (See Plate 63.) Acquired by Mr. W. Thornton at Milingimbi between 1948–51, and purchased by the Art Gallery of New South Wales in 1959.

Plate 62

This bark, from Milingimbi, combines western with north-eastern Arnhem Land style. It represents the smaller rock pythons which appear in the Wawalag myth. (See Plates 55 and 68.) After Julunggul had swallowed the two sisters, he returned to the waterhole and stood erect. *Dua* moiety pythons from the Wessel Islands and other places saw him, erected themselves, and asked what he had eaten. Finally, Julunggul confessed that he had swallowed the Wawalag. As he said this, he made a tremendous noise—which became part of the bullroarer's sound when it is swung. (See Warner, 1937/58: 250–9; R. Berndt, 1951a: 18–32.)

The bark painting contains, in addition to the snakes, stringy-bark flowers (black ovals surrounded by white dots) from trees growing around the sacred waterhole; they float on the surface of the pool. (See R. Berndt, 1951a: Plate 11.) It has been illustrated in McCarthy (1938/58: Frontispiece, 2). Some bark paintings referring to this myth appear in Mountford (1956). Size, 49 × 17; artist, unknown, but possibly Lialauwamiri, Liagalwamiri, or Brangu linguistic unit. This bark painting was collected by Professor W. L. Warner during his field-work in northern Arnhem Land, 1926–9. It is now in the Australian Museum, Sydney.

Plate 63

This beautiful bark painting, from Milingimbi, also combines the style typical of north-eastern Arnhem Land with that of western Arnhem Land where a plain, open background is preferred (see Preface).

Male and female freshwater goanna face one another across a vertical bar. On their bodies are clan designs of the *jiridja* moiety, such as are painted on the chests of participants in the corresponding sacred ritual; there is also a small, unexplained tortoise on the right-hand side.

According to the annotation supplied by the Methodist Overseas Mission, some mythical goanna people dug themselves into the ground during a drought until, when they came to rock (the central bar), they themselves turned into stone—a goanna-shaped mountain or hill at Arnhem Bay. The right-hand goanna are females, and the linked oval designs on their bodies are said to be eggs. (See Australian Aboriginal Art Catalogue, 1960–61, No. 46.)

Mountford (1956: 371, Plate 118) illustrates and mentions very similar, but poorer paintings from Yirrkalla and from Milingimbi. He also speaks of these as freshwater goanna associated with a mythical site named Gurunga, at Caledon

Bay. (See Chapter Two.) In this case the designs on their bodies represent various kinds of ochre removed from Gurunga by a *jiridja* moiety *mogwoi*, or spirit, named Wirili; Gurunga is an important site for obtaining these ochres. In Elkin and R. and C. Berndt (1950: 105–6), mangrove goanna (*djalga*) are mentioned as being associated with the *jiridja* moiety, Mararlba-speaking group. The painting illustrated here is said to have been used in an increase ritual, and as a teaching-aid to novices learning about the relevant myth.

Size, 30·5 × 14·125; artist, Djawa (or Djalwar), born 1905 (?), *gadjag* subsection, Gubabingu linguistic unit, *jiridja* moiety. Djawa, from Buckingham Bay, is widely acknowledged as an outstanding artist. This bark painting was acquired from the Methodist Overseas Mission in 1959 by Dr. S. Scougall, who presented it to the Art Gallery of New South Wales. (New South Wales Art Gallery Catalogue, 1959, No. 183.)

Plate 64

This magnificent example of western Arnhem Land bark painting was obtained by Sir Baldwin Spencer at Oenpelli in 1912, either directly from the Kakadu (Gagadju) artist, or as a gift from Mr. P. Cahill, who was then running this pastoral station, later to become a Government venture and then a mission station. Several such bark paintings are illustrated in Spencer (1914; 1928) and in McCarthy (1957a): this particular specimen, however, was shown in the Jubilee Exhibition (1951: No. 6).

The painting depicts a spirit being, of which there are a number of categories. The name of this one is unknown, but is possibly a *mam* or a *namandi*, a spirit often antagonistic to man (sometimes a human ghost). Stories concerning these creatures relate how they attract men to their doom. This painting is of 'incipient X-ray' variety, which is more apparent in representations of animals: the central vertical lines from neck to bottom of trunk represent vertebrae; horizontal white bands on the right are rib-bones, and on the left internal organs are added; on the thighs and upper part of the spirit's legs the designs indicate slices of flesh. Frontal and side views are combined in this painting. The penis is elongated, a common feature of such spirits who have a reputation of raping human women prior to killing them. From the elbow-bands hang dead men's bones; a beard is indicated, along with a heavy crop of hair. (See Chapter Two.)

Stories concerning such spirits are distinct from those of a historical, totemic, or mythical nature. Some are mild and timid, avoiding human beings. Others, directly malignant, are usually credited with being physically abnormal, with long penes, insatiable lusts, and sadistic tendencies. The people of this region believe in their presence, and are ready to relate alleged experiences on the part of others, if not of themselves. Of course, with the coming of the mission and other European authorities, these spirits show a tendency to retreat from the settlement areas. In the bush, however, they are still prevalent and may be encountered by the unwary. (See R. and C. Berndt, 1951: 150–78.) Traditionally, such paintings were drawn on the walls of bark shelters or in caves, or made by an artist to illustrate a story or 'authenticate' a personal experience.

Size, 46 ×18; artist, unknown, Kakadu tribe; now in the National Museum of Victoria.

Plate 65

In this bark from Yirrkalla are human footprints, handprints, and (extreme right) a row of stingray livers. (See Chapter Two.) The footprints and handprints have been made in wet sand, and the lines of dots represent water emerging and filling the tracks. Such prints often appear in bark paintings, and for that matter in cave paintings, in association with other subject-matter, but rarely as a complete composition; Mountford (1956: Plates 101 A, 107 D, 108 D) gives some examples. Compare, too, with Plate 12 in Elkin and R. and C. Berndt (1950). With its clear space between the prints, this is not typical of the art style of north-eastern Arnhem Land. The tracks themselves are possibly those of a spirit being; and stingray liver is a highly prized delicacy in this region.

Size, 26·5 ×15·75; artist, unknown, but possibly a Gumaidj or Waramiri man. Collected by the Reverend W. Chaseling, it was purchased by the Australian Museum, Sydney, in 1939.

Plate 66

This extremely interesting bark painting is said to show scenes from the life of Mimi spirits. (See also Plates 17, 36 and 37, although the style of these is markedly different.) It may represent a combination of styles, because Beswick Creek Government settlement, where it was obtained, serves as a 'melting-pot' for Aborigines from the Oenpelli, Roper, Katherine and even, much farther and only occasionally, the central coastal Arnhem Land area. The arrangement of panelling is like that of north-eastern Arnhem Land; the figures closely resemble Oenpelli painting, especially that of, for example, the Mangeri and some of the Gunbalang; the subject-matter is certainly western Arnhem Land. It is attributed to an artist of the Maiali tribe. Maiali is said to refer to stony or rocky country, and people calling themselves by this name include not only some Gunwinggu and Dangbun, but also Rainbarnga (or Rembranga), who originally occupied the country toward the source of the Liverpool River, inland toward the Bulman Gorge and Creek, in south-western Arnhem Land. They also come into Oenpelli. There are three panels, the bottom one divided into two sections. The top figures are (from left to right) a didjeridu player, a singing man with clapping-sticks, and four dancers: the cross on the chest of one possibly indicates a woman, since this closely resembles what is called a *maidga*, or breast girdle, in north-eastern Arnhem Land (see Plate 68). In the middle panel are (from left to right) a seated woman, a didjeridu player, four female dancers and one male. The bottom-left panel shows (from left to right) four dancers, two male and two female. In the remaining section are a didjeridu player and a songman with his clapping-sticks, both seated. For notes on the Mimi, see annotations to Plates 36 and 37; and Chapter Two. See also Art Gallery of New South Wales, Acquisitions (1960: No. 135).

Size, 31·75×19; artist, 'Spider', Maiali tribe. (It is possible that this 'Spider' is Spider Namirgi, a Dangbun man who has ties not only with the Pine Creek-Katherine area, but also with Oenpelli, where he has lived from time to time.) Purchased by Dr. S. Scougall from Beswick Creek Settlement in 1960, and presented to the Art Gallery of New South Wales.

Plate 67

This bark from Yirrkalla also diverges in treatment from the majority of paintings of that area. It seems to be a combination of traditional and outside, possibly mission, influence; it resembles some which were collected by Mountford (1956), but even then the drawing of the human figures and the treatment of the faces are different.

Unfortunately, no information was obtained with the painting. The annotation in the *Australian Aboriginal Art Catalogue* (1960–61: 29, No. 76) states that it refers to 'a big feast'—the fishermen return with a large sail-fish and sit down to eat it. The left-hand panel, according to this annotation, depicts 'women and children awaiting their turn to eat what is left of the fish, after the men have finished'.

This identification is open to question. In the first place, unless the fish were declared tabu for religious reasons, it would possibly be cooked by women, if these were present, and they would share in it without having to wait until the men had eaten. Secondly, there is no indication that the fish is being eaten: it would need, first, to be cut up and shared out. The right-hand panel shows eight men facing one another in two rows across a long-nosed fish (sail-fish?): those at the bottom are sitting cross-legged: surrounding them is the typical criss-crossing design used as background in north-eastern Arnhem Land, and here representing the ground or sand. The fish shows the incipient or pseudo-X-ray treatment; and the men are drawn in a similar way, with ribs showing. In the left-hand panel are two women (with ribs showing), sitting before a fire with rising flames or smoke: at each side is a child.

It is not clear what the scene represents. It could be a scene from the Land of the Dead, with skeletons (cf., the hollow eye-sockets) around a sawfish coffin; or men sitting around their catch singing the clan songs associated with this creature, before passing it on for cooking and preparation by the two women; or a mythical scene involving spirits; or the fish could represent a sacred *rangga* emblem, around which the men sing, while the left-hand scene shows the main camp. There are other possible interpretations, too, but these seem the most likely. Size, 17·25×9; artist, unknown. Acquired from the Methodist Mission, Perth, 1959. Now in the Western Australian Art Gallery.

Plate 68

Carved Wooden Figures of Sacred Beings.

As noted in the annotations to Plate 69, human figures of relatively realistic design are derived directly from the post-figures. They have been discussed and illustrated by R. and C. Berndt (1948: 309–26, Plate 1), Elkin and R. and C. Berndt (1950: 50–8, Plates 1, 7, 8), Elkin (1938/56: facing 175), and in Chapter Two. Other human figures of this variety are illustrated and discussed by Mountford (1956).

The three figures here are sacred beings, and are occasionally used as *rangga* emblems: exhibited to postulants, kept in a sacred storehouse, and used in dancing. (See R. Berndt, 1958a: 260.) From left to right:

a The younger Wawalag sister of the myth mentioned in the annotations to Plates 55, 62 and 73. (See Chapter Two.)

The treatment of sacred figures as shown in this group differs from that of others, such as the *wuramu*. In this particular case the sacred designs are painted directly onto the trunk on a red-ochred background. The carved breasts are those of a young girl, and the ridge between is cicatrization. Arms are carved solidly against the trunk, while vulva (hidden by a pubic covering) and buttocks are raised and not patterned. The figure originally included a feathered pendant, which encircled the forehead and hung down at one side: this is now missing. She wears also a *maidga* of red-ochred jungle fibre, a breast girdle which young girls wear for decoration and to 'strengthen' the breasts.

On the forehead a headband is painted: curved lines from the headband to the jawline below the ears outline the cheek or the groove between nose and eye. The design under the chin represents *durilji* gum-tree flowers: horizontal lines of dots above and below the breasts signify rain made by Julunggul. Curved vertical bands represent boomerangs and the dots, rain. Below the second series of curved vertical bands is a design signifying menstrual blood. Horizontal lines on the thighs (not seen) are cuts, referring to the circumcision of her husband.

Size, 32 inches in height; artist, Mauwulan, Riradjingu, *dua* moiety. Collected by R. Berndt at Yirrkalla in 1947, and originally in the collection at the Department of Anthropology, University of Sydney; in 1957, when this was dispersed, it went on permanent loan to the Australian Institute of Anatomy, Canberra.

b This is the elder Wawalag sister, broadly similar in design to the younger. Here, however, the pattern was first incised on a red-ochred background and then painted. Arms stand out from the trunk, and breasts are elongated to signify that she has borne, and is breast-feeding, a child. The designs are similar to those on her younger sister: horizontal lines between and above the breasts are cicatrizations; marks on the forearms are scars for a brother's circumcision, and dots on the chest are rain sent by Julunggul.

Size, 36 inches in height; artist, Mauwulan (as above). Collected by R. Berndt at Yirrkalla in 1947, and originally in the collection of the Department of Anthropology, University of Sydney; in 1957, when this was dispersed, it went on permanent loan to the Australian Institute of Anatomy, Canberra.

c This is a remarkably fine and unusual figure of the *jiridja* moiety being Laindjung. (See also Plate 35, and Chapter Two.) His face is white with the foam which marked it as he emerged from the sea at Blue Mud Bay. On his body are watermarks forming patterns, which he gave to various *jiridja* linguistic units and clans. Laindjung and his son Banaidja, and the myth associated with them, serve to substantiate the *jiridja*

nara rituals, counterpart of the *dua nara* rituals inspired by the Djanggawul.

Arms stand out from the main trunk; the top of the head is flat, and has human hair fastened on with blood. The feathers at the top, seen in the present illustration, were not there in the original: they have (apparently) been broken from the feathered ornament suspended from the chin, and representing a beard; initially, this extended to a point below the shoulders. The original beard had two bunches of feathers, the first of red parakeet feathers, the second (now, wrongly, on top of the head) of seagull feathers. At each corner of the mouth are parakeet feathers suggesting a moustache (the upper lip being bare of hair, with long tufts left at each side). On the head are a red-ochred headband and a facial decoration (a band of red ochre from ear to ear, across the nose). On the left arm is a parakeet-feathered armband.

The sacred patterns (or watermarks) on the body are as follows. At neck, freshwater weed design (Dalwongu). First section, from shoulders, Dalwongu-Mararlba. Second section to navel, Mararlba, fire and ashes inside seaweed and mud; Ridarngu-Wonguri-Manggalili, hollow log under water; Gumaidj, stripped bark, red ochre, and cliffs. From navel to top of pubes: Ridarngu-Wonguri, spring-water; continuation of Manggalili design; Manaidja clan, wild bees and honeycomb; Wonguri, mangrove worm and hollow log. On left and right thighs: Gumaidj-Ridarngu, wild bees, ashes, and honeycomb.

Size, 36·5 inches; artists, Liagarang, Dalwongu linguistic unit, and Munggaraui, Gumaidj linguistic unit: *jiridja* moiety.

Collected by R. Berndt at Yirrkalla in 1947, and originally in the collection of the Department of Anthropology, University of Sydney; when this was dispersed in 1957, the figure was taken to the Australian Institute of Anatomy, Canberra, where it is now.

Plate 69

Carving and Moulding.

Realistic and conventionalized wood carving in the round has been discussed and recorded by R. and C. Berndt (1948; 1949), Elkin and R.

and C. Berndt (1950: Chapter IV, Plates 1, 3 B, 7, 8, 9), R. Berndt (1958*a*: 259–60), Elkin (1938/56: facing 175), Mountford (1956: 415–37, with illustrations; 1958*a*; 1961*a*), and McCarthy (1938/58: 36–6, Fig. 22). A number of these figures have legs and arms, but some retain their traditional form as post-figures.

These figures cover a very wide range of spirits, creative and mythical beings, historical and pseudo-historical characters, and even contemporary persons, particularly those recently dead. They are (or were) used in mortuary ritual, as grave-posts, in secular ceremony, as well as occasionally in sacred ritual. Many of the highly stylized posts traditionally used in Melville and Bathurst islands (see, for example, Spencer, 1914; Mountford, 1958*a*) represented human beings. There is no reason to suppose that they were not indigenous and traditionally inspired, since somewhat similar constructions of various kinds are found throughout the continent, although Macassan contact over a long period was quite possibly responsible for their elaboration and development. In contrast, the realistic examples with arms and legs and increasing remoteness from the simple post-figure style are fairly recent innovations. The carved heads were made for me, for the first time, in 1946–47. (See Chapter Two.)

From left to right:

a A carved wooden head, previously illustrated in Elkin and R. and C. Berndt (1950: 59, Plate 9 c), is of Ranjara, identified with the female Kultana (Guldana). (See also R. and C. Berndt, 1948: 323–5, Plate II, 1 and 2; Elkin and R. and C. Berndt, 1950: 54, Plate 7.) Guldana is associated with the *jiridja* moiety Land of the Dead. With her husband she usually lives on Mudilnga, north of the Wessel Islands, and lights large grass-fires to attract spirits of the dead. Ranjara also sends the 'cold' north winds to the mainland. There are no actual ceremonies or rituals connected with these spirits; but songs referring to them are sung during mortuary rituals, and a Guldana or Ranjara post could be erected at such a time—either for the purpose of the ritual, or to mark the grave of the person concerned.

The main design painted on the head represents wind and clouds. The height of the head is 10·5 inches; diameter at top (slightly domed), 5·25; and circumference of neck, 8·25 inches. Artist, Munggaraui, Gumaidj linguistic unit. Collected by R. Berndt at Yirrkalla in 1947, and originally in the collection of the Department of Anthropology, University of Sydney; when this was dispersed, the object was taken (with others) in 1957 to the Australian Institute of Anatomy, Canberra, on permanent loan.

b A moulded ochre head from Oenpelli, western Arnhem Land. Such heads are extremely rare in Aboriginal Australia. (See Chapter Two, and also L. Adam, 1954: Fig. 41.) Examples of this form, from Oenpelli, have been illustrated and discussed by R. Berndt (1951*b*: 350–3, Plates 1 to 10). The Gunwinggu and neighbouring tribes traditionally made roughly moulded heads and figures from pipeclay (or white ochre), which were used for sorcery. (See R. Berndt, 1951*h*: Plate 3.) These, however, were eventually destroyed or disintegrated. At my suggestion, therefore, when I was carrying out field-work in the Oenpelli region in 1950, some examples of these were prepared (fifteen, including the roughly moulded sorcery head, were collected).

The specimen illustrated here is of a man's bust: triangular face, with eyes and wrinkles marked by scratching, as well as a moustache, beard, and teeth. It was said to represent a local Aboriginal, whose name (for obvious reasons) was not supplied.

Size, 6·5 inches in height; artist, Joshua Wurungulngul, Gunwinggu. Collected by R. Berndt at Oenpelli in 1950 and originally in the collection of the Department of Anthropology, University of Sydney; in 1957, when this was dispersed, it was placed on permanent loan in the Australian Institute of Anatomy, Canberra.

c A post-figure from Yirrkalla, north-eastern Arnhem Land, illustrated and discussed in R. and C. Berndt (1949: 213–22, Plate II, Fig. 4). The *wuramu* or 'collection' figures are said to owe their origin to Dutch custom officials, who levied taxes on the Macassan praus when they returned from the Arnhem Land coast. Alternatively, *wuramu* are said to have been 'wild natives', or bandits, who came down occasionally to Macassan towns on pillaging expeditions. Arnhem Landers who were employed on the praus are reported to have seen these people, and later to have recorded these events by making *wuramu* posts and instituting a collection ceremony. (See R. and C. Berndt, 1954.) On the other hand such posts, it is said, were made by Macassans themselves for the graves of their own dead on this north coast. In present-day mortuary ritual such a post is made, representing either the dead person, or one of the relevant spirits, or a Macassan; attached to it are long feathered strings representing its arms and hands (the traditional *wuramu* does not have carved arms). To the accompaniment of singing the *wuramu*, or collection man, is taken from camp to camp, and everywhere it goes it collects any goods or objects which people have not hidden securely away. By this means food and goods are obtained for the main participants in the mortuary rituals. (See Warner, 1937/58: 412–50.) Finally the post is placed on the grave or erected in the main camp, where it is left to rot. Mountford (1956: Plate 136 c) has mentioned these post-figures. (See Preface and Chapter Two.)

This example is a Macassan *wuramu* man. On the front of the post is the typical *darabu* pattern (possibly derived from batik cloth), variously said to represent Indonesian cloth or clouds.

Size, 18·5 inches in height; artist, Munggaraui, Gumaidj linguistic unit, *jiridja* moiety. Collected by R. Berndt at Yirrkalla in 1947, and originally in the collection of the Department of Anthropology, University of Sydney; in 1957, when this was dispersed, it went on permanent loan to the Australian Institute of Anatomy, Canberra.

Plate 70

Incised Objects.

Australian Aborigines have produced some very beautiful examples of incised, carved, fluted, and pecked work on rock-facings (see Chapter Three), on flat stones, as in the case of *tjurunga* (Chapter Four), on pearlshell (Preface), and on wooden weapons, sacred boards, and other objects.

Stone *tjurunga* come from the Aranda, Central Australian area, although a few examples are reported from the Great Victoria Desert and from the north-west. The best incised work in wood, particularly on shields and boomerangs, is to be found in eastern Australia. But, where incising on sacred wooden boards is concerned, a very large region is involved; the most outstanding specimens come from the desert tribes of north-western South Australia and central Western Australia, from the Kimberleys, and also from the Victoria River area. The pearlshells come mostly from the Kimberleys, particularly the coast, although they have been traded over long distances.

The best discussions, with illustrations, are to be found in Davidson (1937), and McCarthy (1938/58; 1957a).

a, top, is a shield from south-east Australia—a beautifully balanced object, with symmetrical incising of concentric and hollow diamonds: from the lower Darling River, western New South Wales. Such shields were used primarily as protection from spears, the end projections serving to deflect or knock aside a striking spear. The meaning of the design is unknown; but it probably refers to a myth or represents, in a stylized form, waterholes, country, and the tracks of ancestral beings.

b, left, is an ornate fighting boomerang from Lake Narran, northern New South Wales, with a raised double-diamond motif similar to that in *a*, but without the concentric effect. Such decorated fighting boomerangs are found also in western and central Queensland. McCarthy (1938/58: 20, quoting Roth) notes that such designs do have meanings, but none is mentioned specifically for those illustrated here. He adds that 'the designs and their execution . . . equal the finest decorative work produced on the continent. The weapon illustrated here is of the non-returning variety.' Boomerangs were widely, but not universally, distributed throughout the continent; the returning boomerang was largely confined to eastern and western Australia.

c, left middle, are three engraved pearlshells smeared with red ochre to make the incising stand out. These come from the northern Kimberleys, and two have attached necklets or waistbands (the darker one of human-hair twine). They are occasionally called phallocrypts, since they were often worn by initiated men suspended from a human hair waistband as a pubic covering, as decoration rather than protection. They are also worn as necklets—not, however, as everyday ornaments, but mainly for ceremonial and ritual occasions. They are highly valued, and in some instances, especially in far distant places to which they have come by trade, are used for magical purposes: at Ooldea, on the transcontinental railway-line, they were used for rain-making. Some from, say, Wyndham, have found their way as far south-east as Port Augusta, as well as into Central Australia and to Darwin.

The designs vary considerably; but among the commonest, traditionally, were maze, key pattern, and angular meandering groups of parallel lines. Some of these last represent waves, tidal marks on a beach, clouds, pools of water, rain, or the tracks of ancestral beings, rivers, and so forth. Others (like the bottom left-hand one) are highly stylized human figures, although in the example illustrated here animal tracks are shown as well. The pearlshells illustrated here come specifically from Wyndham (top left), Sunday Island (bottom left), and the Admiralty Gulf (right).

d, middle, third from right, is a wooden sacred board from the Laverton area of Western Australia, and would belong to the Bidjandjara-speaking people of that region. It is used in sacred ritual, when it is either sung over and handled; or it might be decorated with designs in ochre or in feather down (in much the same way as noted in Plate 16).

Designs of this nature vary a great deal in meaning, but each represents part of the wanderings of some mythical being, or beings (see Chapter Four), much as the Aranda *tjurunga* do. This could refer to a range of places and a number of sacred beings—the Wadi Gudjara (Two Men),

for instance. When the boards are sung over or used in ritual, only the parts relevant to that being are sung or performed. The object itself is a representation of that being, and consequently embodies part of his power.

e is a hunting, or fighting, fluted boomerang, which could well come from Central Australia. This type has a wide distribution: in the southern Kimberleys, for instance, throughout the central-western part of the Northern Territory, and even into the Daly River and Arnhem Land areas. It can be a dangerous weapon in fighting: when thrown with force, its sharp end can cut open a man's belly. It is also used as a musical instrument; a singing man holds one in each hand, clapping and rattling them, or beating on the ground, according to the rhythm. The meaning of the design is unknown, but in this case probably represents a creek, with channels, and no doubt has mythical significance. The particular specimen illustrated here was collected at Caledon Bay, eastern Arnhem Land, and probably entered that region as a trade item via the Rose and Roper rivers.

f, extreme right, is a well-incised spearthrower from Peak Hill, north Murchison district, Western Australia, of a type used fairly generally throughout the Western and Great Victoria deserts, and into Central Australia. The incised section is the inner part along which the spear rests, fitted into its peg (top); at the bottom of the handle is a resin knob, into which a stone flake has been fitted, thus making the 'thrower into an adze; the outer surface is usually plain. The flat, carved section can serve also as a platter for mixing ochres, or ash for chewing native tobacco, or for holding food. The design has been variously interpreted: more commonly it is said to represent mythical snakes; the tracks of mythical beings; and creeks.

g At the bottom of this plate (left and right) are two stone *tjurunga*, both Aranda. Strehlow, in Chapter Four, discusses these objects and their significance. Spencer and Gillen (1938: 128–66) give the meanings of some of them.

The right-hand *tjurunga* closely resembles one which was described in the *Australian Aboriginal*

Art Catalogue (1960–61: 33, No. 110) as being of the marsupial mole totem of Ltalaltuma (Gilbert Springs): the concentric circles represent the holes of this creature, the rectangles with parallel lines being air-holes in the ground and the parallel lines tail-marks. Ltalaltuma is identified by Strehlow (1947: 60, 65, 66, 102, 119, 154–5) as a spring on the northern slopes of the Krichauff Ranges, the location of a ritual ground occupied by a wild-cat totem band. McCarthy states that this design represents a sacred *waningga*, or *wonigi*, but its mythical significance is unknown.

The *tjurunga* on the left, according to McCarthy, refers to the caterpillar totem, Ngurungatja, which lives on the leaves of the *ngurunga* bush. The concentric circles signify its camps, the rows of dots and sets of parallel lines its tracks, and the sets of sinuous lines the way in which this insect lies along the twigs of the *ngurunga*. All examples in this plate are from the collections of the Australian Museum, Sydney.

Plate 71

Baskets and Painted Objects.

Top row, from left to right:

a A beautifully made dilly-bag or basket of fine twine, or pandanus fibre, painted in clan and linguistic unit patterns at the top, with pendants of red parakeet feathers, and equipped with a carrying string. This is a man's sacred spirit bag for keeping his private and usually sacred and magical possessions. It is from Milingimbi, north-central coast of Arnhem Land. Similar bags of this type, with and without feathered pendants, have been illustrated by Spencer (1914: Plates XXII, XXIII, XXIV), Warner (1937/58: III A), and McCarthy (1938/58: 43, facing contents, Figs. 23 and 52; 1957a: 68). Similarly shaped baskets, finely made, are used for carrying liquid honey or even water.

Bags like this one are usually carried by men under one arm, with the string flung over the same shoulder. Some have an overstitching of human hair, outlining coloured feathers which have been worked into the main body of the basket. The pendants may incorporate nobs of hard beeswax, encasing the foreskin of the basket's owner, or of a close relative, usually of his own or his mother's linguistic unit. Part of their making is done ritually on the men's sacred ground to the accompaniment of singing. They are sometimes used as items of trade, and are looked upon as extremely valuable. (See Elkin and R. and C. Berndt, 1950: 103–6.)

There is also a great deal of symbolism associated with them. *Dua* moiety bags, for instance, are said to have been brought originally by the Djanggawul (see Plate 25), and are worn during certain rituals. Although such baskets are sacred they are not secret: they are worn in the camp and, in fighting or serious arguments, may be held in the teeth, if a small padded fighting-bag is not available. The basket itself symbolizes the uterus of one of the Djanggawul sisters: and the red parakeet feathered pendants are rays of the sun, or umbilical cords. (See R. Berndt, 1952: 4, etc.)

b Another sacred spirit bag, bearing diamond-shaped designs ochred and outlined with an overstitching of twine; there is a fringe of red parakeet feathers, with pendant drops of red parakeet feathers and (possibly) seagull feathers. This basket is from Yirrkalla. The design suggests that it represents wild honey, and is of the *dua* moiety. On the other hand, it resembles quite closely the design on a sacred Fire Dreaming *rangga* illustrated in Elkin and R. and C. Berndt (1950: 42, Plate 18 B [c]), of the *jiridja* moiety.

c A bark armlet worn by women in the *bugamani* mortuary rituals of Melville and Bathurst islands. It has a binding of human hair around the middle and at one end, and is decorated with parakeet feathers.

Such bark armlets have been discussed and illustrated by Spencer (1914: Plates VIII, XXIX, XXX), McCarthy (1957a), and Mountford (1958a). Spencer (1914: 233, Fig. 52) mentions that they are kept in place by holding the arms close to the side. At the end of the rituals, performers remove their armlets and leave them on the grave as a present for the spirit of the dead.

Left, middle row:

d A woman's seed-winnowing dish of wood,

nicely decorated with snake and lizard motifs: from the Victoria River region, Northern Territory. In treatment this dish is not unlike the shield illustrated in Plate 28. It has been illustrated in McCarthy (1938/58: Fig. 42). It is possible that this example was used for ritual purposes (as a substitute for a ground drawing), because the design would not have lasted for long, if it were in everyday use; the painted area would usually rest on the ground.

e is a cane basket, made and decorated by men, but used by women for carrying vegetable foods. It is from the Cairns district, north-eastern Queensland. See also McCarthy (1957a: 66, 68).

f is a further basket made of stringy-bark, and used by women for carrying vegetable foods. It is from Melville Island. (See Spencer, 1914: Plates XXV, XXXIV, and XXXV.) The meaning of the design is not recorded.

g, below *e*, is a bark armlet from Melville and Bathurst islands: see *c*, above.

From left to right, bottom:

h is another bark armlet from Melville and Bathurst islands: see *c*, above.

i is a sacred bullroarer, with broken swinging twine, from Milingimbi. The painting represents wild-honey bees (white dots). Warner (1937/58: 502) mentions these. The one illustrated here is of the paddle or bird type; its sound is said to be the cry of a bird. R. Berndt, (1951a: Plate III) has discussed the significance of the bullroarer in the Kunapipi (Gunabibi) rituals.

j is a bark belt worn by men on the South Alligator River, western Arnhem Land. Spencer (1914: 402, Fig. 71) illustrates some of these. They are made from the bark of cypress pine. (Gagadju and Jiwadja tribes.)

k A long Malay or Macassan-type pipe from Yirrkalla, incised and decorated. These cylindrical pipes were introduced by Macassan traders to the northern Arnhem Land coast. (See Elkin and R. and C. Berndt, 1950: 102, Plates 3 A [b], 20 B; and R. and C. Berndt, 1954. Mountford, 1956: 389–400, Figs. 59, 60, 62, 63, and Plate 128, illustrates and discusses various pipe designs. McCarthy, 1957a: 108, and Elkin, 1938/56: facing 63, give photographs of these pipes in use.) Such pipes are usually made from the hollow, pithy stem of the *lungin* (pipe) bush. Some are undecorated, but the majority are incised (and sometimes painted, as in the example illustrated); the whole stem is first red-ochred, so that the incising stands out against the white underwood. Sacred and secular patterns are used, and the former are often wrapped in paper-bark, or rag, when the pipe is being smoked in the main camp.

All specimens from the Australian Museum collections, Sydney.

Plate 72

This plate shows a variety of decorated spears, a fighting-club (centre), and four spearthrowers (below).

The two spears on the outer left and the two on the outer right are from Melville Island. Mainland Northern Territory Aboriginal spears usually consist of a hollow shaft, mostly of eucalyptus, from five to nine feet in length; the peg of the spearthrower fits into the hollow end of the spear, and not only enables the spear to travel further, but gives it more force and ensures a more accurate aim. In contrast, the spears of Bathurst and Melville islands are made from very hard wood, with ornately carved barbs: they are from six to eleven feet in length, and are thrown by hand. (See McCarthy, 1938/58: 45–7, Fig. 36; 1957a: 73; Spencer, 1914: 357, Plates XIII, XIV, XV, who gives a number of examples of these Melville Island spears; and Mountford, 1958a: 98, Plate 32.) Mountford speaks of two varieties of carved ceremonial spear: the male *bugamani* (mortuary festival) spear, called *dungaringa* (barbs at one side only), and the female *dungaguni* (with barbs at both sides). These, he says, are made solely as gifts to the dead, and are used in mortuary ritual. The barb cutting was done with cockle-shells.

The other eight spears are from Yirrkalla, and were used in ritualized avenging expeditions, or during the *magarada* peace-making ceremony, or 'trial by ordeal'—when an accused man runs the gauntlet of his opponents, who are lined up at one side of a cleared ground facing his supporters. (See Warner, 1937/58: 174–6.)

After the Macassan traders on this north coast brought iron, shovel-bladed (shovel-nosed) spears became popular, and remain so until the present day. Warner (1937/58: 485–9, Plate II B) describes the variety of spears used in this region, each with its special name.

The flat-bladed club (centre) is from Milingimbi. Warner (1937/58: 489–90) notes that such clubs are used for striking a direct blow, and the type illustrated here is used only for hand-to-hand encounters. It is used mostly by men, but also occasionally by women.

The four horizontally arranged spearthrowers are also from Arnhem Land. The first three are from Groote Eylandt; Mountford (1956: Plate 146) illustrates six. The second from the bottom bears a north-west wind design, and the bottom one (from Yirrkalla) is decorated with a line of turtles. (See also Warner, 1937/58: 483–5.) All examples in this plate are from the collections of the Australian Museum, Sydney.

Plate 73

Painted objects from Arnhem Land. From left to right:

a A sacred board used in the Arawaldja rituals at Groote Eylandt. (See Mountford, 1956: 21–60; P. Worsley, 1955: 860.) These rituals are made up of a series of totemic performances, associated in part with circumcision, but primarily with the increase of the natural species with which they deal. Sacred 'houses' or shelters, and painted poles and boards, are used. An object similar to the one illustrated here appears in Mountford (1956: Plate II A, and a description of the relevant dancing on pp. 49–50). The figure drawn on the board represents Aidja, a creative totemic being who formed the Amakula River on Groote Eylandt, along with others.

b A hollow-log coffin from Yirrkalla, north-eastern Arnhem Land. Similar coffins have been illustrated and discussed by Elkin and R. and C. Berndt, 1950: Plates 5 (b), 18 B (b), Chapter VII; and by Warner, 1937/1958: Chapter XII; and others. (Mountford, 1956: 311–32, Plates 102 to 105; McCarthy, 1957*a*: 157; 1938/58: 40, Fig. 21.)

After a corpse has been exposed for a time on a mortuary platform, the bones are collected and ritually broken up (except for the skull), and then placed in a long, hollow log called *nganugu laragidj*: this is red-ochred, and carefully painted with the deceased's clan and linguistic unit patterns. The painting is done in sections, and several artists may take part, for the usual length of such a post is twelve to twenty feet. The pole itself may also represent, for the *dua* moiety, a whale, sawfish, porpoise, shark, snake, or stone; for the *jiridja* moiety, a mast, ship's funnel, cloud, wild honey, and certain varieties of fish.

The specimen illustrated here is a model; but in traditional times bark coffins too were used, of about this size, and after the mortuary rituals were either carried about by a close relative, or stored in a tree. This example is of the *jiridja* moiety, and the painting on it is of a Macassan prau. Special mortuary songs tell of the departures of these praus from the north coast, and the erection of their masts: in this case the log itself represents such a mast, symbolizing the departure of the spirit for the *jiridja* land of the dead.

c Another log coffin, in this case closely resembling a didjeridu or drone-pipe used in sacred ritual. It is from the McArthur River, Northern Territory, and was possibly associated with the Binbinga, Wadari, Janjula, and Ngewin tribes. The log, with its stopper of bark (protruding from the top), was first red-ochred; then white and reddened feather down, or wild cotton, was stuck on with blood. The patterning represents a kangaroo's hind and front paws and tail—marks made as it walks on all fours.

d This object resembles closely a hollow-log gong called *uwar*, which is used in sacred ritual. The Wawalag mythology (see R. Berndt, 1951*a*; also Chapter Two) substantiates three ritual cycles; the third of these, now only rarely performed, is the *ngurlmag*, in which such an object is used. Warner (1937/58: 311–29), describing this ritual, notes that the gong or drum is beaten with a pandanus stump: the object itself represents Muid or Julunggul, the great rock python, and the sound of the drum is his voice. In western Arnhem Land such a drum is called *ubar*: among the Gunwinggu at Oenpelli it is a female rainbow snake (*ngaljod*); at Goulburn Island it represents the body of the Fertility Mother. (See R. and C. Berndt, 1951; also Elkin and R. and C. Berndt, 1950: 39, 41, Plate 4A,a.)

However, according to McCarthy (1938/58: 40–2, Fig. 33) this particular object is a hollow-log coffin; in the design, a man wearing a pubic fringe has a spear over one arm and a spear-thrower under the other, with small baskets attached to his shoulders: on the right-hand side is an emu, on the left a large snake. A similar object, collected at Milingimbi, is mentioned by Mountford (1956: 456) as an *uwar*, the human figure being Julbaibai, whose wife was said to have been raped by Julunggul at his sacred waterhole. (See McCarthy, 1938/58: Fig. 21.)

e This is a sacred *rangga* used in *dua* moiety *nara* ritual. (See Warner, 1937/58: 39–51; R. Berndt, 1952; Elkin and R. and C. Berndt, 1950:

Chapter III.) It represents Wunungu, the Lightning Snake, one manifestation of Julunggul (above). The top part of the design is Wunungu, surrounded by many younger snakes: the bottom half is the waterhole from which they emerged at Milingimbi.

f below. Two painted skulls from Yirrkalla. Such decorated skulls were much more common in the Milingimbi area, where they were carried about by close relatives of the deceased—worn as a necklet, or hung in camp on a tree. Not only is the skull carried in memory of the deceased, but it is also said to attract his spirit. The painted designs represent the dead person's clan and linguistic unit emblems, and are a form of social identification. (See Elkin and R. and C. Berndt, 1950: 98–9, Plates 3 B, b, 9, g; McCarthy, 1938/58: Fig. 24.) The skull on the left is probably of the Gumaidj linguistic unit; the one on the right, Mararlba.

These seven objects are in the collection of the Australian Museum, Sydney.

ADAM, L. 1943
Introduction to *Primitive Art Exhibition*, Melbourne.
ADAM, L. 1951
'The Bark Paintings of Groote Eylandt (Gulf of Carpentaria) in the Melbourne University Collection', *Südseestudien, Gedenkschrift zur Erinnerung an Felix Speiser*, Museum für Völkerkunde, Basel.
ADAM, L. 1954
Primitive Art, Pelican, London.
ANTHROPOLOGICAL SOCIETY OF WESTERN AUSTRALIA, 1960
A preliminary report of a survey being carried out by the Anthropological Society of Western Australia, relevant to the preservation of Australian Aboriginal sites in Western Australia, Perth. (Typescript: mimeographed.)
ARNDT, W. 1962
'The Nargorkun-Narlinji Cult', *Oceania*, Vol. XXXII, No. 4.
AUSTRALIAN ABORIGINAL ART
An Exhibition arranged by the State Art Galleries of Australia, 1960–61.
BARRETT, C. and CROLL, R. H. 1943
Art of the Australian Aboriginal, Bread and Cheese Club, Melbourne.
BARRETT, C. L. and KENYON, A. C. 1950
Australian Aboriginal Art, Melbourne.
BASEDOW, H. 1925
The Australian Aboriginal, Preece, Adelaide.

BATTARBEE, R. 1951
Modern Australian Aboriginal Art, Angus and Robertson, Sydney.
BERNDT, C. H. 1961
'Art and Aesthetic Expression', Conference on Aboriginal Studies, Canberra, May: data paper.
BERNDT, R. M. 1947
'Wuradjeri Magic and "Clever Men"', *Oceania*, Vol. XVIII, No. 4; Vol. XVIII, No. 1.
BERNDT, R. M. 1948
'A Wonguri-Mandjikai Song Cycle of the Moon-Bone', *Oceania*, Vol. XIX, No. 1.
BERNDT, R. M. 1951*a*
Kunapipi, Cheshire, Melbourne.
BERNDT, R. M. 1951*b*
'Aboriginal Ochre-Moulded Heads from Western Arnhem Land', *Meanjin*, Vol. X, No. 4.
BERNDT, R. M. 1952
Djanggawul, Routledge and Kegan Paul, London.
BERNDT, R. M. 1958*a*
'The Mountford Volume on Arnhem Land Art, Myth and Symbolism: A Critical Review', *Mankind*, Vol. 5, No. 6.
BERNDT, R. M. 1958*b*
'Some Methodological Considerations on the Study of Australian Aboriginal Art', *Oceania*, Vol. XXIX, No. 1.
BERNDT, R. M. 1959
'The Concept of "The Tribe" in the Western Desert

of Australia', *Oceania*, Vol. XXX, No. 2.

BERNDT, R. M. 1962
An Adjustment Movement in Arnhem Land, Cahiers de L'Homme, Mouton, Paris.

BERNDT, R. M. and C. H. 1948
'Sacred Figures of Ancestral Beings of Arnhem Land', *Oceania*, Vol. XVIII, No. 4.

BERNDT, R. M. and C. H. 1949
'Secular Figures of North-eastern Arnhem Land', *American Anthropologist*, Vol. 51, No. 2.

BERNDT, R. M. and C. H. 1950
'Aboriginal Art in Central-Western Northern Territory', *Meanjin*, Vol. IX, No. 3.

BERNDT, R. M. and C. H. 1951
Sexual Behaviour in Western Arnhem Land, Viking Fund Publications in Anthropology, No. 16, New York.

BERNDT, R. M. and C. H. 1954
Arnhem Land, Its History and Its People, Cheshire, Melbourne.

BERNDT, R. M. and C. H. 1957
Introduction to *Australian Aboriginal Art, Arnhem Land Paintings on Bark and Carved Human Figures*, Western Australian Museum, Perth.

BLACK, L. 1942
Cyclons: The Mystery Stones of the Darling River Valley, privately printed, Leeton, N.S.W.

BOAS, F. 1927
Primitive Art, Instituttet for Sammenlignende Kulturforskning, Serie B, Vol. 8, Oslo: 1955 Dover Book, New York.

BUNCE, D. 1857
Australasiatic Reminiscences, London.

CAMPBELL, Major 1834
'Geographical Memoir of Melville Island and Port Essington', *Journal of the Royal Geographical Society*, Vol. IV.

COX, J. C. 1878
'Drawings by Australian Aborigines', *Proceedings of the Linnean Society of New South Wales*, Vol. iii.

COX, J. C. 1888
'Figures. Wax', *Proceedings of the Linnean Society of New South Wales*, Vol. iii (2nd series).

CURR, E. M. 1886–7
The Australian Race . . . 4 Vols., Government Printer, Melbourne.

DAVIDSON, D. S. 1936
'Aboriginal Australian and Tasmanian Rock Carvings and Paintings', *American Philosophical Society*, Memoir V, Philadelphia.

DAVIDSON, D. S. 1937
'A Preliminary Consideration of Australian Aboriginal Decorative Art', *American Philosophical Society*, Memoir IX, Philadelphia.

DU JARDIN, E. 1888
'Le Cloisonisme', *Revue Indépendante* (May, 19) quoted from J. Rewald, 1956.

DUNBAR, G. K. 1943
'Notes on the Ngemba Tribe of the Central Darling River, Western New South Wales', *Mankind*, Vol. III, No. 5.

ELISOFON, E. 1958
The Sculpture of Africa (text by W. Fagg), London.

ELKIN, A. P. 1930
'Rock Paintings of North-West Australia', *Oceania*, Vol. I, No. 3.

ELKIN, A. P. 1938/1956
The Australian Aborigines: How to Understand Them, Angus and Robertson, Sydney.

ELKIN, A. P. 1948
'Grey's Northern Kimberley Cave-Paintings Refound', *Oceania*, Vol. XIX, No. 1.

ELKIN, A. P. 1949
'The Origin and Interpretation of Petroglyphs in South-East Australia', *Oceania*, Vol. XX, No. 2.

ELKIN, A. P. 1952
'Cave-Paintings in Southern Arnhem Land', *Oceania*, Vol. XXII, No. 4.

ELKIN, A. P. 1961
'Art and Meaning: A Review Article', *Oceania*, Vol. XXXII, No. 1.

ELKIN, A. P., and BERNDT, R. M. and C. H. 1950
Art in Arnhem Land, Cheshire, Melbourne.

FIRTH, R. 1951
Elements of Social Organization, Watts, London.

FLANAGAN, R. J. 1888
The Aborigines of Australia, Flanagan and Robertson, Sydney. (Reprinted from the *Empire*, 1853–54.)

GLEESON, J. 1959
in *The Sun* (July 18th), Sydney.

GODDARD, R. H. 1939
'Aboriginal Sculpture', *Australasian Association for the Advancement of Science*, Vol. XXIV.

GOLDING, J. 1959
Cubism, London.

GREY, G. 1841
Journals of Two Expeditions of Discovery in North-Western and Western Australia, London.

HALE, H. M. and TINDALE, N. B. 1930
'Notes on Some Human Remains in the Lower Murray Valley', *Records of the South Australian Museum*, Vol. IV.

HARNEY, W. E. 1943
Taboo, Australasian Publishing Co., Sydney.
HARNEY, W. E. 1960
'Ritual and Behaviour at Ayers Rock', *Oceania*,
Vol. XXXI, No. 1.
HOWITT, A. W. 1904
The Native Tribes of South-East Australia, Mac-
millan, London.
HUYGHE, René 1959
The Discovery of Art, London.
JUBILEE CATALOGUE, 1951
Jubilee Exhibition of Australian Art.
KABERRY, P. 1939
Aboriginal Woman, Sacred and Profane, Routledge,
London.
KING, P. P. 1827
*Narrative of a Survey of the Intertropical and
Western Coasts of Australia*, London.
KUPKA, K. 1958
Kunst der Uraustralier, Führer durch das Museum
für Völkerkunde Basel, Basle.
LEACH, E. R. 1956
In E. E. Evans-Pritchard, *et al.*, *The Institutions of
Primitive Society*, Blackwell, Oxford.
LÉVI-STRAUSS, C. 1958
Anthropologie Structurale, Librairie Plon, Paris.
LÉVI-STRAUSS, C. 1962
Le Totémisme Aujourd'hui, Presses Universitaires de
France, Paris.
LINDSAY, D. 1943
Foreword to Catalogue on *Primitive Art Exhibition*,
Melbourne.
LINTON, R. and WINGERT, P. 1946
(In collaboration with R. d'Harnoncourt) *Arts of
the South Seas*, New York.
LINTON, R. 1958
Preface in E. Elisofon, 1958.
LOMMEL, A. 1952
'Die Unambal ein Stamm in Nordwest-Australien',
Monographien zur Völkerkunde, Hamburg.
LOMMEL, A. and K. 1959
Die Kunst des fünften Erdteils: Australien, Staat-
liches Museum für Völkerkunde, Munich.
LOVE, J. R. B. 1930
'Rock Paintings of the Worora and their Mytho-
logical Interpretation', *Journal of the Royal Society
of Western Australia*, Vol. XVI.
LÖWENFELD, V. 1939
The Nature of Creative Activity, London.
McCARTHY, F. D. 1938/1958
Australian Aboriginal Decorative Art, Australian
Museum, Sydney.

McCARTHY, F. D. 1939
' "Trade" in Aboriginal Australia, and "Trade"
Relationships with Torres Strait, New Guinea and
Malaya', *Oceania*, Vol. X, No. 1.
McCARTHY, F. D. 1941–56
'Records of the Rock Engravings of the Sydney-
Hawkesbury District', *Mankind*, 3–5, and *Records
of the Australian Museum*, Vol. XXIV.
McCARTHY, F. D. 1953
'A Circumcision Ceremony and Stone Arrangement
on Groote Eylandt', *Records of the Australian
Museum*, Vol. XXIII, No. 3.
McCARTHY, F. D. 1957a
Australia's Aborigines, Their Life and Culture,
Colorgravure Publications, Melbourne.
McCARTHY, F. D. 1957b
'Theoretical Considerations of Australian Abori-
ginal Art', *Journal and Proceedings of the Royal
Society of New South Wales*, Vol. 91, Part 1.
McCARTHY, F. D. 1958
Australian Aboriginal Rock Art, Australian Museum,
Sydney.
McCARTHY, F. D. 1960
In C. P. Mountford, ed., *Records of the American-
Australian Scientific Expedition to Arnhem Land*,
Vol. 2, *Anthropology and Nutrition*, Melbourne
University Press, Melbourne.
McCARTHY, F. D. 1960–1
Introduction to *Australian Aboriginal Art*, *An
Exhibition arranged by the State Art Galleries of
Australia*.
McCARTHY, F. D. 1961
'The Rock Engravings of Depuch Island, North-
East Australia', *Records of the Australian Museum*,
Vol. XXV, No. 8.
McCARTHY, F. D. 1962
'The Rock Engravings at Port Hedland, North-
western Australia', *Papers, Kroeber Anthropolo-
gical Society*, University of California, No. 26.
McCARTHY, F. D. and MACINTOSH, N. W. G.
1962
'The Archaeology of Mootwingee, Western New
South Wales', *Records of the Australian Museum*,
Vol. XXV, No. 13.
McCONNEL, U. 1935
'Inspiration and Design in Aboriginal Art', *Art in
Australia*, No. 59.
McCONNEL, U. 1953
'Native Arts and Industries on the Archer, Kendall
and Holroyd Rivers, Cape York Peninsula, North
Queensland', *Records of the South Australian
Museum*, Vol. XI, No. 1.

MACINTOSH, N. W. G. 1951
'The Archaeology of Tandandjal Cave, South-West Arnhem Land', *Oceania*, Vol. XXI, No. 3.
MASSOLA, A. 1958
'A Victorian Bark Engraving in the British Museum', *Victorian Naturalist*, Vol. LXXV.
MATHEWS, J. 1896
'The Bora Ceremony', *Journal of the Royal Anthropological Society*, Vol. XXV.
MOUNTFORD, C. P. 1928 and 1935
'Aboriginal Rock Carvings in South Australia', *Reports, Australasian Association for the Advancement of Science*, Vols. XIX, XXII.
MOUNTFORD, C. P. 1937
'Examples of Aboriginal Art from Napier Broome Bay and Parry Harbour, North-Western Australia', *Transactions of the Royal Society of South Australia*, Vol. LXI.
MOUNTFORD, C. P. 1937, 1938(A)
'Aboriginal Crayon Drawings', *Records of the South Australian Museum*, Vol. VI, Nos. 1 and 2.
MOUNTFORD, C. P. 1937, 1938(B)
'Aboriginal Crayon Drawings', *Transactions of the Royal Society of South Australia*, Vols. LXI, LXII, LXIII.
MOUNTFORD, C. P. 1939a
'Aboriginal Decorative Art from Arnhem Land, Northern Territory of Australia', *Transactions of the Royal Society of South Australia*, Vol. LXIII, No. 2.
MOUNTFORD, C. P. 1939b
'Aboriginal Crayon Drawings, Warburton Ranges, Western Australia', *Oceania*, Vol. X, No. 1.
MOUNTFORD, C. P. 1948
Art of Albert Namatjira, Bread and Cheese Club, Melbourne.
MOUNTFORD, C. P. 1954a
'A Carved Human Figure from the Durack Ranges, North-western Australia', *Transactions of the Royal Society of South Australia*, Vol. LXXXVII.
MOUNTFORD, C. P. 1954b
Australia: Aboriginal Paintings—Arnhem Land, U.N.E.S.C.O. World Art Series, No. 3.
MOUNTFORD, C. P. 1956
Records of the American-Australian Scientific Expedition to Arnhem Land, Vol. 1, Art, Myth, and Symbolism, Melbourne University Press, Melbourne.
MOUNTFORD, C. P. 1957
'Aboriginal Bark Paintings from Field Island, Northern Territory', *Records of the South Australian Museum*, Vol. XII, No. 1.
MOUNTFORD, C. P. 1958a

The Tiwi—their Art, Myth and Ceremony, Phoenix House, London.
MOUNTFORD, C. P. 1958b
'Aboriginal Cave Paintings at Sleisbeck, Northern Australia', *Records of the South Australian Museum*, Vol. XIII, No. 2.
MOUNTFORD, C. P. 1961a
Aboriginal Art, Longmans, London.
MOUNTFORD, C. P. 1961b
In Marian W. Smith, ed., *The Artist in Tribal Society*, Routledge and Kegan Paul, London.
MOUNTFORD, C. P. 1962
'The Aboriginal Art of Australia', in A. Bühler, *et al.*, *Oceania and Australia: The Art of the South Seas* (in Art of the World Series), Methuen, London.
MUNN, N. D. 1962
'Walbiri Graphic Signs: An Analysis', *American Anthropologist*, Vol. 64, No. 5.
NEUMANN, E. 1955
The Great Mother, New York.
NEW SOUTH WALES, 1958, 1960, 1961, 1962, 1963
Purchases and Acquisitions for 1957, 1959, 1960, 1961, 1962, Art Gallery, of New South Wales.
NIETZSCHE, F. 1871
The Birth of Tragedy (reprinted in *The Philosophy of Nietzsche*, Modern Library, New York).
PÉRON, F. A. and FREYCINET, L. 1807–16
Voyage de Découvertes aux Terres Australes, Paris.
PETRI, H. 1954
Sterbende Welt in Nordwest-Australien, A. Limbach, Braunschweig.
PETRI, H. 1957
In *Ferne Völker. Frühe Zeiten*, des Museums für Völkerkunde und des Frobenius-Institutes an der J. W. Goethe-Universität, Frankfurt am Main.
PETRI, H. 1959
'Australiane Culture', in *Enciclopedia Universale Dell'arte*, Vol. II, Instituto per la Collaborazione Culturale, Venezia-Roma.
PRESTON, M. 1925
'The Indigenous Art of Australia', *Art in Australia*, No. 11, 3rd Series.
QUARTERLY
Art Gallery of New South Wales, *Quarterly*, Vol. 1, No. 4.
READ, Sir Herbert, 1961
In Marian W. Smith, ed., *The Artist in Tribal Society*, Routledge and Kegan Paul, London.
REWALD, J. 1956
Post Impressionism from Van Gogh to Gauguin, New York.

ROBINSON, R. 1956
The Feathered Serpent, Edwards and Shaw, Sydney.
ROTH, W. E. 1897
Ethnological Studies Among the North-West-Central Queensland Aborigines, Government Printer, Brisbane.
RUSKIN, J. 1873
Ariadne Florentine, London.
SALMON, A. 1912
La Jeune Peinture Francaise, Paris: quotation J. Golding, 1959.
SCHULZ, A. 1946
'North-western Rock-Paintings', *Memoirs of the National Museum of Victoria*, Vol. 20.
SMITH, Marian W. (ed.) 1961
The Artist in Tribal Society, Routledge and Kegan Paul, London.
SMYTH, R. Brough, 1878
The Aborigines of Victoria . . ., 2 Vols., Government Printer, Melbourne.
SPENCER, B. 1914
Native Tribes of the Northern Territory of Australia, Macmillan, London.
SPENCER, B. 1928
Wanderings in Wild Australia, 2 Vols., Macmillan, London.
SPENCER, B. and GILLEN, F. J. 1899/1938
The Native Tribes of Central Australia, Macmillan, London.
SPENCER, B. and GILLEN, F. J. 1904
The Northern Tribes of Central Australia, Macmillan, London.
STEWART, D. 1959
In *Bulletin* (July 1st.), Sydney.
STIRLING, E. C. 1896
Report on the Work of the Horn Scientific Expedition to Central Australia, Part IV, Mullen and Slade, Melbourne.
STIRLING, E. C. and WAITE, E. R. 1919
'Description of Toas, or Australian Aboriginal Direction Signs', *Records of the South Australian Museum*, Vol. I, No. 2.
STOCKDALE, J. (ed.) 1789/1790
The Voyage of Governor Phillip to Botany Bay, London.
STOKES, J. L. 1846
Discoveries in Australia, 1837–43 . . ., London.
STREHLOW, C. 1907–20
Die Aranda-und Lortija-Stämme in Zentral-Austra-

lien, Frankfurt.
STREHLOW, T. G. H. 1947
Aranda Traditions, Melbourne University Press, Melbourne.
STREHLOW, T. G. H. 1951
In R. Battarbee, *Modern Australian Aboriginal Art*, Angus and Robertson, Sydney.
THOMSON, D. F. 1933
'The Hero Cult, Initiation and Totemism on Cape York', *Journal of the Royal Anthropological Institute*, Vol. LXIII.
TINDALE, N. B. 1932
Manuscripts, a Miscellany of Arts and Letters, Adelaide.
TINDALE, N. B. 1940
'Distribution of Australian Aboriginal Tribes: A Field Survey', *Transactions of the Royal Society of South Australia*, Vol. LXIV, No. 1.
TINDALE, N. B. 1959
'Totemic Beliefs in the Western Desert of Australia, Part I. Women who Became the Pleiades', *Records of the South Australian Museum*, Vol. XIII, No. 3.
TINDALE, N. B. and BIRDSELL, J. B. 1941
'Tasmanoid Tribes in North Queensland', *Records of the South Australian Museum*, Vol. VII, No. 1.
WARNER, W. L. 1937/58
A Black Civilization, Harper, New York.
WEBSTER, W. J. E. 1962
'Techniques of Field Photography for Archaeological Purposes', *Oceania*, Vol. XXXIII, No. 2.
WHITE, J. 1790
Journal of a Voyage to New South Wales, London.
WORMS, E. A. 1942
'Die Goranara-Feier im Australischen Kimberley', *Annali Lateranensi*, Vol. 6.
WORMS, E. A. 1954
'Prehistoric Petroglyphs of the Upper Yule River, North-Western Australia', *Anthropos*, Vol. 49.
WORMS, E. A. 1955
'Contemporary and Prehistoric Rock Paintings in Central and Northern North Kimberley', *Anthropos*, Vol. 50.
WORSLEY, P. M. 1955
'Totemism in a Changing Society', *American Anthropologist*, Vol. 57, No. 4.
WORSNOP, T. 1897
The Prehistoric Arts, Manufactures . . . of the Aborigines of Australia, Government Printer, Adelaide.

Index

113

This book was designed by Hal Missingham. It was set in Monotype Times New Roman, and the typesetting and printing of the text and plates were by Waite & Bull Proprietary Limited, Strawberry Hills, Sydney. The book was bound by Stanley Owen & Sons Proprietary Limited, of Sydney, in Australian-made Brella cloth. All the plates were made by Colour Engravings Proprietary Limited, Surry Hills, Sydney. The grey broad-laid text paper was made by Associated Pulp and Paper Mills Limited, of Burnie, Tasmania. The case was silk screen printed by Royelltone Prints Proprietary Limited, Sydney.

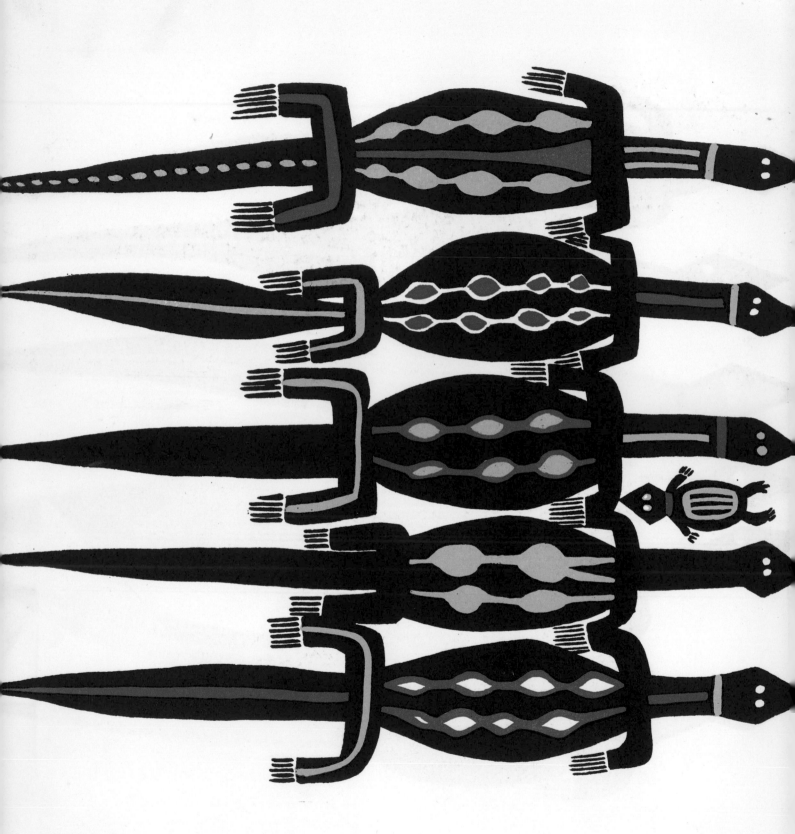